ISBN 978-0-282-54071-5
PIBN 10818643

REPORT OF THE FIFTH THULE EXPEDITION 1921—24
THE DANISH EXPEDITION TO ARCTIC NORTH AMERICA IN CHARGE
OF KNUD RASMUSSEN, PH. D.
VOL. VII. NO. 1

INTELLECTUAL CULTURE OF THE IGLULIK ESKIMOS

BY

KNUD RASMUSSEN

GYLDENDALSKE BOGHANDEL, NORDISK FORLAG
COPENHAGEN 1929

Edited with the Support of the Ministry of Education.
Translation Expenses defrayed by the Rask-Ørsted Fund.

Translated by W. WORSTER
from the Danish original.

PRINTED IN DENMARK
GYLDENDALS FORLAGSTRYKKERI
KØBENHAVN

TO MY FRIEND

WILLIAM THALBITZER

PROFESSOR OF ESKIMO LANGUAGE AND CULTURE
IN THE UNIVERSITY OF COPENHAGEN

General Plan and Methods of Work.

The work of the Fifth Thule Expedition was divided up between us so that Kaj Birket-Smith and Therkel Mathiassen dealt with the material aspects of the Eskimo culture, while I took the intellectual side. My principal objects of study under this head comprised:

1) The natives in the vicinity of our headquarters at Danish Island, or in other words, the Aivilingmiut, Iglulingmiut and the immigrant Netsilingmiut. The Aivilingmiut and Iglulingmiut constitute, together with the Tununermiut at Ponds Inlet, the Iglulik group.

2) The Inland Eskimos of the Barren Grounds, which we have agreed to call the Caribou Eskimos.

3) The Netsilingmiut, Ilivilermiut and Utkuhikjalingmiut, who are akin by intermarriage, and occupy, roughly speaking, the region between Bellot Strait, Back River and Adelaide Peninsula.

4) The Umingmaktôrmiut, between Kent Peninsula and Bathurst Inlet.

5) The Mackenzie Eskimos.

6) The Alaskan Eskimos, especially comprising the inland tribes between Colville and Noatak River, Point Hope, Nome, the islands in the Bering Strait and finally the fairly isolated population on Nunivak, south of the Yukon Delta.

It may be as well here further to explain that the terms used for the various tribes and settlements are to be understood as follows:

Iglulingmiut, plural of Iglulingmio, a man or woman from Iglulik, an island in Fury and Hecla Strait.

Amitjormiut, plural of Amitjormio, one living at Amitjoq (sometimes also pronounced Amitsoq), a name for Melville Peninsula. The territory here more particularly concerned is that between Usugârjuk and Lyon Inlet. They are part of the Iglulik tribe in the wider sense of the word.

Aivilingmiut, plural of Aivilingmio, one living at Aivilik, the old name for the region round Repulse Bay.

Netsilingmiut, plural of Netsilingmio, one living at Netsilik. the original name for the great lakes of Boothia Isthmus. The term Netsilingmiut however is now used for all coming from the eastern part of the Northwest Passage territory, many of these having for several generations taken up their quarters at various points between Lyon Inlet and Chesterfield Inlet.

Saglermiut, plural of Saglermio, one living on the island of Sagleq, i. e. Southampton Island. These are for the most part former members of the Aivilingmiut, and a few Iglulingmiut, who, attracted by the favourable conditions for hunting, settled here early in the 20th century, after the original Saglermiut had become extinct.

Finally may be mentioned the Igluligârjungmiut, or dwellers at Igluligârjuk, the native name for Chesterfield. These are not a tribe but consist of a mixture of the groups already mentioned with a further contingent of Inland Eskimos from Baker Lake and Kazan River.

There is no very marked difference between the Aivilingmiut and the Iglulingmiut. The dialects are so alike that it is difficult for a stranger to tell the difference. There is a more pronounced dissimilarity, however, between these dialects on the one hand and that of the Netsilingmiut on the other, the latter having a more emphatic sibilant than the former. The pronunciation of the Greenland "s" sound itself, however, which sometimes becomes h, sometimes j, is often so much a matter of accident and individual peculiarity, that it is hard to lay down any thoroughly consistent method of spelling for words in which the letter occurs. Reference may here be made, for further information, to Birket-Smith's Five Hundred Eskimo Words Vol. III, No. 3 of this series.

The above-mentioned distribution of our work among our party whereby Mathiassen and Birket-Smith took the entire material culture and I attended to the intellectual has, of course, the advantage — which indeed was the reason for the arrangement — that it gave each one more time to go into details than would have been the case had one had to consider both aspects together. On the other hand, I feel obliged to point out one difficulty involved by such an arrangement, in keeping the intellectual culture distinct from the material. It will always be natural for an explorer first to describe the geographical environment of any particular tribe or people, and the material culture whereby they maintain themselves in the struggle for existence, the two being closely connected; and with these factors to start from, one can then later endeavour to show forth the manner of their intellectual life and its manifestations.

It seemed to me therefore that it might be helpful to the general understanding of the position if I were to give, by way of introduction, a few brief sketches of the conditions under which I first encountered the people whom I shall endeavour in the following pages to describe. These brief sketches should thus give their views of everyday life and their attitude towards life and destiny. I hope that such an introduction may contribute towards a more intimate appreciation of the material and problems subsequently to be dealt with.

It was necessary for me first of all to gain the complete confidence of my Eskimo collaborators before I could begin the work at all. And this was only to be achieved by sharing their daily life, living with them under precisely the same conditions as they themselves. That I was able to do so with complete success was due to the fact that I could speak their language, and, from my knowledge of their kinsfolk in Greenland, was already familiar with their ideas and habit of mind.

And it has always been one of my main objects, in the portrayal of primitive culture, to get the natives' own views of life and its problems, their own ideas expressed in their own fashion. This was often quite as important to me as eliciting new elements in their religious and spiritual life.

I therefore think it will not be out of place to commence this book with an account of my method of work and the manner in which I first gained the confidence of my Eskimo collaborators.

I.

Eskimo Life: Descriptions and Autobiographies.

Our first meeting with the Aivilingmiut near Repulse Bay.

Our first encounter with these natives took place on the 4th of December 1921. More than two months had passed since our arrival at Danish Island, and up to now we had not set eyes on a single human being of the tribes we had come all this way to visit. Work of various kinds had kept us busy at headquarters, and the state of the ice had hitherto precluded excursions of any length. By the end of November, however, all the fjords were frozen hard enough for us to set out for Repulse Bay, where we knew there should be one of the Hudson Bay Company's trading stations. We could there obtain information as to the distribution of the population between Iglulik and Chesterfield Inlet.

Peter Freuchen, the Polar Eskimo Nasaitsordluarssuk and I were at last on our way to the north-west in search of natives. We had followed the northern coast of Vansittart Island through the mouth of Gore Bay, and making a wide detour where the strength of the current prevented the formation of winter ice, had gone overland past the south-western coast of Melville Peninsula; we were now on the sea ice in Haviland Bay. We had had an accident to one of the sledges, which had suffered damage among the pressure ridges, and Freuchen and Nasaitsordluarssuk were consequently a little way behind.

It was about noon, the red of the sun tinged the horizon out towards Rowe's Welcome. The sky was perfectly clear, and it was bitterly cold. A faint breeze blowing right in my face stung so that I could hardly keep my head to the front as I drove. It was fine, level fjord ice underfoot; we were some distance from the edge of the ice, which was just visible with its pressure ridges to the south, and as the way was clear ahead, I had turned my back to the wind for a moment, to thaw my face. I had only been sitting like this for a moment, when I started up at a sudden sound. I had heard it quite distinctly, and the dogs too must have noticed; they began to sniff eagerly about, and I was thus sure I had made no mistake. The sound I had heard was that of a shot fired not far off; there was no mistaking it. I glanced back towards my companions, thinking they had fired as a signal to me to wait. I soon descried them, but they were driving up at a good pace, and as far as I could see, overtaking me; it could not be from them. I then looked out ahead, and perceived, some four kilometres distant, a black line extending across the ice midway out in the bay. It could not be bare rock. I stopped the team at once and got out my glass; and now I could plainly distinguish a whole line of sledges with a great number of dogs. They had halted, as I myself had done, and were watching me intently. One man broke away from the rest, and came running across the ice at right angles to the line I was following. I realised that he was making for me, and with the excitement natural to a first meeting with human beings in these wilds, I at once jumped on the sledge and gave my dogs the signal for full speed. It was not long before they too sighted the man as he ran, and regarding him as game in flight, set off in chase. In a few minutes I had come up with him, and the dogs, themselves excited by the strange smell of him, and his unfamiliar dress, would have attacked him had I not shouted to him to stand still. I stopped the team at the same moment, cracked my whip over their heads, and leaped clear of the sledge in front of the dogs, so as to place myself between them and the stranger. I had made a long jump, and with such impetus that to avoid knocking him over I was obliged to throw my arms round his neck. So there we stood, laughing and shaking each other, while the dogs, crestfallen, lay down on the ice, as if ashamed at having mistaken a friend for an enemy.

The first thing that struck me when I had recovered a little was that the man understood all I said; and I understood him in turn when he spoke. He was a tall, well-built fellow, his face and long hair covered with rime after his run, which had made him so hot that his cheeks were literally steaming. He explained that his name was Papik ("Tail-feather") and he had his autumn quarters by Nivfâvik, which I later ascertained was up at the head of Lyon Inlet. I was so eager to get into touch with the natives that I did not wait for my companions to come up, but went across at once to the group, now quite near. The men came forward to meet us without hesitation, but the women and children remained lying by the sledges, stretched at their ease in the sun, as if there were no such thing as cold. Several of the women were nursing half-naked infants at the breast. The light fell on their brown smiling faces, and my first impression was that they must be uncommonly hardy folk. I considered myself fairly accustomed to the climate of these latitudes, but only a moment ago

I had suffered so from the icy wind that I had been forced to turn and let my face thaw. Yet here were these women and children sitting about as if altogether unaffected by the cold.

These, then, were the people whom the Greenlanders called Akilinermiut ("those who dwell in the land beyond the great sea"); the people I had heard about ever since, as a boy, I had first begun to listen to the Eskimo folk tales. I could not have found a more picturesque setting for a first impression. Here was a whole caravan out in the midst of the ice, men and women in curious dresses of skins, like living illustrations to the Greenland story-tellers' tales of the terrible "inland folk". Every stitch of their clothing was of caribou skin, fine, short-haired skins of animals killed at the opening of the autumn hunting season. The dresses of the women especially rendered them altogether shapeless — very wide in the upper part, with a big fur hood falling from the shoulders down over the back, and long loose coat tails coming down over the breeches before and behind, edged with white skin. The footwear also was peculiar, the actual boots being apparently covered with an outer envelope, commencing in a long tongue right up on the thigh, and terminating just below the calf in a sort of bag; a most comical arrangement, serving as far as could be seen no useful purpose whatever.

The curious fur dresses of the men were as if made for running; they were not so long as those of the women, but had the same tail fashioning front and back. The tails were either of equal length, divided up the thigh, or comparatively short in front with a longer tail behind.

Many different impressions passed rapidly through my mind at this first meeting, but there was one thing which moved me beyond all else, and almost at once made a bond between us, as if we had been old acquaintances, and that was the language. True, I had always known that the natives here spoke the same tongue, but I had never imagined there would be so little difference that we could enter into converse at once without the slightest hindrance. Owing to the similarity of language, they took us at first for distant tribal kinsmen from Baffin Land. They themselves had just started off with their loads on the sledges, on the way to their snow huts a few days' journey away. But like all Eskimos, they were so swayed by the impulse of the moment that all thought of proceeding on their way was abandoned for the present. As soon as they saw we were friendly folk, as interesting to them as they were to us, they went wild with delight. There was a shouting and laughing and cracking of jokes which further raised their spirits, and as there happened to be some big deep snowdrifts close at hand, we moved over to them at once to set about building snow huts, where we could spend the rest of the day and the night in improving our acquaintance and celebrating the occasion. This frank, spontaneous friendliness was a great pleasure to me, for I realised that among such people I should find no difficulty in learning from them, later on, all they could tell about themselves and their past.

Meeting an unknown tribe is rather like travelling through unknown country; one is, so to speak, prepared for surprises. And so it was with us. The surprises were not wanting. The faculty of observation is of course most alert at the first meeting. The common, everyday business of building a snow hut, which we ourselves had had to do hundreds of times, was now something extraordinary; and quite exciting to watch. Never had we seen a house spring up so rapidly out of the snow as under the snow-knives of our new friends here. Among the Polar Eskimos of North Greenland, the building of a fair-sized snow hut is reckoned a good hour's work for two men. One cuts the blocks from a snowdrift lying outside the ground plan of the house, and hands them, unless there happens to be a third man on the job, to the one who is building the hut. Here however, one man cut the blocks and built the hut at the same time. Selecting a portion of a snowdrift where the snow was of the right degree of firmness for his purpose, he marked out a circle in it, the snow within the circle being reckoned to suffice for the entire hut. To make a calculation of this sort in a moment calls for a great deal of experience and practice. Actually, then, our native architect here builds his wall and the selfsupporting roof up over the space left by the blocks cut out of the drift as he works. He must therefore cut down to the full depth of the drift, working his way to the bottom, whereas the Greenlanders cut the blocks they need from the surface. It was a simplification of the process amounting to genius, and labour-saving to such a degree that one man here could cut the blocks, set them in place and trim them off with his knife all in about the same time that a Greenlander would take to cut the blocks alone. As the hut grew up out of the drift, one of the women, taking a big flat wooden shovel, spread loose snow over the wall from the outside. This layer of loose snow fills in any cracks and crevices, making the house thoroughly sound and warm inside, however hard it may be blowing without. The remarkable skill here displayed was evidently the result of many generations' technical experience, and we at once realised that we had come upon a system of winter housing, and a capacity for utilising available material, superior to that which we knew from Greenland. These men were experts in the use of snow as building material. In three quarters of an hour, three large snow huts were ready; and almost as soon as the snow bench inside was cut to shape, the blubber lamp was lit and the interior warmed up. I and my two companions quartered ourselves in different huts, so that we might make the most of our new acquaintance. Before long, all our baggage was stowed on high platforms built of oblong snow blocks, and as soon as the dogs had been fed, we could go in and settle down among our friends. Snow was melted in pots hung over the lamp, and our hosts boiled caribou meat from the store they had with them. We had walrus meat, but were not allowed to cook any, as this was strictly taboo in a house where caribou meat was to be eaten at this time of year.

My host was a genial, kindly fellow named Pilakapsak; his wife Hauna was untiring in her efforts to make us comfortable, and it was not until all had eaten their fill that we settled down to talk.

We now learned, to our great satisfaction, that there were native settlements in nearly all directions from our headquarters on Danish Island. The population was not overwhelming in numbers, but the more interesting in point of composition. A couple of days' journey from our house we could come into contact not only with Iglulingmiut, but also with Aivilingmiut and Netsilingmiut.

The conversation was of a very general character, we on our part feeling our way carefully at first, to learn how far we could go in our questionings without appearing too inquisitive. Thanks to our speaking the language, however, and the confidence this inspired in our hosts, we were able even to touch upon matters of religion, in regard to which I very soon ascertained that these people were still entirely primitive in their views and unaffected by outside influences.

On the day following this first meeting, we arrived at Repulse Bay while it was still daylight, and made the acquaintance here of Captain George Cleveland, an old whaling captain, now in charge of the Hudson's Bay Company's trading station there. Captain Cleveland received us with great hospitality, and most willingly furnished us with a great deal of information that proved very valuable in arranging our plans of work. We stayed here a few days, and made several other acquaintances, including that of one old man in particular with whom I was to have further dealings in the course of my work later on. His name was Ivaluardjuk; he had a long white beard and red, rheumy eyes, worn dim with over many blizzards. He was, it appeared, the geographer of his tribe, and was remarkably well up in the country and its inhabitants throughout the entire range between Ponds Inlet and Chesterfield. When I brought out a pencil and paper, he drew, to my astonishment, the whole coastline from Repulse Bay to Ponds Inlet, without hesitation, and though the proportions of

Ivaluartjuk, the old story-teller and ballad-singer.

The shaman Padloq.

Takornâq, the shy one.

course could not be correct, the map yet gave such a good general view that we were now able to fix a number of the Eskimo place-names. This was a very essential point for us, as we should have to discuss the various localities with natives who knew nothing of the English names given to parts of their own territory by Parry and Lyon a hundred years before, while on the other hand they had an abundance of names of their own for fjords, lakes, mountains and all characteristic features. I was thus able to note, on the map drawn for me by Ivaluardjuk, somewhere about a hundred Eskimo names, which I shall refer to later on.

I discovered at once, in the course of our first talk, that Ivaluardjuk, though very careful about what he said, was remarkably well acquainted with the ancient traditions of his tribe. In order to draw him out a little, I narrated a few of the stories common in Greenland. These proved to be well-known here, and the surprise of the natives at finding a stranger from unknown lands able to relate old tales they fancied were exclusively their own, was such that in a short time the house was filled with inquisitive listeners. Thus I gained the old man's confidence, and we were soon discussing the folk-lore of his people as experts, the reserve he had shown at first being gradually discarded. He is the oldest member of the household I am visiting, and is indeed one of the oldest members of his tribe. He himself might have stepped out of some old, weird story, with his strange, worn look, and the quiet, steady manner of his own narration makes a deep impression on those around. After a while he tells me something of his own family affairs. He ought long since to have been a widower, he says, a poor old fellow with no authority among his neighbours; for his first wife had died many years before, and all his children of that marriage grown up. But he dreaded the loneliness and helplessness that are always the lot of a wifeless man in his country, and had therefore married an adoptive daughter of his own, and bought her a child, paying for it with one of his dogs. He laughs in his quiet, kindly fashion as he tells the story, and adds:

"Thus men can better their existence and soften the harshness of fate. Now I no longer feel alone, and my old age is a restful time. But when I chance to think of my childhood and recall all the old memories from those days, then youth seems a time when all meat was juicy and tender, and no game too swift for a hunter. When I was young, every day was as a beginning of some new thing, and every evening ended with the glow of the next day's dawn. Now, I have only the old stories and songs to fall back upon, the songs that I sang myself in the days when I delighted to challenge my comrades to a song-contest in the feasting house".

Hardly had he finished speaking when all present begged him to sing a song; he made no objection, but drew back a little on the bench. His wife then chanted in a clear voice a monotonous air, consisting of but a few notes constantly repeated. The other women at once joined in, and Ivaluardjuk himself, thus supported, delivered a peculiar song which I afterwards wrote down. The ideas and expressions, and the general effect, of Eskimo songs are so unlike anything we are accustomed to in our own that it is not always possible to translate literally. The following is, however, as close a rendering of the original as can reasonably be given when endeavouring at the same time to reproduce something of the charm and the unconscious art displayed in the utterance of the Eskimo singer:

Cold and mosquitoes,
These two pests
Come never together.
I lay me down on the ice,
Lay me down on the snow and ice,
Till my teeth fall chattering.
It is I,
Aja — aja — ja.

Memories are they,
From those days,
From those days,
Mosquitoes swarming
From those days,
The cold is bitter,
The mind grows dizzy
As I stretch my limbs
Out on the ice.
It is I,
Aja — aja — ja.

Ai! but songs
Call for strength
And I seek after words,
I, aja — aja — ja.

Ai! I seek and spy
Something to sing of,
The caribou with the spreading antlers!

And strongly I threw
The spear with my throwing stick (sic!).
And my weapon fixed the bull
In the hollow of the groin
And it quivered with the wound
Till it dropped
And was still.

Ai! but songs
Call for strength,
And I seek after words.
It is I,
Aja, aja — haja — haja.

This utterance of an old man, who recognised that for him the joyous days of life were long since over and past, brought the noisy listeners to silence. And I saw that these people I had come to study were not unacquainted with the virtues of piety and reverence. I realised that if I could only go the right way to work, I could learn from them something that might show others at home something of the Eskimo mind.

Takornâq and her husband Padloq.

My visit to Repulse Bay proved of the greatest importance in the subsequent arrangement of my work. The natives here were frank and genial folk, with whom it was easy to enter into conversation on ordinary matters of everyday life. Nor had they any reluctance to tell a story, or sing a song accompanied by the whole household as chorus. But as soon as I ventured to touch on more serious themes, they showed more reserve. There were great and difficult questions here which were best left alone. Only when actual happenings called for some decision, some course of action in face of threatening circumstances, would the subject be discussed with the wise men of the tribe. The earth grew angry if men out hunting worked too much with stones and turf in the building of their meat stores and hunting depots; so also the spirits that guided men's fate might be offended if men concerned themselves over much with such things. Men knew so little of things apart from their food and sleep and rest; it might easily seem presumptuous if they endeavoured to form any opinion about hidden things. Happy folk should not worry themselves by thinking.

And old Ivaluardjuk held to this view at first, maintaining a profound reserve when I endeavoured to draw him out. Moreover, apart from this innate reluctance to speak of such things as life itself and the purpose of life, and its guiding powers, the Eskimos of these regions were extremely cautious in expressing their views at all when dealing with white men. True, no missionaries ever came here — save for a few brief visits — to condemn their religion, but the little they knew of "that sort of white men", who were so unlike the traders and whalers, was not calculated to render them more communicative. As far as they could understand, it seemed that the strangers regarded them pityingly on account of their belief in such unreasonable things as their wise men maintained to be the foundations of all wisdom. A kind of spiritual shyness, not unmixed perhaps with a certain sense of dignity, made them reticent on the subject; they merely acknowledged that the missionaries otherwise appeared to be good men in their daily life.

"The other sort" of white men comprised the traders and whalers. These were bright, smart fellows, caring only for their hunting and trading. But when any of them occasionally happened to be present at the solemn seances of the angákut, they would merely shrug their shoulders, or make some scornful remark, as to the relations of these shamans with the supernatural. Furthermore, all white men looked with supreme disdain on the system of taboo by which the balance of the Eskimo community was maintained.

I understood then, that if I were to succeed in gaining the full confidence of these people, it was absolutely necessary to place myself in their position. I was not concerned to guide or correct them in any way, but had come to their country expressly for the purpose of learning what they could teach. The thing to do, then, was to make friends with some of the elders, those most familiar with the traditions of the tribe. Once I had won their friendship, the rest would come of itself.

It was not long before I made just the sort of acquaintance I had in mind; it happened indeed on the way back from Repulse Bay to Danish Island. Peter Freuchen had gone on further south to continue his investigations, and Nasaitsordluarssuk and I were driving home alone to inform our companions of all that we had learned. In order to save time, we decided to make a short cut from Haviland Bay down to Gore Bay. We had not got far inland when we came upon an old woman fishing for trout in a lake. The ice was thick already, and she lay half hidden among broken hummocks, with her head bent over the hole where her line was down. We thus took her entirely by surprise. She started up as the dogs gave tongue, and stumbled backward in confusion at the sight of us. We had already been told that the natives here were not usually pleased to encounter strangers unawares; there was no knowing whether it was friend or enemy. We were not surprised then, that the old woman endeavoured to run away; in this, however, she was unsuccessful; in fact, a moment after she was sitting on my sledge — albeit much against her will — and driving down towards the place where she lived, our dogs having already scented human dwellings near. She had with her a little puppy, that she had not wished to leave behind, and held it in her lap with a convulsive clasp, looking up at me at the same time with such an expression of terror in her eyes that I could not help laughing. She had heard nothing of our arrival in the district and saw now only two men and two sledges, every detail revealing the stranger. The fashion of our clothes, the build of our sledges, the dogs' harness, and even our manner of speech. She was sitting behind me, and as I bent down to explain who we were and what we wanted, I suddenly noticed a sound I had not perceived before, and now discovered, tucked away down at the back of her behind the fur hood, a little naked infant with its arms round her neck, squealing in concert with the puppy. I now hastened to mention the names of all the new friends I had made during my stay at Repulse Bay, and this, as showing that I was well known to people she knew as neighbours, changed her attitude entirely. So delighted was she to find herself among friends that her eyes filled with tears. As soon as she had calmed down a little, I explained where we had come from. It was easier now to do so than in the case of our first meeting with natives at Haviland Bay, for I could now give the Eskimo names of the places. I knew that Ponds Inlet was called Tununeq, and explained therefore that we came from a country beyond the great sea that washed the shores of Baffin Land. Hardly had I finished speaking when she told me that she herself was called Takornâq ("the recluse" or "the one that is shy of strangers") and came from Iglulik. She had moved down to Repulse Bay with her husband, Padloq, expressly in order to be near white men and all the wealth which one could obtain by bartering with them. She had often been to Ponds Inlet, and had met Scottish whalers there. They had told her of the people from whose land we came, who spoke the same language as she did, and lived over on the other side. So pleased was she at finding that we belonged, as it were, to her own world after all, that she became frankly communicative, not to say garrulous herself. It was not long before we had the village in sight and soon came up to the three snow huts which were all it amounted to. They were built close to a lake where trout were to be caught. The inhabitants came running towards us but without knowing quite how to receive us, for they also had recognised at once that we were strangers. But on catching sight of Takornâq, who was laughing delightedly, they came up and gathered round us. Takornâq certainly did not bear out the character implied in her name. She chattered away, recounting all the information she had just acquired, and pointing to us, explained that we were real live human beings, from a country far, far away beyond the sea from Tununeq.

Takornâq was consious of her position at the moment, as the principal actor in the scene, and when I asked her the names of those about us, she took me by the shoulder and led me, laughing herself all the time, from one to another, mentioning their names. This one was Inernerunashuaq ("the one that was made in a hurry") an old shaman, and I noticed that he wore, as a mark of his dignity, the belt of office round his waist, consisting of a broad strip of skin hung about with many odd items, bones of animals, little implements, knives and whips cut out of walrus ivory. His wife, who was conspicuously tattooed on the face, was called Tûglik ("northern diver"), a big, fat woman with a whole crowd of little children hanging to her skirts. Then there was Talerortalik ("the one with the forepaws"); his wife was the shaman's daugter, Utsukitsoq ("the narrow vulva"). The young couple stood modestly in the background, but Takornâq, who was not afraid of saying what she thought, declared openly that it was they who kept the shaman and his family alive. Inernerunashuaq might be a great shaman — that was none of her business to say, she put in laughing — but he was certainly a very poor hunter. This lack of respect for a shaman interested me very much, albeit the remark was only made in jest, for I had always understood that the natives were very careful about what they said to the shaman. I learned afterwards that this was indeed the rule, and Takornâq the exception, being not only remarkably free with her tongue, but equally sincere in what she said. She was herself skilled in shamanism, though practising more in secret, and would thus know something of the limitations of the craft. Finally, there was Talerortalik's brother Peqingajoq ("the crooked one"), who was actually a cripple, with a pronounced hunchback figure. Takornâq informed me that he was a most hardworking fellow, and so keen on his fishing that there was always ice on the front of his dress — from lying face downward on the ice at his fishing hole. There were other natives in the party, but it would take up too much space to mention every one.

Takornâq, maintaining that she had a sort of right to us, as having been the first to meet us, now invited us in to her house. It was a well-kept snow hut, but rather cold until we got the blubber lamp going. Nasaitsordluarssuk and I clambered up on to the bench, which was completely covered with warm skins of caribou, a pot of meat was set to boil, and these domestic preparations finished, our hostess sat down between us and declared that now she was married to both of us, for her husband was away on a journey. She burst out laughing herself at this observation, and seemed to enjoy her own joke immensely. It was indeed, not to be understood in any ill sense, for she added directly after that she knew no better man than her husband. It was only her fun, she said, and there was no harm in talking nonsense when one felt a little jolly.

As soon as the place was warmed up a little, she pulled out the infant from her amaut, and laid it with motherly pride in a sleeping bag of hare's skin. The child's name was Qahîtsoq, it had been called after a mountain spirit. It was not her own child but one of twins, belonging to a certain Nagjuk ("deer's horn") of the Netsilingmiut, and Takornâq had bought it of him as it would otherwise have been killed. "Twins", she added, "are hardly ever allowed to live in our country, for we are always travelling about, and a mother cannot carry more than one in her amaut". The price paid for Qahîtsoq was a dog and a frying pan; really too much for such a skinny little bit of a thing. Takornâq was evidently sore at the recollection that Nagjuk had cheated her, and kept the fatter of the twins for himself.

Takornâq talked incessantly, and it was not long before we were quite like old acquaintances. There was no need for me to say much, a grunt here and there, an encouraging remark, sufficed to keep her going. She was proud of her descent, for the Iglulingmiut, which of all the tribes has had least to do with white men, is reckoned as having the cleverest hunters and the best women. She was therefore anxious that we should not mistake her birthplace for that of the others in the village, these being all Netsilingmiut. They were dirty with their clothes, she said, and not at all clean in their houses. She and her husband, now, had special vessels for urinals indoors, which showed how cleanly they were even when living in snow huts, whereas the Netsilingmiut did not hesitate to make water on the floor, or even on the bench under their pillows, simply lifting up the skins that covered it.

When the talk began to quieten down a little, I told her about my own childhood in Greenland, that she might understand how I came to speak her language, and having ended my story, I declared that I would rather listen to others than talk myself. At this she burst out laughing, and observed that it was just the other way with her; she would much rather talk herself than listen to other people. I therefore took her at her word and begged her to tell me about her own life, as far as she could remember, from her earliest childhood. And now for the first time since we had entered the hut, Takornâq seemed inclined to talk seriously. She closed her eyes and sat for a long time without speaking; then when at last she began, she gave us the whole story of her life, all her experiences recounted without hesitation, in clear and fluent language.

"My father and mother often had children that died. My father was a great shaman, and as he was very anxious to have children, he went up inland to an ice loon and asked it to help him. My father and mother say that it was with the aid of this creature that I was born; a strange creature it was, half bird, half human. So it was that I came into the world. And I lived.

"Some time after I was born, there came a season of scarcity, and all were in want of food. My father had gone out to a hole in the ice, and here, it is said, he spoke as follows:

" 'If my daughter is to live, you will remain as you are. If my daughter is to die, you will close over, and keep away all the seal. Now give me this sign.'

"The hole in the ice did not change, there was no movement in the water, and my father began to catch seals, and he knew that I was not to die.

"When he came home in the evening, he said to my mother:

" 'Today a sign has been given to tell me that our daughter is not to die like the others. Therefore you need no longer trouble about all those rules for women who have had a child.'

"And though it is the custom among our people for women with young children to refrain from many kinds of food which are considered harmful to the child, my mother now ate whatever she liked, and nothing was forbidden to her. But then it came about that I fell ill after all, and they thought I should die. Then my father said to my mother:

" 'Take the meat fork and stand it up in the pot! If it falls down she will die; if it stays upright she will live.'

"The fork was laid across the pot, and slipped down of its own accord and stood upright. Thus once more they learned that I was to live, and my mother again took to eating whatever she liked.

"Thus I began to live my life, and I reached the age when one is sometimes as it were awake, and sometimes as if asleep. I could begin to remember and forget.

"One day I remember I saw a party of children out at play, and wanted to run out at once and play with them. But my father, who understood hidden things, perceived that I was playing with the souls of my dead brothers and sisters. He was afraid this might be dangerous, and therefore called up his helping spirits and asked them about it. Through his helping spirits my father learned that despite the manner in which I was born, with the aid of a magic bird, and the way my life had been saved by powerful spirits, there was yet something in my soul of that which had brought about the death of all my brothers and sisters. For this reason the dead were often about me, and I could not distinguish between the spirits of the dead and real live people. Thus it was that I had gone out to play with the souls of my dead brothers and sisters, but it was a dangerous thing to do, for in the end the dead ones might keep me among themselves. My father's helping spirits would therefore now endeavour to protect me more effectively than hitherto, and my father was not to be afraid of my dying now. And after that, whenever I wanted to go out and play with the spirit children, which I always took for real ones, a sort of rocky wall rose up out of the ground, so that I could not get near them.

"The next thing I remember is hearing people talk of evil spirits, which were said to be about us; evil spirits that would bring misfortune and spoil the hunting. When I heard this I was very much afraid, for I was now old enough to understand that our life was set about with many perils, and I fell to crying. Then I remember we all went away, to escape from that dangerous place, and travelled long and far until we came to Qiqertaq (Ship Harbour Island, near Haviland Bay). It was here that I first saw the white men, and I learned later on that they were whalers. I remember some curious things from those days. There was an old woman who wanted to sell a puppy to the white men, but they would not buy it, and I thought how hard it was on the old woman, for she was very poor. I remember she tried to work magic and do the white men harm because they would not help her.

"Another thing I remember about the white men is that they were very eager to get hold of women. A man with a handsome wife could get anything he wanted out of them; they never troubled much about what a thing cost as long as they could borrow the wife now and again. And they gave the women valuable gifts. I was only a little girl myself at that time, and had but little knowledge of what took place between man and woman when they were together, but I remember there were some of our men who would have no dealings with the white men, because they did not wish to share their wives with them. But most of the men did not mind; for it is quite a common thing among us to change wives. A man does not love his wife any the less because she lies with someone else now and again. And it is the same with the woman. They like to know about it, that is all; there must be no secrets in such matters. And when a man lends his wife to another, he himself always lies with the other man's wife. But with white men it was different; none of them had their wives with them to lend in exchange. So they gave presents instead, and thus it was that many men of our tribe looked on it as only another kind of exchange, like changing wives. And there were so many things in our way of life that did not agree with the white men's ways, and they did not feel obliged themselves to keep our rules about what was taboo, so we could not be so particular in other matters. Only the white men had less modesty than our own when wishing to lie with a woman.

Our men always desired to be alone with the woman, and if there was no other way, they would build a snow hut. But the white men on the big ship lived many together in one place, lying on shelves along the steep sides of the ship, like birds in the face of a cliff. And I remember a thing that caused great amusement to many, though the ones to whom it happened were not pleased. One evening when a number of women had gone to the white men's ship to spend the night there, we in our house had settled down early to rest. But suddenly we were awakened by the sound of someone weeping outside. And this was what had happened. A woman named Atanarjuat had suddenly fallen through the shelf where she was lying with one of the men on the ship, and rolled stark naked on the floor. She burst out crying for shame, put on her clothes in a great hurry and went home weeping, saying that she would never again lie with a white man. It was she whom we had heard outside our house, and as I said before, these things took place at a time when I did not rightly know what went on between man and woman. But all the same, when I heard about this, a thing most of the others laughed at, I could not help feeling that the white men must have less sense of decency than we had.

"Then I forgot all that happened at that place, and did not remember again until we came to Malukshitaq (Lyon Inlet), where we had taken land. One thing I remember from that time is that my mother always had a urine bucket for a pillow when she lay down to sleep. This she did in order that my father might be successful in his hunting. Thus she helped the hunters, and they killed a walrus. There was a great feast, and I was there, and I remember there was a fight between father and son. I was afraid, and ran away.

"All this that I have told you I remember only as in a mist. My first clear remembrance is of the time when we lived at Utkuhigjalik (Wager Bay); my father died there. Soon after his death, my mother married Mánâpik ("the very much present") but they could not live together, and it was not long before they separated, and my mother was married to a man named Higjik ("the marmot"). Shortly after, we went away from there, and lived at Oqshoriaq (the word means quartzite; it is the Eskimo name for Marble Island). There were many people there at that time, and life was very amusing. The men often had boxing matches, and there were great song feasts at which all were assembled. It was there I saw for the first time an old woman from Qaernermiut (Baker Lake). I was told that this old woman was the first who ever saw Oqshoriaq. Before that time, it was nothing but a heap of pressure ridges in the ice. It was not until later that the ice turned to the white stone we call Oqshoriaq. I remember the first time we came to that island, we had to crawl up on to the land, and were not allowed to stand upright until we reached the top. That was done then, and it is done to this day, for the Island is a sacred place; magic words made it, and if we do not show respect for it by crawling it will change to ice again, and all the people on it will fall through and drown."

— At this point in Takornâq's story the meat in the pot began to boil, and she interrupted her narration to serve up a meal. Tea was made from our own supply, and the old woman was so pleased at this little trivial courtesy, that she at once improvised a song, the words of which were as follows:

Ajaja — aja — jaja,
The lands around my dwelling
Are more beautiful
From the day
When it is given me to see
Faces I have never seen before.
All is more beautiful,
All is more beautiful,
And life is thankfulness.
These guests of mine
Make my house grand,
Ajaja — aja — jaja.

We then settled down to eat, but Takornâq herself would not join us, for in order to preserve the life of the delicate infant she had bought, she was obliged to refrain from eating any food cooked in a pot with meat intended for others; she must have her own special cooking pot, and eat from no other.

As soon as we had finished, she went to a store chamber at one side of the hut, and dragged out the carcase of a caribou, which she gave us with the following words:

"Go out and give this to your dogs. I am only doing as my husband would have done had he been at home."

We then went out and fed our dogs, and when we re-entered the hut, the talk naturally turned upon her husband, Padloq (properly, "he who lies face downwards"). She had already told us that she had been married several times before. She now resumed her story where she had left off, as follows:

"When I was old enough to begin taking part in games with the young men, I was married. My first husband was called Angutiashuk ("one who is not a real man"). We were only married a very short time. I did not care for him, he was no good, and so we separated. He died of hunger shortly after.

"It was not long before I was married again, this time to one named Quivâpik, but everyone was afraid of him, because he was always threatening to kill people if he did not get exactly what he wanted. He went up inland hunting caribou, and I went with him to help carry the meat. We lived quite alone, far from any people, and I often wept with misery at our loneliness. I felt the need of being among others, and having someone to talk to, for Quivâpik was a man who hardly ever spoke. We stayed up inland all that summer. The only means we had of getting fire was by using firestone (pyrites) but once we could not find any, and could make no fire. Then Quivâpik called up his helping spirits, and while doing this he cried to me suddenly:

"'Close your eyes and clutch at the air!' And I did so, and a piece of fire-stone came flying through the air and I caught it, and we were able to make a fire once more.

"Summer came to an end, and autumn set in, and when the darkness came, we could sometimes see beings in human form, but we did not know what they were. We were afraid of them, and returned home to our own place, where at that time there was scarcity of game and great want of food. Before long a walrus was captured, and then there was meat for all once more.

"Real knives of iron and steel, such as we use now, were very rare in those days, and the men often lost them. Then my husband would hold a spirit calling, and in that way recover the lost knives.

"Once while we were at Southampton Island, Quivâpik was attacked by some of his enemies, and wounded by a harpoon in one eye and one thigh, but so great a shaman was he that he did not die.

"Quivâpik once tried to catch a dead man who was trying to return to his village. A corpse thus trying to come to life again is called an aŋ̣ᴇrlᴀrtukxiᴀq. They are persons at whose birth magic words have been uttered, so that if they die, they can come to life again and return to their place among men. But it was a hard matter for Quivâpik to catch this one, so he got another shaman to help him, and even then they did not succeed. Quivâpik said it would have been easy to bring the dead man to life again if only the moon had given leave. But the dead man's mother had sewn garments of new caribou skin on the island of Oqshoriaq, and that is not allowed there, so the moon would not let her son come to life again.

"Another time we were out after salmon, and I could not catch any. But my husband came and took the fish hook and line from me and held the hook between his legs, and after holding it there a while, he swallowed it, and drew it out from his navel, and the line the same way. After that I caught plenty of salmon.

"I was married to him for seven years, but then he was killed by some people who were afraid of him. A man named Ikumaq ('the flame') stabbed him with a snow knife, and took me to wife himself. He was not my husband for long, and when I married again, it was Padloq. It is not our custom to call our husbands by their names. I call Padloq o'maga ("the one that keeps me alive"). From the day I married him, my life became restful.

"In the course of my life, from childhood to old age, I have seen many lands, and lived in many different ways. There were times of abundance, and times of dearth and want. The worst thing I remember was when I found a woman who had eaten her husband and her childern to save herself from starvation.

"Ûmaga and I were travelling from Iglulik to Tununeq when he dreamed one night that a friend of his had been eaten by his nearest kin. Ûmaga has the gift of second sight, and always knows when anything remarkable is going to happen. Next day we started off, and there was something remarkable about our journey from the start. Again and again the sledge stuck fast, but when we came to look, there was nothing to show what had stopped it. This went on all day, and in the evening we halted at Aunerit ('the melted place', in the interior of Cockburn Land). Next morning a ptarmigan flew over our tent. I threw a walrus tusk at it, but missed. Then I threw an axe, and again missed. And it seemed as if this also was to show that other strange things were to happen that day. We started off, and the snow was so deep that we had to help pull the sledge ourselves. Then we heard a noise. We could not make out what it was; sometimes it sounded like a dying animal in pain, and then again like human voices in the distance. As we came nearer, we could hear human words, but could not at first make out the meaning, for the voice seemed to come from a great way off. Words that did not sound like real words, and a voice that was powerless and cracked. We listened, and kept on listening, trying to make out one word from another, and at last we understood what it was that was being said. The voice broke down between the words, but what it was trying to say was this:

"'I am not one who can live any longer among my fellows; for I have eaten my nearest of kin'.

"Now we knew that there should properly be no one else in this part of the country but ourselves, but all the same we could distinctly hear that this was a woman speaking, and we looked at each other, and it was as if we hardly dared speak out loud, and we whispered:

"'An eater of men! What is this we have come upon here!'

"We looked about us, and at last caught sight of a little shelter, built of snow with a piece of a skin rug. It lay half hidden in a drift, and was hardly to be noticed in the snow all round, which was why we had not made it out before. And now that we could see where it was the voice came from, it sounded more distinctly, but still went on in the same broken fashion. We went slowly up to the spot, and when we looked in, there lay a human skull with the flesh gnawed from the bones. Yes, we came to that shelter, and looking in, we saw a human being squatting down inside, a poor woman, her face turned piteously towards us. Her eyes were all bloodshot, from weeping, so greatly had she suffered.

"'Kivkaq,' she said (literally, 'you my gnawed bone,' which was her pet name for Padloq, whom she knew well) 'Kivkaq, I have eaten my elder brother and my children.' 'My elder brother' was her pet name for her husband. Padloq and I looked at each other, and could not understand that she was still alive and breathing. There was nothing of her but bones and dry skin, there seemed indeed hardly to be a drop of blood in all her body, and she had not even much clothing left, having eaten a great deal of that, both the sleeves and all the lower part of her outer furs. Padloq bent down quite close, to hear better, and Ataguvtâluk — for we knew her now, and could see who it was — said once more:

"'Kivkaq, I have eaten your fellow-singer from the feasting, him with whom you used to sing when we were gathered in the great house at a feast.'

"My husband was so moved at the sight of this living skeleton, which had once been a young woman, that it was long before he knew what to answer. At last he said:

"'You had the will to live, therefore you live.'

"We now put up our tent close by, and cut away a piece of the fore curtain to make a little tent for her. She could not come into the tent with us, for she was unclean, having touched dead bodies. When we went to move her, she tried to get up, but fell back in the snow. Then we tried to feed her with a little meat, but after she had swallowed a couple of mouthfuls, she fell to trembling all over, and could eat no more. Then we gave her a little hot soup, and when she was a little quieter, we looked round the shelter and found the skull of her husband and those of her children; but the brains were gone. We found the gnawed bones, too. The only part she had not been able to eat was the entrails. We gave up our journey then, and decided to drive back with her to Iglulik as soon as she felt a little stronger. And when she was once more able to speak, she told us how it had all come about. They had gone up country hunting caribou, but had not been able to find any; they then tried fishing in the lakes but there were no fish. Her husband wandered all about in search of food, but always without success, and they grew weaker and weaker. Then they decided to turn back towards Iglulik, but were overtaken by heavy snowfalls. The snow kept on, it grew deeper and deeper, and they themselves were growing weaker and weaker every day; they lay in their snow hut and could get nothing to eat. Then, after the snow had fallen steadily for some time there came fierce blizzards, and at last her husband was so exhausted that he could not stand. They kept themselves alive for some time by eating the dogs, but these also were wasted away and there was little strength in them as food; it simply kept them alive, so that they could not even die. At last the husband and all the children were frozen to death; having no food, they could not endure the cold. Ataguvtâluk had been the strongest of them all, though she had no more to eat than the others; as long as the children were alive, they had most. She had tried at first to start off by herself and get through to Iglulik, for she knew the way, but the snow came up to her waist, and she had no strength, she could not go on. She was too weak even to build a snow hut for herself, and the end of it was she turned back in her tracks and lay down beside her dead husband and the dead children; here at least there was shelter from the wind in the snow hut and there were still a few skins she could use for covering. She ate these skins to begin with. But at last there was no more left, and she was only waiting for the death to come and release her. She seemed to grow more and more dull and careless of what happened; but one morning, waking up to sunshine and a fine clear sky, she realised that the worst of the winter was over now, and it could not be long till the spring. Her snow hut was right on the road to Tununeq, the very road that all would take when going from Iglulik to trade there. The sun was so warm that for the first time she felt thawed a little, but the snow all about her was as deep and impassable as ever. Then suddenly it seemed as if the warm spring air about her had given her a great desire to go on living, and thus it was that she fell to eating of the dead bodies that lay beside her. It was painful, it was much worse than dying, and at first she threw up all she ate, but she kept on, once she had begun. It could not hurt the dead, she knew, for their souls were long since in the land of the dead. Thus she thought, and thus it came about that she became an inukto·majɔq, an eater of human kind.

"All this she told us, weeping; and Padloq and I realising that after all these sufferings she deserved to live and drove her in to Iglulik, where she had a brother living. Here she soon recovered her strength, but it was long before she could bear to be among her fellows. It is many years now since all this happened, and she is married now, to one of the most skilful walrus hunters at Iglulik, named Iktukshârjua, who had one wife already; she is his favourite wife and has had several more children.

"That is the most dreadful thing in all my life, and whenever I tell the story, I feel I can tell no more."

— With these words she set about arranging a sleeping place for Nasaitsordluarssuk and myself on the bench, and for a long time did not speak. Quietly she prepared a little meal for herself, after having entertained us so lavishly, and always taking great care that none of her food came in contact with any we had left; for that might have been dangerous to the adopted child that she was vainly endeavouring to keep alive. She then crawled up on to the bench behind her lamp and soon fell asleep.

Takornâq was the first of all the Hudson Bay Eskimos whose confidence I gained. In her narrative that first evening we were together she gave me, as it were, in a single sum, the life I had now to investigate in detail. Early next morning we set off again, but not before extracting a promise from Takornâq to come and stay with us for a while as soon as her husband returned.

She kept her word. Padloq proved to be just the right sort of husband for her. He was a quiet and persevering hunter, and a good traveller, and we afterwards arranged for them to assist us in the work of the expedition; they took up their quarters on Danish Island and stayed with us throughout one winter. My intercourse with them was of great importance to my work, for Padloq was a shaman, and from him and Takornâq together I obtained much valuable information.

Padloq and I often made excursions together, and on one of our many journeys an event occurred which showed him in such a characteristic light that I include the story here. It happened during a walrus hunt on the edge of the ice, out in Frozen Strait.

Padloq might fairly be said to be of a humble, religious turn of mind, and it was his firm belief that all the little happenings of everyday life, good or bad, were the outcome of activity on the part of mysterious powers. Human beings were powerless in the grasp of a mighty fate, and only by the most ingenious system of taboo, with propitiatory rites and sacrifices, could the balance of life be maintained. Owing to the ignorance or imprudence of men and women, life was full of contrary happenings, and the intervention of the angákut was therefore a necessity. Padloq himself was always most concerned about the adopted child, Qahîtsoq, on which he and Takornâq alike

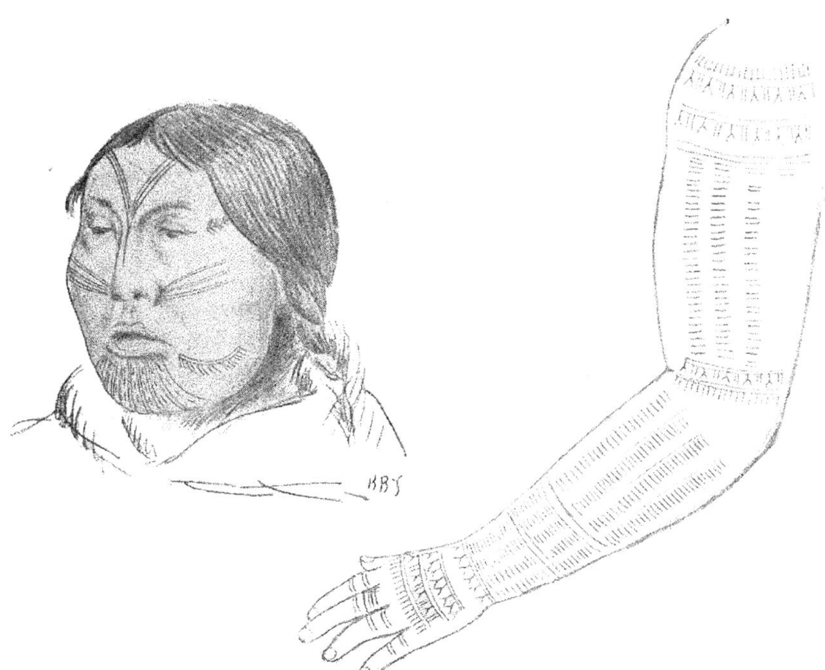

Above: The shaman Unaleq, called Inernerunasuaq. — Below: Unaleq's wife, Tûglik and her arm, showing her tattooing. Drawings by Kaj Birket-Smith.

The spirit-drawer Anarqâq.

Usugtâq, the animal-drawer.

lavished all their affection. The poor, emaciated creature, a boy, seemed hardly capable of life, and despite all the efforts of Takornâq to feed him and fatten him, with constant meals of seal-meat soup and blubber from her own mouth, he was always whining, even in sleep. Padloq himself once said of the poor little weakling — which after all lacked nothing but its own mother's milk — that "he was as a guest among the living". By way of linking him more strongly to life, they had him betrothed to a fine healthy little girl, who was, like himself, less than a year old. But all efforts were unavailing, the boy died ere the winter was out. During his lifetime, however, the little fellow had furnished material for many conversations, and in the course of these talks with Padloq I could not but think, many a time, how unjust it is to accuse primitive peoples of being only concerned with their food and how to get it with least trouble. True, they say themselves that a man's only business is to procure food and clothing, and while fulfilling his duties in this respect he finds, in his hunting and adventures, the most wonderful experiences of his life. Nevertheless, men may be to the highest degree interested in spiritual things; and I am thinking here not only of their songs and poems, their festivals when strangers come to their place, but also of the manner in which they regard religious questions, wherein they evince great adaptability and versatility. This it is which always gives their accounts that delightful originality which is the peculiar property of those whose theories are based on experience of life itself. Their naturalness makes of them philosophers and poets unawares, and their simple and primitive orthodoxy gives to their presentment of a subject the childlike charm which makes even the mystic element seem credible.

One evening, Padloq, who was an enthusiastic angákoq, had been particularly occupied in studying the fate of the child. We were lying on the bench, enjoying our evening rest, but Padloq stood upright, with closed eyes, over by the window of the hut. He stood like that for hours, chanting a magic song with many incomprehensible words. But the constant repetition, and the timid earnestness of his utterance, made the song as it were an expression of the frailty of human life and man's helplessness in face of its mystery. Then suddenly, after hours of this searching in the depths of the spirit, he seemed to have found what he sought; for he clapped his hands together and blew upon them, washing them, as it were, in fresh human breath, and cried out:

"Here it is! Here it is!"

We gave the customary response:

"Thanks, thanks! You have it."

Padloq now came over to us and explained that Qahîtsoq had been out in a boat the previous summer, the sail of which had belonged to a man now dead. A breeze from the land of the dead had touched the child, and now came the sickness. Yes, this was the cause of the sickness: Qahîtsoq had touched something which had been in contact with death, and the child was yearning now away from its living kind to the land of the dead.

We settled down then all together on the bench, waiting for the meal that was cooking. It was midwinter, the days were short, and the evenings long. A blubber lamp was used for the cooking, the pot being hung over it by a thong from a harpoon stuck into the wall. Suddenly the pot gave a jump, and rocked to and fro, as if someone had knocked it. The heat had melted the snow at the spot where the harpoon was fixed, the harpoon had slipped down a little, jerking the thong, and making the lumps of meat hop in their soup. Padloq, still under the influence of his trance, leapt up from his place and declared that we must at once shift camp, and move up on to the firm old winter ice; for our hut here was built among some pressure ridges forming a fringe between the old ice and the open sea. We had taken up this position in order better to observe the movements of the walrus, but Padloq now asserted that we were too near the open sea, and were filling the feeding grounds of the walrus with our own undesirable emanations. They did not like the smell of us. And the sea spirit Takánakapsâluk was annoyed, and had just shown her resentment by making our meat come alive in the pot. This is said to be a sign often given to people out near the fringe of the ice, and we were obliged to accept it. But the rest of us were not at all inclined to turn out just at that moment, all in the dark, and shift camp. It would be several hours before we got into new quarters, and hours again before we got anything to eat. Therefore, despite Padloq's protest, we stayed where we were, and when we had eaten our fill, crept into our sleeping bags. None of us dreamed how nearly Padloq had been right until next morning, when to our horror we found a crack right across the floor. It was only a narrow one, but wide enough for the salt water to come gurgling up through it now and again. The roof of the hut was all awry over by the entrance, and on knocking out a block of snow, we saw the black waters of the open sea right in front of us. The young ice on which the snow hut was built had broken away, but instead of being carried out to sea, it had drifted in at the last moment among some high pressure ridges kept in place by a small island.

After that I was obliged to promise Padloq that I would in future have more respect for his predictions as a shaman, should we again be out hunting on the ice-edge; for, as Padloq put it, the spirits can, at times, speak through some poor ignorant fellow otherwise of no account, and that to such purpose that even those far wiser may be well advised to heed what is said.

Inernerunashuaq the shaman and his wife Tûglik.

One bitterly cold day in March, during our first winter, a sledge suddenly appeared from behind some drifts at the back of the house, and pulled up a moment later at the door. The driver was an old shaman named Inernerunashuaq, whom I had met previously, at Takornâq's village; he had come down to us now with his whole family, in the hope of living for some indefinite period in abundance on our supplies of meat. He was beyond all comparison the most unskilful hunter of his tribe, and all that winter he had only managed to kill one caribou. He had thus no meat for food, and no skins to clothe his wife and children. The entire band were also in such a pitiably ragged state that it was a marvel they could travel at all in the cold wind. As it was they looked almost perishing. Almost all the natives we had encountered up to now had been more or less well off, or at least adequately clad, and in these regions that is the main thing, or nearly so. It was painful to us all, therefore, to see this naked poverty in the midst of winter. I had already heard, up at one of the villages, where everybody knows all about everybody else, that Inernerunashuaq had lived for the past month, with his wife, his children and his dogs, on the meat of a single bearded seal given him by the ever generous Padloq.

While sympathising heartily with their plight, however, I was obliged to welcome them with some reserve. We had already learned by experience that undue hospitality might bring down upon us visitors of the poor relation type whom we could not afford to keep, but found it almost impossible to get rid of. In several cases we had been forced to ask them, in so many words, to leave, as we were obliged to husband our stores for the many journeys to be made. And the family which now appeared on the scene was; I knew, one of the worst of its kind.

As soon as the miserable equipage had halted, and the wretched dogs sought shelter close to the house, Inernerunashuaq came running up to me, uttering a jumble of incoherent sounds that no one could be expected to understand. I fancied for a moment he must have lost his senses. And my companions were equally mystified, when Tûglik came up and explained that one of her husband's principal helping spirits was the spirit of a white man, and that this had now, on our arrival at the white men's dwelling, entered into him, and was talking white man's talk in our honour. The old shaman himself played his part with force and conviction, and when I, entering into the game, addressed him in Danish, he showed not the slightest confusion, but answered again in his own made-up gibberish, as if he understood every word I said. All this made a certain impression on some Eskimos of Inernerunashuaq's own tribe who were present; they actually believed that their shaman was speaking a language which I understood. I was anxious to make the man's acquaintance, and was therefore obliged to back him up. Accordingly, I refrained from any exposure of his trickery, but when I felt he had exerted himself sufficiently, broke in upon his inspired nonsense and informed him that we were unfortunately on the point of setting out on a journey ourselves, and would not be able to entertain visitors for any length of time; they could, however, stay a few days if they liked, provided he would undertake to answer various questions I wished to ask him. The poor fellow, doubtless accustomed to be received with far less consideration elsewhere, was sufficiently delighted at this. I told him that I knew he was a great shaman, and wished to learn something of his art. This further increased his satisfaction, and he went off very cheerfully to set about building a snow hut close to our house. As soon as this was done, and the family with their few miserable belongings had moved in, I invited the whole party to a feed of frozen caribou meat and boiled walrus. It was really a delight to give these hungry people food, though they devoured it with a greediness that seemed almost inhuman. It looked as if their stomachs could never be filled; and I called to mind an old Greenland proverb which runs: "A dog is always ready to eat; for it never eats so much but that it can begin again; only a hungry human being eats beyond reason."

Next day we started work. I got Inernerunashuaq into the little apartment I used as a study, and questioned him as to all he might know regarding the traditions of his people. Unfortunately, I soon found that his brain was too confused for me to take his statements as generally valid. Nor was he altogether reliable in himself; if he found any difficulty about the question, he was not afraid to invent an answer on the spur of the moment, and though his explanation of the matter might be interesting enough, it was not what I wanted.

I take this opportunity of drawing attention to a point of importance in connection with this work. I have often been asked how I manage to check the accuracy of statements made in the course of such conversations. Many people are in opinion that artful shamans would very often try to deceive me with false information. This might perhaps happen, but I would point out that if one has but the right sort of relations with the Eskimos, and understanding of their ways, with a thorough knowledge beforehand of their religious ideas and how their imagination expresses itself therein, it will never be difficult to distinguish between information derived from their ancient traditions and the unscrupulous invention or embroiderings of irresponsible individuals. I have never questioned a native on serious matters, things of life and death, unless I knew him well enough to judge as to the value of what he might tell me. Inernerunashuaq was not a liar or a humbug, but a man of weak intellectual capacity, and in the course of our talks, he felt he was called upon to maintain his dignity as a shaman; he was, indeed, really afraid that a confession of ignorance might offend the spirits on whom his whole art depended. It was therefore he so often tried to make do with nonsensical meanderings, to such an extent that his wife, who, though not an angákoq, was an intelligent woman with plenty of sound common sense, had to intervene with an explanation of her own. And though Tûglik herself could not but be aware that her husband was by no means brilliant, she had nevertheless the greatest respect for his magic powers.

Inernerunashuaq, or, as he requested us to call him, Unaleq, the Cree Indian, had immigrated from the west some twenty years before, from the neighbourhood of Pelly Bay, where the nearest of the Netsilik Eskimos are established. I was anxious to learn something as to the views of these people, but after we had spent a whole day trying to solve the mystery of how the first human beings appeared on earth, it was as usual Tûglik who related the following, which she had heard from her great-grandmother:

"There was once a world before this one, and in that world lived human beings who did not belong to our tribe. The earth at that time rested on pillars, but one day the pillars gave way, and all things disappeared into nothing, and the world was emptiness. Then there grew up out of the earth two men; they were born and were grown up all at once, and they wished to beget children. By means of a magic song, one of them was changed into a woman, and they had children. These were our earliest forefathers, and from their offspring all the lands were peopled."

— — —

There was no denying the fact that Unaleq was a foolish and ridiculous old fellow, but since he nevertheless enjoyed a considerable reputation as a shaman, I was interested in him as a phenomenon. For the Eskimos hold that spirits will often show a deliberate preference for one otherwise incapable, and express themselves through such a medium. Unaleq was not brilliant, and he was a wretched hunter, who, unless helped out by others, let his family starve and go about in rags. All the same an atmosphere of mystery surrounded him. People who were really in trouble often applied to him, possibly considering that a man who knew so little about the everyday things of life might perhaps for that very reason have special knowledge of matters hidden and mysterious to his fellows.

Unaleq had ten helping spirits, and when I asked him for their names, he was greatly upset at such a want of respect. I pressed him nevertheless to tell me; but he insisted then on our shutting ourselves up in my little study, when he drew pictures of these helping spirits for me, and whispered their names in my ear. They were for the most part deceased Eskimos and Indians that he had met on solitary hunting expeditions up in the hills, he could not say how it had come about. The mightiest and most influential of them all was Nanoq Tulorialik ("The Bear with the fangs"). This was a giant in the shape of a bear, who came as often as he called. There were also the following deceased members of the Netsilik tribe; Angusingarna and Alu, both men, Arnagnagluk and Kavliliúkâq, both women. Then there were two nameless Indians of the Chipewyan tribe, two mysterious mountain spirits of those which are called Norjutilik, the name being derived from a peculiar tuft at the end of a stiff thong extending up above their heads from the point of the hood. Finally, there was a woman of the Tuneq tribe, or the people that inhabited the country before the present Eskimos made their way to the coasts; this woman's name was Kamingmalik.

Otherwise, he could tell me nothing more definite about these spirits. He merely said that their power lay in their own unfathomable mysteriousness. They had appeared to him in the first instance without his asking, he had touched them, and they had thereby become his property or his servants once and for all, coming to help him whenever he called. We agreed that Unaleq should give a demonstration of his art the same evening. I was just then making preparations for a sledge journey down to the Inland Eskimos west of Chesterfield, and the purpose of his seance, or to'nrinEq, as he himself called it, was to ensure a free passage for our party, with plenty of game and no misfortunes on the road. He would ask the advice of the Giant Bear, Tulorialik; when that particuliar spirit deigned to occupy his body, he, Unaleq, could transform himself into a bear or a walrus at will, and was able to render great service to his fellow men by virtue of the powers thus acquired. In payment for the seance, he was to have one of the biggest and handsomest of our snow knives; for a shaman would insult his helping spirits if he were to invoke them without adequate remuneration from the persons on whose behalf they were asked to intervene. And Unaleq had never possessed such a snow knife as we had.

In the evening, after dark, he came in, followed by his whole family, ready to fulfil his promise. The spirits, however, were not called upon until after he, assisted by his wife and children, had devoured a mass of walrus meat sufficient, in his judgement, to act as ballast in his inner man. Not until then did he declare himself ready to begin. There were several Eskimo visitors present, and all were eager to see what the evening would bring forth. We had hoped that Unaleq could have his trance in the mess room, where all could be present and witness his transformation to Tulorialik, but the old man declared very firmly that the apartment in question, being used by all, was too unclean for his spirits to visit. The invocation must take place in my little study, for he took it for granted that I, when I shut myself up there alone, would be occupied with lofty thoughts, like himself. He then required all the lamps to be put out, and crawled in under my writing table. His wife carefully hung skins all round the table, so that her husband was now hidden from all profane glances. All was in darkness, we could only wait for what was to come. For a long time not a sound was heard, but the waiting only increased our anticipations. At last we heard a scraping of heavy claws and a deep growling. "Here it comes" whispered Tûglik, and all held their breath. But nothing happened, except the same scraping and growling, mingled with deep, frightened groans; then came a fierce growl, followed by a wild shriek, and at the same moment, Tûglik dashed forward to the table and began talking to the spirits. She spoke in their own particular spirit language, which I did not understand at the time, but will give later on. The spirits spoke now in deep chest notes, now in a high treble. We could hear, in between the words, sounds like those of trickling water, the rushing of wind, a stormy sea, the snuffling of walrus, the growling of bear. These however, were not produced with any superlative art, for we could distinguish all through the peculiar lisp of the old shaman acting ventriloquist. This sitting lasted about an hour, and when all was quiet once more, Tûglik informed us that her husband, in the shape of the fabulous bear, had been out exploring the route we were to follow on our long journey. All obstacles had been swept aside, accident, sickness and death were rendered powerless, and we should all return in safety to our house the following summer. All this had been communicated in the special language of the spirits, which Tûglik translated for us, and at last, when this was done, Unaleq crawled out from under the table, exhausted by the heat.

Despite the extreme naïveté of the whole proceeding, this spirit seance was to me of great interest. For it was one of the first at which I was present, and I could not but feel astounded at the manner in which it impressed the Eskimos themselves. They were altogether fascinated, as if they really felt a breath of some supernatural power in the pitiful acting which any critical observer could see through at once. I saw here how great was the faith of these people in their wizardry, and how even the most mediocre practitioner can gain adherents, because all are ready to believe without question. And, as I was to learn in a moment, the old shaman himself believed in his helping spirit. He was a poor ventriloquist, but no humbug all the same; and this was proved in rather curious wise.

There was a little shed outside where we kept our trade goods, and when the general excitement after the seance had subsided, Unaleq and I went out to get the snow knife I had promised him. It was wonderful weather, perfectly calm and still, for once, without a cloud in the sky, and bright moonlight. The soft light had something of that unreality which always lies in the yellowish gleam of the moon over white, dazzling snow, the very light that spirits of the air would choose to come forth in, according to the Eskimo account. The charm of the winter evening seemed also to have made an impression on Unaleq, and the dogs, when they saw us come out, threw back their heads and uttered a monotonous howl that produced a strange, uncanny effect in the quiet of the night. The Eskimos always believe there are spirits about when the dogs howl in unison.

We stood still for a moment, affected by the beauty that surrounded us. Then suddenly Unaleq asked a question.

"Can you also call up spirits?"

"Just as well as you can" I answered quite sincerely.

"What would happen if you did" he enquired eagerly.

Half thoughtlessly, half on purpose, I answered:

"The roof of my house would fly up to heaven and with it whichever of us two is the poorer shaman."

To my great astonishment, Unaleq leapt aside so suddenly that he fell down into a deep hollow in the snow just behind us, and lay there jerking his limbs about, half senseless, until I helped him up. I laughed, and tried to explain that my answer was only meant in fun, and that I had not the slightest pretensions to any power over spirits. But his own conviction was so strong, his will to believe so thoroughly sincere, that nothing could now efface his first strong impression. Whatever I might say now, Unaleq fully and firmly believed that I was a great shaman. So impressed was he indeed, that when we reentered the house shortly after, he could not refrain from telling the others at once all that had passed. And the funny thing about it was that while all the others thoroughly understood my joke, the shaman himself alone maintained that I must be a great shaman all the same, and that his own power over the helping spirits had really been in serious peril.

I willingly admit that it was not very considerate of me thus to play upon the old man's simplicity; on the other hand, it was my business to study his mind in its natural state, and that was my excuse. And it certainly led me to understand that these Eskimos really believe one shaman can steal another's helping spirits; for all through that winter, whenever Unaleq was unsuccessful in his operations with the spirits, he declared to his fellows that it was my fault; his helping spirits were with me. This was due partly to the fact he had described them to me by his drawings, and had mentioned their names. I was loth to hurt the simple old man to no purpose, and therefore, in the following year, I went to his village and there declared solemnly that I had come to give him back all his helping spirits; I had forbidden them to follow in my footsteps, and they were now his once more, wholly and entirely. This was the second lie I told Unaleq, but I lied this time with a good conscience, for it made him happy, and freed him from the fear which had plagued him, that I should have taken away his power.

Tûglik, who, unaffected by all minor failings, was a blind admirer of her husband's art, now proposed that we should finish up the evening by playing children's games. She was anxious that I should forget all about her husband's passing weakness as soon as possible, and like a wise woman, chose an old dance song. She had long since discovered that when I touched on the question of Unaleq's relations with the spirits, it was always more self-interest than faith. But she knew that I was very fond of songs and stories, which they themselves did not rank so high as gifts of the spirits. So she drew forth a couple of little girls, little bundles of skins with ruddy cheeks, and placed them one opposite the other. Then, as soon as she started the song, which was sung at a breathless rate which left her gasping, the little girls joined in, crouching down and hopping with bent knees in time to the music:

Aja· — ja· — japape!
Aja· — ja· — japape!
  Bring out your hair ornaments!
  We are but girls
  Who will keep together.
Aja· — ja· — japape!
Aja· — ja· — japape!

  Hard times, dearth times
  Plague us every one,

Stomachs are shrunken,
Dishes are empty.
Aja· — ja· — japape!
Aja· — ja· — japape!

Joy bewitches
All about us,
Skin boats rise up
Out of their moorings,
The fastenings go with them,
Earth itself hovers
Loose in the air.
Aja· — ja· — japape!
Aja· — ja· — japape!

Mark you there yonder?
There come the men
Dragging beautiful seals
To our homes.
Aja· — ja· — japape!
Aja· — ja· — japape!

Now is abundance
With us once more,
Days of feasting
To hold us together
Aja· — ja· — japape!
Aja· — ja· — japape!

Know you the smell
Of pots on the boil?
And lumps of blubber
Slapped down by the side bench?
Aja· — ja· — japape!
Hu — hue! Joyfully
Greet we those
Who brought us plenty!

— Unaleq is surely the most credulous man I have ever met. Despite the fact that he himself was one of the poorest and most helpless wastrels in the district, he firmly believed that he had, through the medium of his helping spirits, the power of helping others.

Anarqâq and his spirit drawings.

In the neighbourhood of our winter quarters, sometimes at one place, sometimes at another, there lived that winter a young man named Anarqaq, who resembled Unaleq to some extent in his reliance on the credulity of others. He also was by no means distinguished as a hunter, and had been something of a vagabond all his life. He had come originally all the way from King William Land and Back River, and while there already acquired his first grounding in the art of shamanism. He was a man of highly nervous temperament, easily affected, and his strong point accordingly consisted in his having a multitude of weird visions as soon as he was left alone on hunting expeditions in the interior. His imagination peopled the whole of nature with fantastic and uncanny spirits, which appeared to him as soon as he lay down to sleep, or while still awake and wandering, tired and hungry, in search of caribou. In some fashion he could not explain, they increased his power of penetrating into all secrets, and though his explanations often sounded naîve, or worse, he was nevertheless, in the eyes of his fellows, surrounded by an atmosphere of inexplicable mystery, precisely as with Unaleq; only Anarqâq managed most skilfully to encourage it.

I find myself repeatedly obliged to note the astonishing credulity with which all messages and communications from the spirit world are received among the Eskimos. Though in truth it may doubtless be said that this trait is not peculiar to the Eskimos, but may be observed among all who concern themselves with spirits. I give here a couple of examples from Anarqàq's practice as a medicine man and spiritual adviser.

One day a little boy came into the hut, crying, but unable to say what he was crying for. Such an occurrence is not unusual or remarkable with children, but Anarqâq at once perceived a chance of making an impression. As if driven by a sudden impulse, he dashed out of the hut without a word and raced off over the ice and was lost to sight. It was a dark evening, and very cold, Anarqâq was away for more than half an hour, and when he came back, the sleeves and lining of his fur were torn, and his arms and hands covered with blood. He breathed heavily, in great gasps, as if throughly exhausted, and without a word of explanation, sank down to the floor and lay there, apparently unconscious. All sat speechless, gazing at him with the greatest astonishment and respect, and no one present thought for a moment of doubting his word when he shortly after came to his senses and explained that the child had been attacked by an evil spirit, which he, Anarqâq, had now vanquished after a hard fight. It never occurred to anyone that he could have snatched up a lump of seal's blood out in the passage, where some had been set out to freeze after the day's hunting; nor did it enter anyone's head to suppose that he might have torn his clothes himself. It was taken for granted that he really had fought with an evil spirit and thus saved the child's life. The boy's father was a skilful hunter, and as Anarqâq was poorly clad, in old, worn skins, which had, moreover, suffered damage in the struggle, the grateful parent presented him with a supply of furs for a new outfit.

One day I asked Anarqâq if he would try to draw for me some of his spirit visions. He hesitated at first, for fear of offending the spirits, but when I promised him payment enough to content his helping spirits into the bargain, he agreed, on the condition that I might do as I pleased with the drawings in the white men's country, but undertook not to show them about among his own people. He had of course never before drawn with a pencil on paper, but it must be said that he set about the new method of work with the true humility of an artist. There was no careless scratching or scribbling; he would sit for hours with closed eyes, solely intent upon getting the vision fixed in his mind, and only when this was done would he attempt to put it into form. Sometimes the recollection of the event affected him to such a degree that he trembled all over, and had to give up the attempt. These inspirations gave me a distinct impression that Anarqâq had faith in his own power as a shaman; he might, no doubt, on occasion make use of some trickery in order to convince others of his relations with the spirits, but strange as it may seem, I believe he was always honest and sincere. Even that time when he went off with a piece of seal's blood and smeared himself with it, I am perfectly convinced that while out in the dark and the cold he had worked himself up to such a state of mind that he ended by actually thinking he had fought a battle with spirits who were endeavouring to harm the child. It is just this sort of thing which makes it difficult in many cases for a "civilised brain" to judge the untutored mind fairly. But if we put ourselves in the place of the primitive man, and accept inspirations and visions as something we cannot explain, we shall as a rule be better able to understand how a shaman can commit a deliberate fraud in making use of certain tricks, and yet never cease to believe that he is really honest with his fellows.

All Anarqâq's drawings were uncommonly rich expressions of Eskimo imagination, and need no explanation beyond that which he himself gave me with each one, setting forth in the first place how he encountered the spirits and then the peculiar characteristics of the spirits themselves. I always wrote down these explanatory notes of his on the spot, and the text here given with the drawings is thus a translation of Anarqâq's own words.

Aua and his wife Orulo.

All study of folk-lore is solely and entirely dependent on the sources from which the material is derived; it is necessary to find narrators not only gifted with knowledge and imagination, but thoroughly interested in the work as well. And they must be sufficiently reliable for the listener to take what they say without reserve, and without over-much criticism. Only thus is it possible to get the right colour and atmosphere; to give life to all the alien material in the mind of the reader. At the very beginning of the first winter, I had the good fortune to make the acquaintance of an old couple who possessed in an unusual degree the qualifications already noted as requisite for effective co-operation. They were Aua and his wife Orulo. I will begin by stating briefly how I first met them, and the manner in which they lived.

It was towards the end of February 1922. The country in which we were to spend the winter was still quite new to us, and as we had a great number of dogs that needed plenty of food, we could not follow the example of the local Eskimos and make do with caribou meat. which is very wasteful in use, and does not contain sufficient fat for dogs kept hard at work. We were therefore constantly going off with our Polar Eskimo hunters in search of grounds where we could get walrus. which is the best food for dogs. On one of these hunting expeditions we had come up to the neighbourhood of Cape Elisabeth, north of Lyon Inlet, where, as we had been told, there were walrus to be found out on the young ice beyond the fringe of the old. We had had a long day's journey in the cold, and were now, in the fine starry night. just ready to set about building a snow hut, when suddenly, out of the darkness ahead, there appeared a long sledge with one of the wildest teams I have ever seen. Fifteen white dogs were racing along at full gallop with one of the big Hudson Bay sledges, at least 7 metres long, and six men on it. They sighted us, and came sweeping down right on top of us, and a little man with a big beard, his face covered with ice, leapt down and came running towards me. He stopped, and after shaking hands in white men's fashion, pointed up inland towards a hollow where, he explained, he and his party had their dwelling. His keen eyes rested on me, full of life and spirits, and he greeted me with a ringing: qujäŋnamik "Thanks. thanks to the guests who have come."

This was Aua the shaman.

Noticing that my dogs were tired after their long day's run, he invited me to join him on his sledge, and quietly, but with an air of authority, told off one of the young men to drive my team. Aua's dogs set up a howl of hunger and homesickness, and we were soon racing away towards land. We drove across a broad bay and made the shore close to a small watercourse; then, after a brief but breakneck run arrived on the shore of a great lake, where the gut windows of the snow hut shed a warm, reddish yellow glow towards us.

The women received us cordially, and Aua's wife Orulo at once led me into their house. This was the first time I had seen one of these large groups of dwellings, where the huts are built together so as to form one connected whole, and here for the first time I saw the true snow architecture of the Hudson Bay natives. Five domed huts rose up in bold curves, with communicating passages in one long line, and numerous outbuildings or store sheds set a little apart from the rest. Each section is linked up by a system of passages with the rest, so that one can go visiting without having to step out into the cold. Sixteen persons occupied the five main buildings. Orulo goes from one family seat to another, and tells me who are the occupants. They have been living here for some time now, and the heat from the blubber lamps has melted the inner layer of snow to a hard crust of ice. Icicles hang down by the entrances, gleaming in the soft light from the lamps. All the sitting places look comfortable and inviting, well furnished as they are with handsome soft caribou skins from the last autumn's hunting. We pass through winding labyrinths, all lit by small, faintly burning lamps, going from one apartment to another and greeting those within; one large and smiling family. There was Aua's eldest son Nataq ("the bottom") and his young wife Kigutíkârjuk ("The one with the small teeth"), and the youngest son Ujarak ("the stone"), living with his fifteen-year-old sweetheart, Eqatdlijôq (named after the father of salmon). Then there was Aua's aged sister Natseq ("the fjord seal"), with her son and daughter-in-law and their children, and finally, out in the farthest end of the passage lived Kuhlo ("the thumb") with his wife and their newborn child.

This was my first visit to a large Eskimo family, and I was greatly interested in the patriarchal conditions apparently prevailing.

Aua was the undisputed master of the establishment, everyone and everything being at his command, and the general tone of the house was set by the cordial, jesting manner in which he and his wife addressed each other and ordered the others about.

We had come to hunt walrus, and when this was made known, there was general rejoicing. The party had already been thinking of shifting from their autumn quarters and giving up land meat in favour of sea food; they now agreed to go off with us and build huts at Cape Elisabeth. They had spent the summer hunting inland, and had plenty of good meat depots in the neighbourhood. We spent one day in making preparations and bringing in a quantity of caribou meat from the nearest depots. When at last the actual move was to take place, all were early afoot. Pots and dishes and all manner of utensils were tumbled out through the passages, all the skins in use within doors were dragged out into the open through holes cut in the walls, as the rules of taboo forbid the transport of caribou skins through the house entrance. The sledges were piled with goods to the height of a man, and just as we were about to start, I had an opportunity of seeing how a new-born infant enters upon its first sledge journey. A hole was cut in the wall from within at the back of Kublo's house, and his wife crawled out through it with her little daughter in her arms. Then she stood in front of the snow hut, waiting, and Aua, who as the angákoq had to see that all needful rites were properly observed, went up to the child, bared its head, and with his lips close to its face recited a magic prayer as follows:

"I arise from rest with movements swift
As the beat of a raven's wings
I arise
To meet the day
Wa — wa.
My face is turned from the dark of night
To gaze at the dawn of day,
Now whitening in the sky."

— This was the child's first journey, and the little girl, whose name was Kâgjagjuk (named after Aua himself), had to be introduced to life by means of the magic formula here given. Men's and women's names are here used indiscriminately. We came down without mishap to Cape Elisabeth, and I lived here for some considerable time in the same hut with Aua and his wife. The days were still short, and in order to make the most of them at our hunting on the ice-edge, we drove out and back in the dark. We caught some walrus, and distributed the meat throughout the community in accordance with the custom of sharing which prevails in these parts. The evenings were spent in lively conversation within doors, and I was fortunate enough here to collect a great deal of interesting material regarding the life of the people in its spritual aspect. All that concerns Aua himself belongs more properly to the section on the angákut, and I will therefore here confine myself to what Orulo told me about her own life, which furnishes, moreover, an excellent illustration of the manner in which the natives here look upon existence and its phenomena.

Aua's wife was one of those women who give themselves up entirely to the care of their house and those about them. She was never idle for a moment during the day, and the amount of work she managed to get through was astonishing. She liked needlework best, but there was certainly no lack of that, in the repairing of all the garments worn and torn in the daily hunting expeditions. And there were many other duties to attend to. She had to fetch in snow for melting, and see that the bucket was always full. Meat had to be thawed on the side bench, where a portion must always be in readiness, dog food must be cut up and kept ready for the teams on their return, there was blubber to be frozen and beaten to make the oil run of itself ready for the lamp, and the lamp in turn had to be carefully tended so that it did not smoke. If the heat in the hut rose beyond a certain limit. the snow on the inside of the roof would melt and drip; this had to be stopped by the application of fresh lumps of snow from without, plastered on to the weakening spots. Should an actual hole be thawed in roof or walls, she had to go outside herself and trim the opening, filling it up then with fresh blocks of snow. Raw sealskins had to be scraped free of blubber and stretched out to dry over the lamp, slabs of hide for sole leather, hard as wood, had to be chewed till soft. All these household duties however, were cheerfully taken as part of her busy day, to the accompaniment of scraps of song; and one could always be sure of hearing the music of cooking pots joined to Orulo's contented humming when the hunters were expected home.

Thus the hours passed, and withall she found time to glance in now and again at the other houses and help out any little scarcity, a portion of meat here, a lump of blubber there, wherever any might be running short. I had often asked her to tell me something about her life and such events as had made any impression on her mind, but she always turned it off with a joke; there was nothing to tell. I would not leave her in peace, however; for this seemed to me an amusing fashion in which to get a glimpse of Eskimo life. A last one day when we were all alone in the house, and the others out hunting, she began to talk. She was sitting in her usual workplace behind the lamp, with her bare legs crossed, sewing at a pair of waterproof boots, when suddenly she herself interrupted me in my work, breaking out without the least introduction into a flow of old recollections:

"I am called Orulo ("the difficult one"), but my name is really Aqigiarjuk ("the little ptarmigan"). I was born at the mouth of Admiralty Inlet. While I was still a little child carried on my mother's back, my parents left Baffin Land and settled at Iglulik.

"The first thing I can remember is that my mother lived quite alone in a little snow hut. I could not understand why my father should live in another house, but then I was told that it was because my mother had just had a child and was therefore unclean and must

Aua and his wife Orulo.

The story-teller Inugpasugsjuk.

Orulo.

not be near the animals killed for some time to come. But I was allowed to visit her when I liked; only I could never find the entrance to that hut. I was so little that I could not see over the block of snow the others stepped across as they went in, so I had to stand there calling out 'Mother, Mother, I want to come in!' until someone came and lifted me over into the passage. And then when I was inside, the snow bench where she sat looked so high, so high, I could not get up there myself but had to be lifted. I was no bigger than that when I first began to remember things.

"The next thing I remember is from Piling, a big hunting ground in Baffin Land. I remember gnawing meat from the leg of a bird, a huge big thighbone, and I was told it was a goose. Up till then I knew nothing bigger than ptarmigan, and thought it must be a terribly big bird.

"Then all my memories disappear, until one day as it were, I wake up again, and then we were living at a place called The Mountain. My father was ill, all the others in the place had gone off hunting inland, and I was left alone. Father had pains in his chest and lungs, and grew worse and worse. We were quite alone, my mother, my two little brothers and I, and mother was very unhappy.

"One day I came running into the tent and called out: 'Here are white men coming!' I had seen what I thought must be white men; but when my father heard it, he gave a deep sigh, and said, 'Alas I thought I might yet live and breathe a little while; but now I know that I shall never go out hunting any more'.

"The men I had seen were i^{j}Erqät, or mountain spirits; no white men ever came to our country in those days, and my father took it as a warning that his death was near.

"Quite without thinking, I made no secret of what I had seen. But my little brother Sequvsu kept it secret, and died of it shortly after. One must never keep the matter secret when one has seen spirits.

"My father grew worse and worse, and when we realised that he had not long to live, we set off and carried him on a sledge to a neighbouring settlement, where there lived a man named Qupanuaq ("young snow bunting") with his wife Qiqertaunak ("great island"). Father died there. I remember he was tied up in a skin and dragged away from the village, and left lying out in the open with his face turned towards the west. My mother told me that was because he was an old man; and such must always be set to face the quarter whence the dark of night comes; children to face the morning, and young people towards the spot where the sun is seen at noon. That was the first time I learned that people were afraid of the dead, and had special customs on that account. But I was not afraid of father, who had always been kind to me. And I thought it was hard that he should lie all uncovered out in the open like that; but mother explained that I must thenceforward never think of my father in the body; his soul was already in the land of the dead, and he would feel no more pain there.

"After my father's death we went to live with an old man who took mother to be one of his wives. A little after that my brother Sequvsu fell ill; his liver swelled up and he died. I was told it was because he had seen i'erqät just before my father's death, the same ones I had seen. But he had kept the vision secret, and if you do that you die.

"In the autum, when the first snow had fallen, Qupanuaq decided to go up country with his wife Qiqertaunak and their son Tôrngraq ("the helping spirit"); my brother Qajakutjuk ("the little kayak") was to go with them. I remember my mother was very distressed about it, for she did not think the old man, armed as he was only with bow and arrows, would ever get any game. But she was not able herself to keep us, and had to agree to my brother's going with them.

"Then a little while after, a strange thing happened. Mother had cooked some ribs of walrus, and was sitting eating, when the bone she held suddenly began to make a noise. She was so frightened, she stopped eating at once, and threw down the bone. I remember her face went quite white; and she burst out: 'Something has happened to my son!' And so indeed it was; soon after, Qupanuaq returned late one night, and before entering the house, he went round outside to the window and called out 'Dear Little Thing. It is my fault that you no longer have a soin!'. 'Little Thing' was a pet name Qupanuaq used for mother. And then he came in and told us how it had come about. They had killed nothing, and had for several days been obliged to live on caribou dung; they were sadly worn out when at last they came to a place where he had stored away the carcase of a caribou he had killed some time before; but now they could not find the cache. They divided into two parties, his wife going one way and Qupanuaq with the two boys another. They searched and searched all about, but could not find the spot. The first snow had fallen, it was autumn, with a cold wind and driving snow, and they were poorly clad; so they lay down behind a shelter of stones to rest; all were much exhausted. The day was short, and the night very long, and they had to wait for daylight before they could begin searching again. Meantime, Qiqertaunak had found the cache, but she did not know where to look for the rest of the party, and being anxious about them, she ate but little herself, and gave the child she was carrying a small piece of meat to suck. She had made a stone shelter like the others, and lay half dozing when suddenly she awoke, having dreamed of my brother. She dreamed that he stood there quite plainly before her, pale and shivering with cold, and spoke to her and said: 'You will never see me again. It is because the earth-lice are angry at our having eaten their sinews and their dung before a year had passed since my father's death'.

"I remember this quite distinctly, because it was the first time I realised that there were certain things one must not do after anyone had died. The caribou are called 'earth-lice' in shaman language.

"So lifelike was the dream that Qiqertaunak could not sleep any more that night. My brother Qajakutjuk was her favourite, and she used to say charms over him to make him strong.

"Next morning, when it was light, and Qupanuaq was ready to start, my brother was so weak that he could not stand, and the others were too exhaused to carry him. So they covered him with a thin, worn skin and left him. Later on they found the meat, but they did not go back to Qajakutjuk. He was frozen to death.

"My stepfather had an old mother named Ísangiaq ("thaw"); she was blind, and I remember I was greatly afraid of her because I had heard that she had once, in a time of famine, eaten human flesh. A shaman had worked magic over her to restore her sight, and she had indeed begun to make out a little, but then she ate some blubber, and that is a thing one must not do when undergoing any magic cure, and so she had become quite blind again, and no one could do anything for her now.

"Next spring we left there and went to Admiralty Inlet. We reached there just at the time when folk were laying up their sledges and belongings before going up country to hunt caribou. There was a man named Kipumên ('the crooked one'); his wife Kunualuk had given birth to a stillborn child a little while before, and was not allowed to go with the hunting party. So my mother went instead, and I went with her. We stayed inland all that summer. The men were successful in their hunting, and we helped them to drag the meat and store it in depots or cut off thin slices and laid them on stones to dry. It was a pleasant time; we lived in abundance, with all manner of dainties besides, and the day passed as in play. Then one day I remember we were startled to hear a woman from one of the tents calling out: 'Here, come and look, quick, come and see'. We all ran to the spot, and there we saw a spider letting itself down to the ground. We could not make out where it came from; it looked as if it were letting itself down from the sky. We all saw it, and there was silence among the tents. For when a spider comes down from the sky it means someone is going to die. And true it was; when people came up from the coast, we learned that four men had perished in their kayaks. And among them was my stepfather, and thus we were left alone and homeless once again.

"But it was not long before my mother was married again, this time with a young man, much younger than she was. They lived together until he took another wife, a young one about his own age; then my mother was cast off, and we were alone again. Then my mother was married to a man named Augpila ("the red one") and we had someone to look after us once more. This Augpila wanted to go down to Ponds Inlet to look for white men. He had heard that whalers often came there in the summer. So he went off with my mother, and I was left alone in the care of Amarualik ("the wolf") and his wife Tutuk ("dirt"). But I did not stay with them long, for Amarualik thought he had too many mouths to feed, so I went to live with Kanajoq ("the sea-scorpion"). I was there when Uvitâra ("my new husband") — that is my pet name for Aua — came and fetched me, and that is the end of all my adventures. For one who lives happily has no adventures, and in truth I have lived happily and had seven children".

— — —

Orulo was silent, and sat deep in thought, but I was anxious to learn more, and broke in with a question:

"What is the bitterest memory of all you can remember?"

Without a moment's hesitation she answered:

"The bitterest I have ever known was a time of famine shortly after my eldest son was born. And to make matters worse, all our stores of meat from the previous hunting had been destroyed by wolverines. During the two coldest months of the winter, Uvitâra hardly slept indoors a single night, but was out all the time hunting seal, and made do with a snatch of sleep now and then in the little snow shelters he built by the blow holes. We nearly starved to death, for in all that time he got only two seals. To see him go out cold and hungry day after day to his hunting, in all manner of cruel weather, to see him grow thinner and weaker all the time — oh, it was terrible. But then at last he got a walrus, and we were saved."

"And the happiest thing you can remember?" I asked again.

At these words the old woman's kindly face lit up with a broad smile, and dropping her needlework, she edged up a little closer and began:

"It was the first time I came back to Baffin Land after I was married. I had always been a poor fatherless creature, passed from hand to hand; but now I was welcomed with great festivity by all in the village. My husband had come to challenge one of the others to a song contest, and there were many feasts on that occasion, feasts such I had only heard about, but never taken part in myself."

— — —

Orulo had been thoroughly in earnest in telling me the story of her life, and I had noticed, as she worked herself up, how the memories came crowding in upon her and took possession of her completely. When at last she had finished her story, she burst out crying, as if overwhelmed by some great sorrow. I asked what was the cause of her emotion, and she answered:

"I have today been a child once more. While I was telling you all about my life, I lived it over again, and saw and felt everything in the same way as when it really happened. There are so many things we do not think of until the memoires are upon us. And now you have learned the life of an old woman from the very beginning to this day. And I could not help crying for joy to think I had been so happy ..."

II.

Religion and Views of Life.

"We do not believe, we fear".

The sketches of Eskimo life given in the foregoing show that these people, like so many other children of Nature, accept all pleasant happenings with great and spontaneous rejoicing, while evil times are endured with a surprising and often sublime resignation. But in their autobiographies, the religious ideas expressed are so hesitating and uncertain that it seems at first as if all were confusion and that the contradictions continually met with must almost preclude the finding of any sense in the scheme as a whole. One is here too often apt to forget that one is dealing with primitive minds, and only when one has realised that the mode of thought and the logic of the stone age are not the same as ours can one appreciate the underlying unity in all these apparent inconsistencies.

I once went out to Aua's hunting quarters on the ice outside Lyon Inlet to spend some time with the men I have referred to in the foregoing. For several evenings we had discussed rules of life and taboo customs without getting beyond a long and circumstantial statement of all that was permitted and all that was forbidden. Everyone knew precisely what had to be done in any given situation, but whenever I put in my query: "Why?", they could give no answer. They regarded it, and very rightly, as unreasonable that I should require not only an account, but also a justification, of their religious principles. They had of course no idea that all my questions, now that I had obtained the information I wished for, were only intended to make them react in such a manner that they should, excited by my inquisitiveness, be able to give an inspired explanation. Aua had as usual been the spokesman, and as he was still unable to answer my questions, he rose to his feet, and as if seized by a sudden impulse, invited me to go outside with him.

It had been an unusually rough day, and as we had plenty of meat after the successful hunting of the past few days, I had asked my host to stay at home so that we could get some work done together. The brief daylight had given place to the half-light of the afternoon, but as the moon was up, one could still see some distance. Ragged white clouds raced across the sky, and when a gust of wind came tearing over the ground, our eyes and mouths were filled with snow. Aua looked me full in the face, and pointing out over the ice, where the snow was being lashed about in waves by the wind, he said:

"In order to hunt well and live happily, man must have calm weather. Why this constant succession of blizzards and all this needless hardship for men seeking food for themselves and those they care for? Why? Why?"

We had come out just at the time when the men were returning from their watching at the blowholes on the ice; they came in little groups, bowed forward, toiling along against the wind, which actually forced them now and again to stop, so fierce were the gusts. Not one of them had a seal in tow; their whole day of painful effort and endurance had been in vain.

I could give no answer to Aua's "Why?", but shook my head in silence. He then led me into Kublo's house, which was close beside our own. The small blubber lamp burned with but the faintest flame, giving out no heat whatever; a couple of children crouched, shivering, under a skin rug on the bench.

Aua looked at me again, and said: "Why should it be cold and comfortless in here? Kublo has been out hunting all day, and if he had got a seal, as he deserved, his wife would now be sitting laughing beside her lamp, letting it burn full, without fear of having no blubber left for tomorrow. The place would be warm and bright and cheerful. the children would come out from under their rugs and enjoy life. Why should it not be so? Why?"

I made no answer, and he led me out of the house, in to a little snow hut where his sister Natseq lived all by herself because she was ill. She looked thin and worn, and was not even interested in our coming. For several days she had suffered from a malignant cough that seemed to come from far down in the lungs, and it looked as if she had not long to live.

A third time Aua looked at me and said: "Why must people be ill and suffer pain? We are all afraid of illness. Here is this old sister of mine; as far as anyone can see, she has done no evil; she has lived through a long life and given birth to healthy children, and now she must suffer before her days end. Why? Why?"

This ended his demonstration, and we returned to our house, to resume, with the others, the interrupted discussion.

"You see" said Aua "You are equally unable to give any reason when we ask you why life is as it is. And so it must be. All our customs come from life and turn towards life; we explain nothing, we believe nothing, but in what I have just shown you lies our answer to all you ask.

"We fear the weather spirit of earth, that we must fight against to wrest our food from land and sea. We fear Sila.

"We fear dearth and hunger in the cold snow huts.

"We fear Takánakapsâluk, the great woman down at the bottom of the sea, that rules over all the beasts of the sea.

"We fear the sickness that we meet with daily all around us; not death, but the suffering. We fear the evil spirits of life, those of the air, of the sea and the earth, that can help wicked shamans to harm their fellow men.

"We fear the souls of dead human beings and of the animals we have killed.

"Therefore it is that our fathers have inherited from their fathers all the old rules of life which are based on the experience and wisdom of generations. We do not know how, we cannot say why, but we keep those rules in order that we may live untroubled. And so ignorant are we in spite of all our shamans, that we fear everything unfamiliar. We fear what we see about us, and we fear all the invisible things that are likewise about us, all that we have heard of in our forefathers' stories and myths. Therefore we have our customs, which are not the same as those of the white men, the white men who live in another land and have need of other ways."

That was Aua's explanation; he was, as always, clear in his line of thought, and with a remarkable power of expressing what he meant. He was silent then, and as I did not at once resume the conversation, his younger brother Ivaluardjuk took up the theme, and said:

"The greatest peril of life lies in the fact that human food consists entirely of souls.

"All the creatures that we have to kill and eat, all those that we have to strike down and destroy to make clothes for ourselves, have souls, like we have, souls that do not perish with the body, and which must therefore be propitiated lest they should revenge themselves on us for taking away their bodies."

"In the old days, it was far worse than it is now," put in Anarqâq, "Everything was more difficult, and our customs accordingly much more strict. In those days, men hunted only with bow and arrow and knew nothing of the white men's firearms. It was far more difficult to live then, and often men could not get food enough. The caribou were hunted in kayaks at the crossing of rivers and lakes, being driven out into the water where they could be easily overtaken in a kayak. But it was hard to make them run the way one wished, and therefore rules were very strict about those places. No woman was allowed to work there, no bone of any animal might be broken, no brain or marrow eaten. To do so would be an insult to the souls of the caribou, and was punished by death or disaster. There is an old story, and a true one, showing the danger that lurks in the souls of animals for us human beings, and it is about

The woman who has swallowed up by the earth for having offended the souls of the beasts.

"Once some women were left alone at a spot where the caribou were accustomed to swim across a river. The women were to wait there for their husbands, who were away hunting. But the men were away a long time, and the women had not food enough, and being near starvation, gathered together bones of animals that had been killed there some time before, and to save their lives, boiled fat from the bones and ate it. Thus they managed to save themselves from dying of hunger, but in doing so disobeyed the strict rule that forbids any breaking of bones at the fords.

"At last, after a long time, their men came home from the hunting. and some had found game and others none. One of the men who had got nothing told his wife she had better go away to her elder brother. His comrades tried to persuade her to stay, saying they would willingly feed her now that they had meat enough, but she did as her husband had said and went off to her brother. She reached the place where he was and lived with him. One day her brother's wife asked her to carry their little child in the amaut, as she herself wanted to make a pair of kamiks for her husband. The woman went out with her brother's child, and sat down in a small gully not far from the house. And while she was there, the earth suddenly closed over her and she could not get out. Later in the day, the woman and child were missed, and when some went out to search for them, it was seen that the earth had closed over them, and the child could be heard crying, and the woman singing:

"Little one, do not cry,
Mother will come and fetch you,
When she has finished her sewing.
I am afraid of my husband,
And dare not go home,
I would gladly go home to the two brothers
Who wished me to stay;
I am afraid of my husband
And dare not go home.

I must live all my days a-visiting
Grow old as a woman a-visiting,
And never dare to go home."

"So the woman perished because she had done what was forbidden at the sacred places. The powerful souls of the caribou had killed her."

— — —

The soul and the name.

In all living beings there are forces that render them particularly sensitive to the rules of life that human beings endeavour to follow. These forces lie in the soul and the name.

The soul, tARniŋa or inu'sia, is that which gives to all living things their particular appearance. In the case of human beings it is really a tiny human being, in the case of the caribou a tiny caribou, and so on with all animals; an image, but very much smaller than the creature itself. The inu'sia (meaning "appearance as a human being") is situated in a bubble of air in the groin; from it proceed appearance, thoughts, strength and life, it is that which makes the man a man, the caribou a caribou, the walrus a walrus, the dog a dog, etc. Where any act of violence is committed against this soul, or any offence by breach of taboo, it becomes an evil spirit, wreaking harm and death in return. But it must not be supposed that all animals are angered when they are killed. Animals have in reality no objection to being killed by human beings, as long as the rules of life are observed by the latter. It may even happen, and not infrequently, that an animal will approach a human being, actually desiring to be killed by that particular person. An animal may perhaps be tired of being what it is; and since its soul cannot change its envelope until the body has been killed, it is natural that animals should sometimes wish to die. The great danger in killing animals commonly hunted lies in the fact that there is hardly a single human being who has kept the rules of life and lived throughout in accordance with the laws laid down by the wisdom of his forefathers. Therefore it is said that the greatest danger lies in the fact that unclean and often guilty human beings have to depend entirely on the souls of other beings for food.

But in addition to the soul there is also the name to be considered, and in regard to this it is stated that:

Everyone on receiving a name receives with it the strength and skill of the deceased namesake, but since all persons bearing the same name have the same source of life, spiritual and physical qualities are also inherited from those who in the far distant past once bore the same name. The shamans say that sometimes, on their spirit flights, they can see, behind each human being, as it were a mighty procession of spirits aiding and guiding, as long as the rules of life are duly observed; but when this is not done, or if a man is tempted to some act unwelcome to the dead, then all the invisible guardians turn against him as enemies, and he is lost beyond hope.

Men have their knowledge of the soul, which none can see, and which in itself is so incomprehensible, from the story of the soul which migrated from one animal body to another. This story, which is also wellknown among the Greenland Eskimos, is as follows:

The human soul that lived in the bodies of all beasts.

There was once a woman who gave birth to an abortion, and taking care that none should know, she threw the thing to the dogs, for she did not wish to observe all the troublesome rites imposed on women thus rendered unclean.

The abortion was eaten by a dog, and remaining in its body for some time, was ultimately born of the dog that had swallowed it, and lived as a dog. And when people threw out refuse from their houses, it would run up with the other dogs for something to eat. But it did not rightly understand how to be a dog, it could not push its way to the front, and thus it never got enough to eat. It grew thin, and the woman who had given birth to it at first, said:

"Do not stay behind like that, but push your way to the front, or you will never get anything to eat."

And accordingly, it adopted the custom of the dogs, and pushed its way to the front wherever there was a chance of anything to be got, but often it got only blows for its pains. And at last it grew tired of being a dog, and changed from the body of one animal to another.

At one time it was a fjord seal. It lived down under the ice, and had its blowhole like the other seals. The seals were not afraid of death, and therefore had no fear of man, but would agree among themselves which hunter they would allow to capture them. And then they would lie there under the blowholes waiting till a little thing like a drop of water should fall down on them. It pricked their bodies, and often hurt.

The soul quite enjoyed being a seal, but all the same it felt it would like to be a wolf, and so it became a wolf. It stayed with the wolves for a time, but then it grew tired of that, for the wolves were always moving from one place to another, and never stayed anywhere for long, there was no time to spend in making love; they trotted and trotted about and knew no rest.

Then it became a caribou. The caribou were always feeding, and therefore it was pleasant to live among them, but on the other hand they were always afraid, always in dread of some danger. So it left them and became a walrus. The walrus were good to live with. They too were always feeding; and they never went in fear of anything. But they had a way of beating one another on the snout with their tusks, and because of this, the soul grew dissatisfied with its life among them.

Thus it wandered from one animal form to another, and when it had passed through all of them, it returned to the seals, that it liked so much.

Then one day it allowed itself to be captured by a man whose wife was barren. He took the seal home to his wife, and as she stood over the carcase to cut it up, the soul slipped into her body. The woman became pregnant, and the child within her grew so fast that it made her ill. At last she gave birth to a boy, a fine, well-proportioned child, but when it tried to speak, all it could say was

"uŋa˙, uŋa˙".

The boy grew up and became a skilful hunter. It was not long before he had a sealing float made from the whole skin of a bearded seal, for he was marvellously strong. And he went hunting, killing whale and seal and all manner of beasts.

Thus the woman's abortion became a human being again after having lived in the bodies of all beasts, and the young man proved a good son to his parents, hunting and finding meat for them till the end of their days.

Told by
Naukatjik.

I asked Aua why the soul was always given so prominent a place in their religious ideas, and he answered:

"We ignorant Eskimos living up here do not believe, as you have told us many white men do, in one great solitary spirit that from a place far up in the sky maintains humanity and all the life of nature. Among us, as I have already explained to you, all is bound up with the earth we live on and our life here; and it would be even more incomprehensible, even more unreasonable, if, after a life short or long, of happy days or of suffering and misery, we were then to cease altogether from existence. What we have heard about the soul shows us that the life of men and beasts does not end with death. When at the end of life we draw our last breath, that is not the end. We awake to consciousness again, we come to life again, and all this is effected through the medium of the soul. Therefore it is that we regard the soul as the greatest and most incomprehensible of all.

"In our ordinary everyday life we do not think much about all these things, and it is only now you ask that so many thoughts arise in my head of long-known things; old thoughts, but as it were becoming altogether new when one has to put them into words."

III.

The Powers that rule Earth and Mankind.

It will now be clearly apparent, from the statements of the Eskimos themselves, as above quoted, that the idea of a God, or group of gods, to be worshipped, is altogether alien to their minds. They know only powers or personifications of natural forces, acting upon human life in various ways, and affecting all that lives through fair and foul weather, disease and perils of all kinds. These powers are not evil in themselves, they do not wreak harm of evil intent, but they are nevertheless dangerous owing to their unmerciful severity where men fail to live in accordance with the wise rules of life decreed by their forefathers. The purpose of the whole system is, to use an expression current among the Polar Eskimos of North Greenland, "to keep a right balance between mankind and the rest of the world". The term used by the Hudson Bay Eskimos for the guiding powers is ᴇʀsigiʃavut, "those we fear" or mianᴇʀiʃavut, "those we keep away from and regard with caution". Individually, they are as follows:

Aṛnâluk takánâluk, "the woman down there", the spirit of the sea, the mother of marine animals, living at the bottom of the sea. She is also referred to, almost with a touch of contempt, as Takánakapsâluk: "the bad one" or "the terrible one down there". The immigrant Netsilingmiut call her Nuliajuk, that being the name she bore when she lived as a little girl among men in the days before she became a spirit.

Sila, the spirit of the weather or of the universe.

Aningât or Tarqeq, the general name for the moon; in this connection however, it is through Aningâp inua or Tarqiup inua, the moon's man or the moon spirit, that the various functions of the moon are exercised.

Of these three powers, Takánakapsâluk plays by far the most important part in everyday life, and is, if one may use such an expression, the principal deity, with power in some respects over both Sila and Tarqeq, these latter acting as agents to see that her will is obeyed.

Her supreme power lies in the fact that all the food of all mankind is under her command, and this, it will readily be seen, is a point of importance in a land where the struggle for existence is more acute and merciless than in other regions of the world. Food is only to be obtained under certain definite conditions. The strict rules of the taboo system must be punctiliously kept, and all the wise ordinances of former generations must be obeyed. When any transgression takes place in regard to these, which are expressly laid down as essential to success in hunting, the spirit of the sea intervenes. The moon spirit helps her to see that the rules of life are duly observed, and comes hurrying down to earth to punish any instance of neglect. And both sea spirit and moon spirit employ Sila to execute all punishments in any way connected with the weather.

The sea spirit Takánâluk arnâluk: The Mother of Sea Beasts.

There was once a little girl who would not have a husband. No one was good enough. At last her father grew angry and said:

“Then may she have my dog!”

And then one evening, when they were going to rest, a strange man came in. No one knew who he was. He had the fangs of a dog hanging down on either side of his chest as an amulet. This man lay down beside the girl and took her to wife. It was the father’s dog in human form, and thus the threat was carried out. But when the girl was with child and about to bring forth, her father rowed her across to a small island near by. This island was Qiqertârjuk, close to Iglulik. But the dog swam after them and lived with the girl on the island. It used to swim in to the village for meat, which was set out for it in a pack saddle of the kind used by dogs when carrying loads up country in summer. Thus the girl and the dog lived together. But the time came when the girl was to bring forth, and she gave birth to a whole litter, some as dogs and some in right human form. The dogs were most, there were five of them, and they lived together, the girl and the dog and her young out on the little island. At last the girl’s father began to feel sorry for his child, he wished he had not spoken those words, and one day, when the dog swam in to fetch meat, he laid stones and sand at the bottom of the load, but covered it with meat on top, so that the dog did not notice anything strange. But when it swam out to sea, the load was too heavy, and dragged it down to the bottom and it was drowned. But the girl was angry with her father for having caused the death of the dog, and she said one day to her dog-children: “atago alupiusaŋ·uᴀr^{d}lugo tikip·-

at qaja· nEriniAripse" "When your grandfather comes out here, pretend you want to lick the blood from his kayak and tear the kayak in pieces".

Their grandfather came out as usual, bringing some meat, and the dog-children, pretending they only meant to lick the blood from the kayak, tore the skin of the kayak. But the old man managed nevertheless to escape and got safely to shore, and after that he never dared to go out again in his kayak.

Now the girl and her young often suffered want. At last she decided to send her children away; she laid all the dog-children in the sole of a kamik, and setting three straws in it for masts, said:

"sA·rqutikʃäpsin·ik sanavagumA·rpuse" "You shall be skilful in the making of weapons".

And then they drifted out to sea.

It is said that the white men are descended from these dog-children. But those of her children that were born in right human form she placed on an alAq: a piece of sole leather that goes under the sole of the kamik proper, and these she sent drifting over to land. From these, it is said, are descended all the itqili·t, the Chipewyan. When the girl had thus sent away her young ones, she returned home to her father and mother and lived with them once more. But one day when her father was out hunting, there came a kayak and made fast close to the village, and the man in it called up to the house:

"taina uʷiniqümasuic·ɔq qaile" "Let the girl who does not want to be married come down here".

"That must be me, I suppose" said the girl, and she took her ikpiArjuk, a sewing bag made from the membrane of a walrus' kidney, and went down to the stranger in the kayak. He seemed to be a fine big man, for he looked tall sitting down, but he had spectacles on, covering his eyes.

"Aquᵛnut ik·i·t" "Sit up here in the stern of my kayak". And sat up behind him in the kayak and he rowed away with her.

When they had rowed some distance, he laid the kayak alongside an icefloe, and stepping out, thrust his great spectacles aside and said:

"igja·k·a takuᵛigit iʲARA-RARa! ikɔrfak·a takuᵛigit iʲAR-RA-Ra!" "Can you see my spectacles, ha, ha, ha; can you see the stool I was sitting on, ha, ha, ha!"

And now for the first time the girl saw that his eyes were red and ugly, and that he was a little puny figure of a man. He had looked tall sitting in the kayak, but that was because he had made a high seat to sit on. The girl was so disappointed at this that she burst out crying, but the man only laughed:

Types of dress from Iglulik. The woman at the bottom to the right from Cumberland Sound. Drawing by the Eskimo girl Eqatliôq.

A family going visiting. At the bottom to the left two female types; to the right a man's dress. Drawing by the Eskimo girl Eqatliôq.

"iʲAR-RA-Ra": "Ha, ha, ha!" and rowed off with her again.

The man who had thus carried her off was a qAqugluk: a stormy petrel in human form. He rowed home with her to his own place, and led her into a nice little tent, light and comfortable inside and made entirely from the skins of young fjord seals. And the girl lived with him there and had a child.

But her father mourned for her, and went off with his wife in a boat to look for her. He found their dwelling, and rowed away with his daughter while her husband was out hunting. But when the husband came home and discovered that his wife had been carried off, he started out in pursuit of the fugitives, taking the shape of a stormy petrel once more. In this way he soon overtook their boat, and flew round it, crying:

"aggA·rzɔqute·k·a takulArᵈlak·a!" "Let me but look at those dear hands that belong to me."

This he said because the girl lay covered up with skins in the middle of the boat, and no part of her could be seen. But the girl's father answered scornfully: "taimaitut-qai aggA·rzɔqutEqArpaktut ikɔrfainait, iksainait": „How can one who is only tall with a stool to sit on, one whose face is covered by spectacles, how can such an one ever have sweet little hands belonging to him?"

At this the stormy petrel grew angry and flew over the boat; it made first some powerful movements with its wings, and then sailed in over the boat, so that a storm arose from the beating of its wings: the waves rose, and the water began to come in over one side. Then again the stormy petrel cried:

"Only her hands, the dear little hands that belong to me; you must let me see them."

But the girl's father took no heed of his crying, and then the bird flew once more furiously round the boat, and gliding over it on stiffly outstretched wings, it sent up such a storm that the boat nearly upset. Then at last the girl's father began to be frightened, and he threw his daughter out into the sea, so that her husband could take her himself. But the girl clung to the side of the boat, and as she would not let go, her father hacked off the top joints of her fingers, and the finger tips fell into the sea, and seals came bobbing up all round the boat. Her finger tips became seals. But again she grasped at the side of the boat, and clung on with the stumps of her hands, and again her father struck at her and cut off the next joints, and the pieces fell into the water, and bearded seals came bobbing up all round; the bearded seals are from the middle joints of her hands. But still she clung to the side of the boat with the stumps of her hands, and then her father struck again, being afraid lest the boat should upset, for the water was now coming in on both sides. This time, the last joints of her hands fell into the sea, and walrus came up all round; the last joints of her hands had turned into walrus. But the girl herself could no longer hold on, the slipped away from the side of the boat and sank down to the bottom of the sea, and there she became a spirit, and we call her Takánâluk arnâluk.

The girl's father rowed home sorrowfully, and so deeply did he mourn for the fate of his daughter that he laid himself down by the water's edge, covered only by a skin, and when the flood tide came and the water rose, the waves bore him away, and so he came down to the bottom of the sea, where his daughter was. And he lived there, and now he is called Takatumâlûp angutialua: the Father of the Woman of the Deep.

And so at last the whole family were gathered together at the bottom of the sea: the dog that was drowned, the girl who sank to the bottom, and the father who was borne away by the waves. They turned into spirits after death. The Mother of the Sea Beasts has a house at the bottom of the sea. In the passage lies the dog that was once her husband; it lies so as to bar the entrance to the house completely, and acts as her watchdog. Only great shamans who fear nothing can pass by it.

But the girl's father lies inside on the bench, covered by a skin, just as he lay when the tide came in and the waves bore him away. He is dangerous, and always in a bad temper, and snaps and strikes at all who enter. We call him Takánâlûp angutialua, the father of the sea spirit; the Netsilingmiut have a special name for him, which perhaps was his name in the days when he lived among men, and that is Isarrataitsoq. Everyone is very much afraid of him, and it is he who mercilessly punishes all those who have trangressed the old rules of life and more especially those who have been guilty of sinful love. Only in his place can they be purified, and must do penance for their sins for a whole year before they are allowed to pass into the land of the dead at the bottom of the sea, which is called Qimiujarmiut. Not far from this land, in the same "underworld" lies the sea spirit's house. All this however, will be dealt with at greater length in the section on shamans.

This is the story of how all the beasts of the sea were formed from the fingers and hands of Takánâluk. She is so fond of them, as being parts of herself, and demands so great respect from mankind for the sacred food, that she will not suffer unclean women to come in contact with them. Hence the strict taboo to be observed if men are to live happily and find seal and other game when they go hunting.

All the beasts of the sea have their place on the right of her lamp when she calls them together; that place is called kaŋia, and is on the right of the lamp when one sits on the bench in the housewife's place facing the passage. Here she assembles and keeps the beasts of the sea when they are to be withheld from mankind. Only the sharks have a special place to themselves; they live in her urine vessel, and that is why the flesh of sharks tastes of urine.

Some old folk believe that the mother of the sea beasts rules over all the animals we hunt, the caribou as well. But others hold a different view. They declare that there were no caribou at the time when Takánâluk lived on earth; and therefore she hates the caribou, and they have another mother, "atianik̤ ikvEqArput": "they have another with whom they are". In the days when Takánâluk lived on earth, men wore clothes made from eider duck and fox, and did not use skins of caribou at all.

This is what is told of the Mother of the Caribou, of "tuktut ikviat": "the one with whom the caribou are":

It is said that at the time when the sea beasts were first made, there were no caribou on the earth; but then an old woman went up inland and made them. Their skins she made from her breeches, so that the lie of the hair followed the same pattern as her breeches. But the caribou was given teeth like other animals; at first it had tusks as well. It was a dangerous beast, and it was not long before a man was killed while hunting. Then the old woman grew frightened, and went up inland again and gathered together the caribou she had made. The tusks she changed into antlers, the teeth in the front of the jaw she knocked out, and when she had done this, she said to them:

"Land beasts such as you must keep away from men, and be shy and easily frightened."

And then she gave them a kick on the forehead, and it was that which made the hollow one can see now in the forehead of all caribou. The animals dashed away, and were very shy thereafter. But then it was found that they were too swift; no man could come up with them, and once more the old woman had to call them all together. This time she changed the fashion of the hair, so that all did not lie the same way. The hair of the belly, under the throat and flanks, was made to lie in different directions, and then the animals were let loose once more. The caribou were still swift runners, but they could not cleave the air as rapidly as before, because the hair stood in the way, and men could now overtake them and kill them when they used certain tricks. Afterwards, the old woman went to live among the caribou; she stayed with them and never returned to the haunts of men, and now she is called, the Mother of the Caribou, "tuktut ikviat" or "the one with whom the caribou are".

Told by
Orulo.

Orulo was, of all the Iglulingmiut I met, the most faithful story-teller and the most patient in answering all my questions. This was partly due to the fact that she was one of those who knew most about the old traditions. I was therefore surprised of find that the myth of the Sea Spirit, as she related it, differed from the versions I had heard elsewhere. Orulo makes the girl who married a dog and the girl who had a stormy petrel for a husband, one and the same woman. In most other places, these two myths are distinct, and regarded as two separate explanations of how the spirit of the sea originated. In both cases, the woman goes down to the bottom of the sea, and the story is content to assert, as its decisive feature, that the woman who was afterwards to obtain such extraordinary and determinative influence on human life, had once been married to an animal in human form, and was changed into a spirit after a violent death.

When I pointed out to Orulo the discrepancy between her description and those I had heard from others, she firmly maintained that hers was the correct one. Another thing I pointed out to her in this connection made not the slightest impression; and as her standpoint here is so characteristic of the Eskimo attitude generally towards myths which are actually of fundamental importance in their religious ideas, I will give our conversation as it took place.

I said to Orulo, that according to her account, all sea beasts originated frem Takánakapsâluk. They were made from her fingers, and it was because she was their mother that human beings had to observe all the numerous and difficult rules of taboo, the purpose of which was to ensure that the thoughts and hands of unclean human beings should never come in contact with the "sacred" food. In a Greenland variant of the story, as I now told Orulo, the Mother of the Sea Beasts could only be the same as the girl who was married to a dog. In the story I knew, the girl let her offspring lick the blood from her father's kayak, with the result that the dog-children at last fell upon the girl's father and tore him to pieces. Their mother had asked them to do so. For she could not forget that it was her father who had degraded her by marriage with a dog, and therefore she wished that the very children of that marriage should themselves be the cause of her father's death. Thus she would be avenged, and her children bit her father to death. The body was thrown into the sea, but afterwards, the girl regretted that she had killed her own father. So great was her feeling of shame at what she had done that she could not bear to live any longer; so she sent her children out into the world, and flung herself into the sea where her father had been cast. She sank down to the bottom, and became a sea spirit. afterwards ruling over all the beasts of the sea.

"But where did the seals come from?" asked Orulo, "If the same girl was not married to a stormy petrel and thrown overboard when her husband was pursuing her, then that could never have taken place which led to the cutting off of her fingers while she clung to the side of the boat. And if that had not happened, the beasts of the sea would never have been made at all."

To this I observed that in that case I also could not understand where the seals came from that lived in the sea long before the Mother of the Sea Beasts ever existed. For in the story Orulo herself had told me, the stormy petrel lived solely on young fjord seals.

At this Orulo laughed, and said:

"Too much thought only leads to trouble. All this that we are talking about now happened in a time so far back that there was no time at all. We Eskimos do not concern ourselves with solving all riddles. We repeat the old stories in the way they were told to us and with the words we ourselves remember. And if there should then seem to be a lack of reason in the story as a whole, there is yet enough remaining in the way of incomprehensible happenings, which our thought cannot grasp. If it were but everyday ordinary things, there would be nothing to believe in. How came all the living creatures on earth from the beginning? Can anyone explain that?"

And then, after having thought for a moment, she added the following, which shows in a striking fashion how little the actual logical sequence counts with the Eskimos in their mythology:

"You talk about the stormy petrel catching seals before there were any seals. But even if we managed to settle this point so that all worked out as it should, there would still be more than enough remaining which we cannot explain. Can you tell me where the mother of the caribou got her breeches from; breeches made of caribou skin before she had made any caribou? You always want these supernatural things to make sense, but we do not bother about that. We are content not to understand.

"I did not tell you all the story before, when I was talking about the mother of the caribou, but now, since you ask such a lot, you may as well have the whole of it.

"At the time when Takánakapsâluk had fashioned the great and meat-giving beasts of the sea, there was an old woman who thought the land ought also to have special animals of its own. So she went up inland, far, far up country, away from the dwellings of men, and here she began uttering magic words to create a kind of animal which might be useful to mankind. By means of strange words and their magic power she gave life to something, the body of which became a caribou. But this caribou was nothing but flesh and blood and bones. It had no hide, no skin. So she could find no better way out of the difficulty than by taking her old breeches, which were made of caribou skin, and over these she worked magic in such a fashion that the caribou got their skins from those breeches. This is why we say that the lie of the hair on a caribou skin is just like woman's breeches of caribou skin. If you take a pair of women's breeches and hold them out in front of you, then you will see they are cut to a special pattern, and the skin used is taken from particular parts of the animal's hide. The upper part of the breeches, over the hips, is taken from that part of the skin which we call ninata qaniŋita — that is, the part near where the legs begin; the hair here is light, though not white. Next to this comes that part of the breeches which has to be darkest. This is taken from the qimᴇrlua; the upper part of the back; and then comes the part which is every woman's pride if it is gleaming white. It is taken from pukᴇq, the white skin under the belly; below this, according to the pattern, there must be a piece that is dark though not so dark as the almost black part above pukᴇq, this is taken from the sanᴇrᴀq or the side of the caribou; and then finally, there is the front part, covering the stomach and lap, which is taken from the quŋasᴇq, or the neck of the caribou, where the hair is longer than on other parts of the body. This is related, perhaps, because people once wanted an explanation of why the caribou had so many colours and patterns in its skin; and then it was said that it was because the caribou got its skin from an old woman's breeches of caribou skin. As to where the woman who afterwards became the mother of all caribou got the caribou skin her breeches were made of — nobody bothered about that".

The whole nature of the Sea Spirit, her functions and manner of ruling and punishing mankind will be further dealt with later under shamans. For the most part, she is regarded by the Eskimos here generally as one with the Mother of the Caribou, so that despite the myths, she appears chiefly as the one ruling over all animals hunted either by land or sea. She is the "food deity" most clearly personified among the Polar Eskimos of the Thule district, who call her Nerrivigssuaq, or "the great meat dish". One of the most oft-repeated accounts of how the Sea Spirit in particular punishes all breaches of taboo, including offences against the caribou, is as follows:

There was once a family that had moved out on to the sea ice to hunt seal. It was early in the winter, and they had just come from those parts of the country inland where they had been hunting caribou since the beginning of autumn. When a family comes down from the interior, they are strictly forbidden to sew new caribou skins on the ice, for all sewing must be done with while they are still on land, in the first snow huts of the autumn. But these people who had now moved out on to the ice failed to observe this important rule, and the wife set about sewing a dress of young caribou calf skins for her son. On the same day, a hurricane burst on them, the ice broke up just behind their snow hut, though it remained firm farther in, where other seal hunters had built their huts; and through the first cracks made by the storm in the ice could be seen a young caribou calf and a marmot swimming about among the breaking pieces. Thus the Sea Spirit made it clear to men that the land animals had been offended by the action of men out on the sea ice. This was her way of showing it, by letting a caribou calf and a little marmot swim about in the rough sea. All the people from the huts near by saw them, and then they disappeared as mysteriously as they had come; but the moment they vanished, the snow hut in which the offence had been committed fell into the sea and was swallowed up, with all who dwelt therein. They were drowned, and their souls went down to Takánakapsâluk, who thus took vengeance upon those that scornfully disregarded the ancient rules of life laid down by their forefathers.

Sila.

Sila is the great, dangerous and divine spirit that lives somewhere "up in the air", out in the universe, between sky and sea, hovering over earth; from there it threatens mankind through the mighty powers of nature, wind and sea, fog, rain and snowstorm. Among the Iglulingmiut and the Aivilingmiut this spirit is regarded more than all else as a personification of the weather, and therefore, instead of sila, the term pErsɔq is used, meaning snowstorm, or even anɔre, the wind.

Inugpasugjuk, an immigrant Netsilingmio, related the following story of the storm spirit Nârtsuk, which was supposed to be silap inua, or the spirit of the air.

Nârtsuk.

There was once a man who was out on a great plain. Here he found a little human being, a child lying on the ground. He thought of killing it, but when the child realised what the man was about to do it found voice, and said:

"If you kill me, then the world will perish" (sila imiktukʃᴀra˙luk: literally, "then Sila, the expanse of heaven, will collapse").

The man would not believe it, and said:

"Well, try to kick that great mountain over there".

The little man answered not a word, but simply lifted one leg and kicked out. And at once the steep mountain collapsed, leaving not a trace behind.

Then at last the man believed the little creature's words, for he understood that it must be possessed of great power and strength. And without a word, he ran away.

This is all that the natives in the neighbourhood of Repulse Bay can remember of the story. By way of further explanation I may add that I later, in the North-west Passage region, was given the following more comprehensive account:

Nârtsuk, also pronounced Nârshuk, was originally the child of a giant and his wife, both of whom were murdered, first the father, then the mother. The murderers left the child to its fate, close to the spot where the parents had been killed. This evildoing turned the child into a spirit, which flew up into the sky and became the lord of the weather. It is always dressed in a full costume of caribou skin — a dress with tunic and breeches made in one piece, and very wide, as worn by children generally. When Nârtsuk shakes his dress, air rushes out from all the loose spaces in his clothing, and the winds begin to blow.

When the spirit of the winds keeps on blowing and there is no peace for men to go out hunting by land or sea, then a shaman has to go up into the sky and beat him, thrash him with a whip, until he calms down and the storms subside. With regard to this, Ivaluardjuk related the following:

The Spirit of the Wind.

It happened once that the Spirit of the Wind kept on blowing, and so a shaman went off up in the air to the place where he was. And this shaman afterwards gave the following account of his visit:

As soon as he reached the spirit, he tore open its clothing and began thrashing it, so that its body shed blood. Not until then did it calm down, and the weather with it. When the spirit of the wind has been given a good sound thrashing, one must wrap its clothes tightly round it, and then the wind will not blow. It is only when its clothing is loose and open so as to make as it were a draught, that the wind comes forth.

The Spirit of the Wind has a face almost like that of a human being, but shamans relate that it has a very thin covering of hair, rather like that of a bear; this hair, however, is found only on the face and hands. Such is the Spirit of the Wind.

The Spirit of the Wind, however, must not be confused with Oqaloraq, as to which Ivaluardjuk states as follows:

Oqalorak, or the Spirit of the Snowdrift.

Oqaloraq is the name given to the firm, sharp edges of a snowdrift. They have a spirit, the Snowdrift Spirit. He lives in the sharp declivities of the snowdrifts, where the wind whines and blows most fiercely. When a blizzard is raging over the country, and the driving snow makes it impossible to see, then this spirit is filled with delight, and if you listen you can hear him laughing in the storm. The wilder the gale, the happier he is and the louder he laughs. He knows that men hate him, and for that reason he persecutes them. He sends down a snowstorm upon them unawares when they are out on their sledges, or on the ice at the blowholes, or in their kayaks, and then he can be heard laughing through the storm when harm comes to the human beings that hate him. He wears close-fitting clothes, made of caribou skin, and does nothing but laugh and chuckle through the blizzard whenever men suffer harm.

Such is the Spirit of the Snowdrift.

The stories I have here given, the only ones known in this district in connection with Sila, show that this spirit here plays a surprisingly small part as an independent force. It is altogether amalgamated with the storm, or foul weather; the one that Takánakapsâluk makes use of when she is angry. Among the Iglulingmiut, it is the Spirit of the Sea which sends Sila to punish mankind. Sila is her agent; but we shall later see, when dealing with the inland folk, that Sila is doubtless the original world power, which at one time, when the Eskimos had not yet become a coastal people dependent on the sea, was the principal spirit, on which all religious ideas were based.

The Moon Spirit.

The Moon Spirit, Aningâp or Tarqip inua, lives with his sister Seqineq in a double house (qᴀrajᴀre·k: a house with two apartments but one common entrance) up in the land of the dead in the sky, the same which is called Udlormiut or the Land of Day. Human beings who perish by drowning in the sea or in a lake, go to dwell with the moon; so also those who are killed by their fellows openly or unawares, those who take their own lives out of weariness or because they are old, and finally, all women dying in childbirth. Human beings going up into the sky enter at once into the eternal hunting grounds, and do not have to purify their minds by a year of penance, as with those who go down to the Sea Spirit. All are loth to go down to her, for fear of the ill treatment meted out to them by her father Isarrataitsoq. A few of the greater shamans can also procure special admission to the Moon Spirit for the dead; this can be done in various ways, e.g. by means of amulets. It is said that the molars of a bear, consecrated by the prayers of a great shaman, are particularly effective in this direction.

The Moon Spirit is one of the great regulating powers of the universe which is not feared. Knowing the view of the East Greenlanders, who regard the Moon Spirit as the most terrible of the punitive deities watching over the deeds of men, I enquired particularly about this point, but was everywhere informed that no one feared the Moon Spirit, only the Sea Spirit was to be feared, and especially her father. The Moon Spirit, on the other hand, is the only good and well-intentioned spirit known, and when he does intervene, it is often more for guidance than for punishment.

People in danger can often hear him calling out:

"Come, come to me! It is not painful to die. It is only a brief moment of dizziness. It does not hurt to kill yourself".

Thus the moon sometimes calls, and it is thus also regarded more particularly as the protector of those perishing by accident or suicide. His house lies midway between the houses of the dead in the Land of Day, and here he lives as a mighty hunter, always willing to share his game with his fellows. It is recognised that the Moon Man has some influence on the sea, as with the tides, and this is why he, alone of all the dwellers in the heavens, can hunt marine animals and procure sea food. All the others up there can only hunt the land fauna. He is also a mighty walrus hunter, and it is when he is out hunting that he is not to be seen in the sky.

The Moon Man has various functions to observe, but in his method of doing so we find, among the Iglulingmiut, often a guiding rather than a punitive element; it seems almost as if he wished to protect the unfortunate or imprudent against the inconsiderate and altogether merciless punishments of the Sea Spirit. He therefore regards it as one of his most important tasks to see that men do not commit any breach of taboo. There is a peephole in the floor of his house, an opening covered with the shoulderblade of a caribou. As soon as this cover is removed, he can look down over all the dwellings of men, and from there, they appear as if quite near, so that nothing escapes his attention. When unclean woman offend against taboo, smoke rises from their bodies. And this foul smoke pours out from the houses where they live, and attracts the notice of the Moon Spirit. This smoke gets into the Sea Spirit's eyes, or falls over her face, hair and body in a mess of dirt. And the Moon Man, loth to see men suffer dearth when the Sea Spirit is roused to anger, therefore hastens down and warns and punishes those who have done wrong.

The Moon Man is not only the moral guardian of mankind, but also the maintainer of fertility. When a woman is barren and cannot bear her husband children, it is the moon that helps her. Sometimes this is done simply by letting the full moon shine on her bare lap, but for the most part, the Moon Man himself goes down to earth' driving across the Land of the Sky with his team of dogs. He races across the clear sky with great speed; the ground here is smooth ice without snow; through the clouds, progress is slower, for here there is snow underfoot. Thus driving, he comes to visit the village where the barren woman lives; sometimes he will lie with her there, and that is all, but it may also happen that he carries her off to the Land of Heaven and keeps her there, until she is with child. Any human being who visits the Moon Man must never make a secret of the fact; to keep it secret would mean death.

In another sense also, the Moon Man is the god of fruitfulness. It is he who sets the currents of the sea in motion, and thus determines the movements of the seal. This gives good hunting to all good men, as the animals are scattered along the coasts; and villages where the ancient rules of life are faithfully observed will never lack food. This is why he is so careful to see that no offence is committed, but he himself is helpless once the mighty Sea Spirit has shut up all the animals in her house.

The Moon is also the well disposed patron of all boys, all great hunters to be, and therefore they sacrifice to him; not because they are afraid of him, but in order that he may bring them luck. And all little boys who wish to become great hunters, sacrifice to the moon in the following manner:

At every new moon, they run out to a spot where the snow is clean and free from footmarks. From here they take a lump of snow, and call up to the moon:

"Give me luck in hunting!" Then they run into the house and put the snow into a water vessel. The reason for this is that the seals, who live in salt water, are always thirsty. And the snow water thus offered is given by the moon to the seals that are to be captured in the future. On the same principle, their mother must sprinkle water out in the direction of the moon, the first time the baby boy in her amaut sees the moon.

All this is done with a view to obtaining success in hunting. And for the same reason shamans often travel through the air to visit the Moon Man, who is always willing to give men good hunting. All hunting on sea or land is reckoned quite as much a matter of luck as of skill. And luck is granted by the Moon Man if only one visits him in his house. Therefore it happens sometimes that the Moon will himself take a hunter up to his house in the sky, out of sheer goodwill towards him. But all who go visiting the Moon must beware of another spirit which it is impossible to avoid meeting in the heavens. Some believe that this spirit lives with the Moon, others that it has its own house just close by. This spirit, which is a woman, is called Ululiarnâq ("the one with the ulo", a knife used by women) and her perculiarity is, that she is always trying to make people laugh. And if they do but smile, she will slit up their bellies and tear out the entrails. She wears a tunic that is too short for her, terminating in a pointed hood. She has tattooed her face in such odd patterns that one can hardly help laughing at that alone. The Moon Man does all he can to keep her out of his house, but nevertheless it happens sometimes that she finds an opportunity of throwing down her dish on the floor; a dish quite white at the bottom from the fat of entrails. And then she herself comes leaping in after it, dancing and hopping and twisting her body in all manner of ludicrous and sensual gestures and movements, ready to fall on any who smile, in a moment, and use her knife. So rapidly is it done, that a man's entrails are dumped down into the dish the very moment his face shows the faintest trace of a smile. Another thing which makes it more difficult to refrain is, that she has always about her a whole crowd of pale and shrunken men, who constantly burst out laughing at everything she does. These are victims whom she has already disembowelled, and who are anxious to see others suffer the same fate.

Thus the Moon Man has his evil Ululiarnâq, just as the Sea Spirit has Isarrataitsoq and the Air Spirit has Oqaloraq. There is this difference, however, that the Moon Spirit always warns people against Ululiarnâq, and turns her out of his house when she tries to do harm, whereas the two other great spirits never hinder their satellites from doing evil to men. Therefore the Moon Spirit is in nearly all respects a kindly spirit, though even he can also be merciless. In a very few cases, he may even have power over life and death. As mentioned elsewhere, there are certain persons who, by virtue of special amulets and spells, are able to come to life again if they happen to die by accident; but where such persons fail to observe their taboo, the Moon Spirit renders all the efforts of the shamans unavailing. Note, for instance, that Takornâq relates how her husband, Quivâpik, endeavoured to catch one such unfortunate in order to restore him to life. But the dead man's mother had made dresses of new caribou skins on Marble Island, which is holy ground, where no woman is allowed to work. Therefore the Moon Spirit rendered all the efforts of Quivâpik unavailing, and no magic sufficed to bring the dead man back to life.

The Eskimo view of the Moon Spirit is best seen through the various legends told about it; and these are also the sources to which the natives themselves refer when asked whence they have their knowledge relating to the moon.

How the Moon Spirit first came.

There was once an old grandmother, who lived with her two grandchildren, a young man and a girl; the young man was named Aningât, the girl Seqineq: The young man was healthy and free from disease at first, but then suddenly he went blind.

They lived alone, poor, and almost without food; and then one day there came a bear to the place where they lived; the bear went straight up to their house and began to gnaw at the frame of the window. Then the old woman took her grandchild's bow and aimed for the blind boy, while he himself drew the bow and loosed the arrow. He struck the bear, and the bear ran away, growling and biting at the wound.

"It sounded as if my arrow had struck a beast" said Aningât.

"No, it was only the frame of the window," said his grandmother.

The grandmother and Seqineq then went out of the house, and saw a bear lying dead on the ice, and now the grandmother suddenly set about building a little house for Aningât. He was to live by himself. And then she killed a dog and let him make do with that, while she and the girl ate delicious bear's meat. But the girl often brought some of the bear's meat to her brother, hiding it in her sleeve.

The old grandmother grew suspicious, and said one day:

"I believe you are taking bear's meat to you brother; otherwise you could not eat up the meat I give you so quickly."

"I eat up so quickly because I am hungry" answered Seqineq.

One day Aningât said to his sister:

"Do you never see a loon up on the lakes here close at hand?"

"Yes, I do" answered Seqineq.

"If only you would take me up to the lakes one day" said Aningât.

And Seqineq did so, and the blind man said: "Will you build a row of landmarks from the lake here down to our house, so that it may not be difficult for me to find my way back?"

And his sister built stone landmarks on the way back.

Now the young man stayed by the lake, listening intently until he heard a splashing of water. It was the sound of a kayak. He waited a little, and then he heard a voice say:

"Come here and sit in the kayak for a moment."

He went towards the sound and sat down in the kayak. He sat down in the kayak and was rowed out to sea, and then suddenly he was taken down under the water. When he came up again, he heard the voice say: "Did you feel dizzy?"

"No" said Aningât. And then once more he was taken down under water, and each time they remained longer and longer under water.

The young man suddenly noticed that he could as it were distinguish things a little, he could see a little, and more and more every time he had been under water.

Every time they had been down under water, the stranger asked: "Can you see anything?"

"I see nothing" answered Aningât, though he could really see a little now.

Now he was taken under water again and this time he was kept there so long that he did feel thoroughly dizzy. "Can you still see nothing?" asked the stranger, when they came up.

"Yes, now I can see" answered Aningât, and he could see even little blades of grass far far off.

After that they rowed in to land and got out of the kayak. The loon flew away, but Aningât cut a piece from his kamiks and made a sling; then he went down towards their house, throwing stones with his sling, finding his way by means of the landmarks his sister had build. Down by the house he caught sight of a bear's skin, and the skin of a dog, stretched out to dry.

"Where did that bear come from?" he asked his grandmother as he entered the house.

"Oh, that must be a skin left behind by the people who came in the umiᴀq; one passed by a little while ago" said the grandmother falsely, and Aningât said no more.

Thus the blind youth regained his sight, and was now able to go out hunting once more. It was spring, just in the time when the white whales were moving along the edge of the ice, and he often went hunting them with his sister, he harpooning them and she helping by holding the end of the harpoon line. One day the old grandmother thought she would like to go with them. She herself would hold the line; and so they went down to the ice-edge. The white whales came swimming in quite close to the firm ice, and the old grandmother cried out: "Here comes a young whale; harpoon it, harpoon it!"

Aningât made as if to strike one of the small whales, but in casting, changed his aim on purpose so as to strike one of the very largest. The old grandmother had the harpoon line fastened round her waist, and when the great whale began to pull, she was drawn over the ice and could not resist, but went sliding out into water. For a moment it looked as if she were running on the surface of the water, then she disappeared.

The white whale remained long under water, and not until it came up again did the old grandmother reappear. And as soon as she had got her head above water, she sang to her grandchild:

"Grandchild, grandchild,
Why do you leash me like a dog?
Have you forgotten that it was always I
Who with never so much as a grimace
Cleaned up dirt and wet after you?
Have you forgotten that it was I?"

Her grandchild answered:

"Grandmother, grandmother,
Why did you give me nothing?
Why was I given nothing of the meat
From the bear that I shot,
The first bear I ever shot?"

His grandmother sang again:

"Grandchild, grandchild,
If only I could reach
Up to that little hillock on dry land!"

— and with that she disappeared under the water.

Thus the brother and sister were left alone. But when the winter came, they left that place, and went out into the world for shame at having killed their grandmother.

The first people they came to were the kukiliqäc'iait, impish creatures with long claws. Here they built a snow hut. While they were building it, Aningât felt thirsty, and said to his sister: "I am so thirsty, go in and get me some water."

Seqineq went to a window and called in "My brother is so thirsty, give me a little water to take to him."

"Come in and fetch it yourself. But it is dripping from the roof in the passage, so you must pull your clothes aside over the hips and come in backwards" said those within. The girl did as they said. But as she was going in backwards, they fell upon her and began scratching her with their long, sharp nails, and Seqineq called out to her brother to come and help her. Aningât ran in at once, taking with him a tent pole, and with this he struck them down one after another; each time he struck, one fell down. Up on the bench lay an old man picking at his nails. He said: "I told you not to hurt the girl or her brother would come and avenge her."

Hardly had he finished speaking when the young man struck him with the tent pole and killed him.

They stayed long in that place, until Seqineq was well again; they then went on again in search of men. They often met with people, but did not stay with them. At last they came to the land of the Rumpless folk, and here they stopped for a time. Round about the houses lay delicious lumps of meat, breasts of caribou, and rich suet. These people could only suck the meat and draw out the juice, they could not swallow it because they had no rump to their backs. Here they stayed, and Seqineq found a husband and Aningât a wife.

These were strange people they had come to, for they had no opening in the body such as ordinary people have, they had no rump, and the women had no genitals, and Aningât could therefore never lie with his wife. One day he suddenly took a knife and made a slit in her lap, such as women usually have, and at once the woman began to sing:

"My husband slit my lap,
I was wounded in the lap,
And it will never close up again".

Seqineq soon found she was with child, and when the time came for her to bring forth, her mother-in-law began plaiting caribou sinew, and when the birth-pangs came on, she began sharpening her knife. When Aningât saw these preparations, he said: "Wait a little, do not slit her up, she can bring forth the child by herself."

And so it turned out. The girl brought forth her child in the natural way. But hardly was the child born than the old mother-in-law began singing for joy:

"My daughter-in-law has brought forth a child,
A little child with a rump,
A little child with genitals;
Now I wonder, how can I
Get a right sort of opening myself?"

With these words she took a meat fork and tried to stick it into herself behind. And all the other women did the same. If they

Snow-house camp. Drawing by Usugtâq.

A boy drawing pictures on the rime of the ice-window with a knife. The picture is of a snow house, lined inside with skin hangings.

Drawing by Taparte. At the top: caricature of Dr. Birket-Smith. Bottom: self-portrait by Taparte, as he sees himself in the bottom of a tin box.

hit the right spot, where the opening should be, they lived, but if they struck in the wrong place, they fell down and died.

While Seqineq lay in the birth hut, it often happened that people assembled in the feasting house to dance and sing. And Aningât often went in to visit his sister and lay with her. But when he came in, he always made haste to put out the lamp, before she could see who it was, and then he would lie with her. His sister did not know who it was, and one evening when he lay with her as usual, she blackened his face with a little soot from the lamp. When he left her, she followed him to the feasting house, and hardly had he entered there when she heard those within laughing: "Look, Aningât has soot on his face!"

But Seqineq was so ashamed at this that she ran back to her snow hut, snatched up her knife and hurried to the dancing house again, and there she hacked off one of her breasts, threw it down in front of her brother, and cried: "You are so fond of my body; eat that too!"

With these words, Seqineq ran out of the feasting house, holding in her hand a torch made of moss dipped in oil. Her brother likewise snatched up a torch and hurried after her. Outside the snow hut they began to run, Seqineq in front, Aningât after, round the hut. But Aningât fell over a block of snow, and his torch went out. Suddenly they both began to rise up from the earth, but moving all the time in a circle round the hut, and thus they rose up in the air, one in chase of the other, moving round the dome of the heavens until they came right up into the sky. And there they became sun and moon. Seqineq with her burning torch was the sun, while Aningât became the moon, with light devoid of warmth.

Told by

Ivaluardjuk.

It has already been noted that the evil spirit which eats men's entrails, and tries to kill all human beings whom the Moon Spirit is seeking to aid, is called Ululiarnâq; the immigrant Netsilingmiut call her Aukjûk. She also, in certain cases, keeps a strict watch to see that men do not commit any breach of taboo, as the following will show. It is strictly forbidden to sleep out on the ice-edge when hunting. Every evening, the hunter must return either to land, or to the old, firm ice which lies some distance back from the open sea. The Sea Spirit does not like her creatures to smell human beings when they are not actually hunting. The following story shows the Moon Spirit and Aukjûk, and finally Aukjûk as the punitive power where men fail to observe the rules of taboo with regard to the creatures of the sea.

The Moon Spirit and Aukjûk.

There was once a man who stood by a blowhole one night waiting for seal. It was moonlight, and he looked at the moon and suddenly it seemed to be coming nearer; growing bigger and coming nearer. Then he caught sight of a sledge driving right under the rays of the moon, and when it stopped, a little way from him, he left his weapons, and the skin he was standing on, and went up to the sledge. The stranger pointed to his sledge and told him to get in and close his eyes. He did so, and was then carried away. He heard only the sound of hard ice underfoot as they drove. Then he opened his eyes a little way to see where they were, but hastened to close them again when the driver cried: "Hei, hei, hei!" Then they drove on again a great way. All he perceived was the wind that blew in his face because they were driving so fast. Then the driver stopped, and said: "Now you may open your eyes."

He opened his eyes, and now discovered that they had come up to the moon. A great number of windows were lit up round about, and many people were running about outside and playing games. Some were boxing; and if they had been real live human beings it must surely have hurt them terribly, for they struck so hard. He would gladly have stayed watching these people, who were playing games and practising various kinds of sport, but the Moon Spirit pointed to the brightest of all the windows, and so he went with him towards it. The man had heard of Aukjûk, who slit up folk's bellies and took out their entrails, and he was prepared to meet her in the house they now came to. At the entrance lay a big live bearded seal, which they had to tread on in order to get in. They trod on the bearded seal and entered the passage, and he heard the bearded seal turn round after they had trodden on it. Then he crept in through the passage and came in to a large double house. As they came into the house, he looked into the second chamber, and such a warmth came out from there that his clothes were moist with sweat at the neck. It was the sun that lived there. A woman came in with the entrails of a caribou, all covered in fat, and invited him to eat, and he put out his hand to take some. But he missed his grasp, and fell out into the passage. He went through the passage, trod on the bearded seal, and when he heard it turn after he had trodden on it, he looked back. And there stood Aukjûk in the house with her dish and her big knife in her hand. He fled away as fast as he could, but she ran after him, and he ran a long way over level ice until suddenly he found himself floating downwards through the air. All he felt was a faint breeze in his face, and he came down at a furious pace on to the ice again, and stood once more by the blowhole where he had been hunting seal. He stood there a little while by the blowhole, waiting for a seal, but he was feeling frightened, and soon went home. When he got in, he ate his meal with the others in the house, saying nothing of what had happened to him, but after a little while found he could not open his mouth. A shaman was called in, and discovered what was the matter with him. He had concealed the fact that the Moon had carried him away, but as soon as this was discovered and talked about, there was no longer anything the matter with him, and he could open and close his mouth once more. But if he had eaten of the food offered him in the Moon's house, he would never again have returned to the dwellings of men.

Told by
Inugpasugjuk.
(immigrant Netsilingmio).

Aukjûk punishes breach of taboo.

There were once three men who went out to the ice-edge to hunt, and they decided to sleep there, although it was forbidden to do so. The oldest of the three men was a shaman.

The hunters had built a snow hut out on the ice, and while they lay there asleep, an old woman came in suddenly through the closed entrance. She got in without any sign to show that the snow block which closed the entrance had been moved. She placed herself in front of the sleeper who lay outermost, and without waking him, robbed him of his entrails. She stood there with her dish in her hand, and her knife, laid down the entrails and went on to the next, whose entrails she likewise took and laid in her dish, but when she came to the shaman, he made as it were an effort, and awoke, and waking his companions, said to them: "I just dreamed that your entrails had been stolen away."

At these words they put their hands to their bellies and discovered that all was empty within; they had no entrails. They got up at once to return to their homes. They went homewards, and the shaman was often obliged to stop and wait for the two who had lost their entrails, as they walked so slowly. The shaman at once went into his house and prepared to call up his helping spirits. The two who had lost their entrails laid their tunics on top of the covered passage to the house and went in. The men came in, and one of those who had lost his entrails said to his wife:

"Go outside and fetch my tunic, which I laid on top of the passage way. Do not be afraid of it, but take it, even though there may be teeth growing out round the neck."

The woman went out to fetch it, but although it was only quite an ordinary garment she was nevertheless afraid of it when she saw that there were ugly teeth growing out round the neck, and she dared not take it, but went in without having accomplished her errand. She said to her husband: "Your tunic looked so dangerous and terrifying that I dared not take it."

The husband answered: "If you do not take it, then I must pass to the realm of death. Do not be afraid of it, but just go and take it."

The woman went out again and tried to take the garment, but it looked so terrible that she dared not take it after all, and a second time she went in without having accomplished her errand. Then the man knew he was lost, and no one could hold him back; he went out towards the ice-edge on his way to the Land of the Dead.

The other man who had lost his entrails now spoke and said to his wife: "I shall suffer the same fate as my companion, who has now passed to the Land of the Dead, if you do not go out and fetch my tunic. Now go out and fetch it. It will not hurt you. Do not be afraid of it, but bring it in."

The woman went out, but when she saw the teeth that had grown out round the neck, she dared not take it after all, and went in again, like the other, without having accomplished her errand, and said: "I dared not take it. It looked so dreadful."

Her husband answered: "Then there is no help for me. I too must now pass to the Land of the Dead."

And then he went out, took up his tunic, and went down towards the ice-edge.

Meanwhile, the shaman had called up his helping spirits, and if only the women had brought in the garments, he could have got the men's entrails back.

After that no one ever dared to sleep on the edge of the ice, for Aukjûk, who lives in the Moon Spirit's house, always steals away the entrails of those who sleep on the edge of the ice.

Told by
Inugpasugjuk.
(immigrant Netsilingmio).

As already mentioned, the Moon Spirit is particularly careful to see that unclean women do not offend the animals in any way. Women with child especially are instructed to observe the greatest possible caution in all respects, and above all else, they must never touch anything taken from a seal. They are therefore strictly forbidden to play any of the games in which the pieces are made from seals' bones, but even in such cases the Moon Spirit never appears as a cruel avenger, but rather indulgent, endeavouring to make people understand that they have done wrong. Often it merely seeks to ward off the disaster which would otherwise occur. The kindliness of the Moon Spirit is especially apparent in the following story, in which, without threats or ill words, it simply takes possession of a woman who might have been a danger to her fellows.

Tutukatuk, who was carried off by the Moon for breach of taboo.

There was once a young woman whose name was Tutukatuk. She was about to have her first child, and although she was with child, she one day played with the pieces of a game made from bones of a seal.

(inuʌrtɔq: playing with a kind of dice made from the small bones of a seal's flippers. The player takes as many pieces as he pleases, shakes them in his hand and throws them down on a flat stone, to see how many lie down and how many stand up. The game is either played for points, or used as a method of divination; for instance, if it is desired to ascertain whether a man has been successful out hunting or not, a piece may be thrown. If it lies flat, he has got nothing, if it stands erect, he has found game.)

One evening when the moon was shining, a sledge was heard approaching. The sledge stopped outside the house, and a man came up to the window and shouted: "Come outside, Tutukatuk, and bring your pieces with you."

Tutukatuk went out, taking the pieces with her, and placed herself on the sledge and drove off with the stranger.

"Now you must not open your eyes" he said. "If you do, you will fall off the sledge."

Suddenly they rose up in the air, for this was none other than the Moon Spirit who had come down to fetch Tutukatuk, and they dashed off now through space at a terrific speed, the sledge bounding every time they passed a star. Across the clear sky the sledge moved evenly, without much shaking, but rapidly. After a long journey, they halted. Now at last Tutukatuk opened her eyes and saw a great number of people playing ball, and the players stopped their game and came forward to greet them. The Moon Spirit said: "It is a live human being I have with me."

Then the others, who were all dead, went away again, and the Moon Spirit led Tutukatuk into his house and set her on the bench. On the floor over at the other side of the house lay a shoulder bone with no meat on. The Moon Spirit lifted it up and said: "Just look down through the opening here, and you can see all the dwellings of men." Some lay far apart, others close together, and looking down on them from the sky, it was as if they had no roofs, for one could see right into the houses. The Moon Spirit opened the peephole every morning, and then Tutukatuk could see that some of the people were asleep, others awake.

(The narrator has here omitted to note the moral of the story, assuming it to be known. The idea, however, is as follows: Pregnant women are not allowed to play with "bones". Such women are unclean and must not have anything to do with seal's bones. It was for this that the moon came and carried off this woman. From his house up above he then shows her, through a peephole, the dwellings of men, and points out all the impurity and filth that rises from a house where a woman has committed any breath of taboo. A woman who does so defiles the universe and frightens the animals away. This also is assumed to be generally known, and therefore not mentioned by the story-teller.)

When the time came for Tutukatuk to bring forth her child, the Moon Spirit brought her back to earth, but before doing so, he said to her: "You must not eat any food procured by human hands. If you do, you will die (for breaking the rules of taboo). But I will bring you food, and you will find it on the drying place above your lamp."

Tutukatuk came home to her own place and gave birth to her child, and all that she needed in the way of food she found on the drying place above her lamp. The lamp itself was filled with oil from there, and joints of caribou meat were ready for her when she felt hungry and wanted something to eat.

The child was born and grew big, and at last Tutukatuk's husband said to her: "Your child is grown big now. There is no need for you to be so careful about what you eat. Why do you never eat any of the meat I bring home?"

But it was in vain that her husband urged her to eat of the meat he brought home from his hunting; she would not do so, and at last the man grew angry. Then his wife dared not refuse to eat of the meat he brought home. As soon as she had eaten of it, the child fell ill and was on the point of death, merely because the woman had broken the taboo which the Moon Spirit had decreed for her. So dangerous a thing is it to break one's taboo. But the visit to the Moon Spirit made such an impression on Tutukatuk that she always in future observed the taboo prescribed for women.

Told by

Inugpasugjuk.

(immigrant Netsilingmio).

The Moon Spirit befriends a woman.

There was once a woman who was very unhappy with her husband. Of an evening, when she went to lie down, he would turn her out of the house, and lie with other women. At last none of the other women would lie with him, but that only made him the more cruel to his wife. He would pull all her clothes off, leaving her stark naked, and then turn her out of doors in all manner of weather.

One evening, when he had done this as usual, she determined never to go back to him any more. It was full moon, and very light. She went over to a place where there were no footprints, where no one had trodden the snow, and here she began walking backwards, very slowly, at the same time wishing for the Moon Spirit to come and carry her off.

"tᴀrqᴇq̃ piᵛʃuma· aiŋa": "Moon, you up there, fetch me" she cried. She was careful not to look up, and kept on walking backwards, very slowly. Then it seemed to her as if the moon came nearer and nearer, but she would not look up, and only kept on walking backwards. And then suddenly there was a sledge just beside her; a man with a sledge and three dogs. The man called to his dogs by name: one was called Teriatsiaq, a white dog, Naluperitsoq, a black dog, and Miglialik. It was the Moon Spirit, a big man with a mighty whip in his hand. He called the woman to him, and told her to get up on the sledge. She did so, and at once the sledge rose up in the air, and they drove up to the sky. As they came near the land of the Udlormiut, the Moon Spirit said: "I live in a double house; be careful not to look into the room next to mine. The sun lives there, and she will burn you. As soon as you come in, Ululiarnâq will be after you to try to make you laugh, but keep away from her. If you feel you want to smile, then bend your head down into your collar and cover your eyes with your hands."

Thus the Moon Spirit warned the woman before they reached the house, that no harm might come to her. And she did as he said. Afterwards she lived with him, and it was not long before she was with child. She felt well and comfortable there, and he was kind to her. One day he showed her, to the right of the lamp, the shoulderbone of a caribou, which was thrust down into the snow as a lid. As soon as he took it away, they could see out over the earth right down to her home. And they could see how her neighbours there were playing the wolf game, the game in which a few are wolves and the rest human beings chased by the wolves. The only one who did not join in the game was her husband. He stood by himself over by his meat stand, sorrowful and with bowed head.

The time came when she was ready to bring forth, and the Moon Spirit now thought it better that she should go down to earth and give birth to the child in her own place. And so he drove her home and built a little house for her. Before leaving, he bade her particularly to remember that she must not eat any meat save of his killing, for he was the child's father. But her husband was jealous of the Moon Spirit, for having begotten a child with his barren wife, and every time the Moon Spirit brought meat, he smeared it with oil from the waste of the lamp, so that it was uneatable. Thus he forced her to eat meat that he himself had killed. And now the Moon Spirit stayed away and never came to visit her again.

This is told of the manner in which the Moon Spirit befriended a woman who was ill-treated by her husband. And he kept the woman with him until her husband repented of his cruelty and felt kindly towards her.

Told by

Ivaluardjuk.

It has now been made clear, through these stories, from the Eskimos' own manner of explaining the position, how the Moon Spirit takes care to see that no breach of taboo takes place. In nearly all the stories here given, the Moon Spirit appears as a good and warning power. It can also show kindness to poor and ill-treated homeless children, who lead a miserable existence owing to their being without relatives. Often it is a case of boys that will not grow, and therefore never get on in the world. They have somehow accumulated in their bodies all the evil, hampering influence arising from breach of taboo on the part of the mother. Then it is that the Moon Spirit appears as a Lord of Power, purifying the outcast and miserable from all evil effects of the offence, and subsequently showing how such a person, freed from all impurity, suddenly begins to grow and becomes a great man among his fellows. This is shown in the following story, which has become almost a national myth both in Greenland and in Canada.

The Lord of Power makes the miserable Kâgjagjuk invincible and mighty among his fellows.

There was once a homeless boy, who would not grow. And for that reason all were unkind to him, and no one would give him anything to eat. The only thing he was given was long strips of thick walrus hide; this he could not swallow, but he had to chew it; and when he kept on chewing it just in the same way as women chew sole leather to soften it for the needle, it sometimes happened that he managed to swallow it after all, so that he got a little meat in his belly. In the same village there lived an old woman who took pity on him, and she would secretly give him small pieces, not too large for him to swallow. She also gave him a little knife, which he could hide about his person in different places, a mere splinter of flint, small enough to be hidden in his ear or under his foreskin. Thus he could always hide it away quickly when unkind people asked him how he managed to eat so quickly, and searched him to see if he had not a knife somewhere. So ill-disposed were all towards him that at last he was forced to lie out in the passage among the dogs.

One evening he was lying out in the passage, asleep, and the moon shone right down upon him. Then he was awakened by the sound of a sledge driving up outside, and he heard a man call to his team to halt, calling the dogs by name as follows: "Teriatsiaq, Kajorshuk and Naluperitsoq". The stranger came to the entrance of the passage and called in through the opening: "Come outside a little", but Kâgjagjuk answered: "I will not come out. You go out, Qaipiarigjualuk" It was one of the dogs he was speaking to. The dog answered: "No, go out yourself."

Then said the voice outside once more: "Kâgjagjuk, come outside a little". And again Kâgjagjuk answered: "No, I will not go out, you go out, Akijaorjualuk". And this time again it was a dog he was speaking to. But the dog answered: "No, go out yourself".

Then said the Moon Spirit again, for it was he: "No, come out yourself Kâgjagjuk."

Well, the end of it was, Kâgjagjuk was obliged to go himself. And hardly had the boy come out when the Moon Spirit took him by the hand and led him to a spot where there were no human footprints to be seen. And here he began beating him, thumping him with clenched fist all over his body. Every time the Moon Spirit struck him, the boy fell down in the snow, and hardly had he got on his feet again when the Moon Spirit once more knocked him down. At last Kâgjagjuk began vomiting, and brought up combings of woman's hair and fragments of skins that had been cut to make women's breeches. Thus the Moon Spirit beat all the impurities out of Kâgjagjuk.

As soon as all the impurity was out of his body, the boy began to grow, and he grew and he grew until he could no longer get into his clothes. Then said the Spirit: "Pull up that stone". It was a big stone that was frozen hard in the soil, and Kâgjagjuk pulled it up. Then the Moon Spirit chose a stone even bigger than the first, and this also Kâgjagjuk pulled up. Then the Moon Spirit took off his own outer garments, his tunic, breeches and kamiks, and gave them to

Kâgjagjuk, and to these gifts he added also a snow beater. And when Kâgjagjuk had received all these things, the Moon Spirit spoke to him and said:

"Tomorrow I will send three bears down to your village. All you have to do is to keep in hiding and not come out until you are called. The three bears will be fierce and dangerous bears."

Morning came the next day, and lo, there came three bears, three big bears, and the people of the village went out to attack. Suddenly they missed Kâgjagjuk; they wanted him to come out that the bears might tear him to death. All looked for him, but no one could find him. At last, however, he came forth and went slowly down towards the ice. The women sang a song:

> "Where is Kâgjagjuk, Kâgjakjuk, miserable wretch?
> Not too good to frighten bears away,
> Not too good to make a morsel for the bears,
> Well and good, let him tease them,
> Well and good, let them eat him up".

Thus the women sang, and it was always the women who were most cruel to Kâgjagjuk. But he went down without fear, and when he came out on the ice, he struck with his snow beater to show how strong he had become. And now he sang:

> "Yes, where is Kâgjagjuk, Kâgjagjuk, miserable wretch?
> Not too good to frighten bears away,
> Not too good to make a morsel for the bears.
> Listen awhile, you that plagued me so,
> You that struck me on hands and feet
> Because you never thought to see me grown up.
> Here I come now as a great man and a fighter,
> You may call names and sing songs of derision,
> But you cannot do me any harm."

With this song he went forward, picking up as he went the men who would have used him as a bait for the bears, and throwing them to the beasts themselves instead, and the bears tore them in pieces. At last he attacked the bears himself and killed them. Afterwards he married the old woman who had always taken his part. That was his way of thanking her.

So the miserable Kâgjagjuk became a strong man and a great fighter, because the Moon Spirit came to him as the Lord of Power and cleansed him from his mother's breach of taboo.

Told by
Ivaluardjuk.

— These, then, are the powers which rule the world and the life of mankind on earth, and they are here presented and characterised just as the Eskimos themselves regard them from the point of view of the precepts laid down, these again having their origin solely in the need for some kind of religious safeguard. Finally, they are described in stories which may often, it is true, — thanks to a poorly developed art of narration — appear insignificant, but which have nevertheless, to the natives themselves, their great power and importance in the fact that they are regarded as historical documents concerning events which once took place, and which are now the source of all information regarding past ages, ancient times when there was hardly any difference between men and animals, and when both men and animals could in some inexplicable way be transformed into mighty and terrible spirits. For they were all, at one time, the Sea Spirit and her father, the Spirit of the Air and the Moon Spirit and the Sun and the Entrail Eater, quite ordinary human beings living on earth like everyone else, without any uncommon attributes whatever.

Mankind would now be altogether crushed by these mighty and unfathomable spirits which, originating from their own race, now occupy the heavens, the earth and the sea, if there were not easily accessible mediators between men and spirits. This office was filled by the angákut, or shamans. But before passing to further consideration of these, we must, in order fully to understand the power and faculties attributed to them, learn something of the manner in which the Eskimos regard that great leap from life here on earth into the vast unknown that comes after death.

IV.

Death, and Life in the Land of the Dead.

In the very earliest times, there was no death among human beings. Men took women to wife, and women bore children, and mankind grew so numerous that at last there was not room for all. The first human beings lived on an island, and there are those who maintain that it was the island of Mitligjuaq, in Hudson Strait. But the people there propagated their kind, and as none ever left the land where they were born, there were at last so many that the island could not support them. Very slowly, then, one side of the island began to slope down towards the sea. The people grew frightened, for it seemed as if they might slip off and be drowned. But then an old woman began to shout; she had power in her words, and she called out loudly: "tɔqu^{w}aglutik pilᴇrlit taʃ·a nuna tat·ɔrtualu·nialᴇra^{p}tigo": "Let be so ordered that human beings can die, for there will no longer be room for us on earth".

And the woman's words had such power that her wish was fulfilled. Thus death came among mankind.

— — —

"Mysterious as the manner in which death came into life, even so mysterious is death itself", says Aua.

"We know nothing about it for certain, save that those we live with suddenly pass away from us, some in a natural and understandable way because they have grown old and weary, others, however, in mysterious wise, because we who lived with them could see no reason why they in particular should die, and because we knew that they would gladly live. But that is just what makes death the great power it is. Death alone determines how long we may remain in this life on earth, which we cling to, and it alone carries us into another life which we know only from the accounts of shamans long since dead. We know that men perish through age, or illness, or accident, or because another has taken their life. All this we understand. Something is broken. What we do not understand is the change which takes place in a body when death lays hold of it. It is the same body that went about among us and was living and warm and spoke as we do ourselves, but it has suddenly been robbed of a power, for lack of which it becomes cold and stiff and putrefies. Therefore we say that a man is ill when he has lost a part of his soul, or one of his souls; for there are some who believe that man has several souls. If then that part of a man's vital force be not restored to the body, he must die. Therefore we say that a man dies when the soul leaves him.

"We have already spoken of how most shamans divide the soul into two parts: inu'sia, of which we say that anᴇrnᴇranut atavɔq: that it "is one with the spirit of life", and the spirit of life is something a living human being cannot do without. The other part of the soul is tᴀrniŋa, perhaps the most powerful part of the soul, and the most mysterious, for while tᴀrniŋa gives life and health, it is at the same time nap'autip ina': the site of disease, or the spot where any sickness enters in.

"We believe that men live on after death here on earth, for we often see the dead in our dreams fully alive. And we believe in our dreams, for sleep has a ruler, a spirit which we call Aipâtle. This spirit would not show us our dear departed if they did not go on living. Aipâtle helps us also in other ways. When we wake in the morning therefore, we pray to him for what we want, and make offerings of meat to him when we are about to eat. We sacrifice to the spirit ,saying: 'aipa'tʟe iluamik piumavuŋa; nᴇrʒutinik tunisigut': 'I wish for what is good, give us luck in our hunting.'

"Old folk declare that when a man sleeps, his soul is turned upside down, so that the soul hangs head downwards, only clinging to the body by its big toe. For this reason also we believe that death and sleep are nearly allied; for otherwise, the soul would not be held by so frail a bond when we sleep. But the Spirit of Sleep is also very fond of the dead, for when we sacrifice meat to him, he gives the souls of the dead meat from our offerings. This also is a sign that death and sleep are nearly allied."

— This account was given by Aua, not, of course, impromptu and all at once, but his explanation is a summary of his own words, in his answers to my numerous questions.

No Eskimo fears death in itself, for all are convinced that it is merely the transition to a new and better form of life. But as mentioned elsewhere, there is also this mystery connected with the soul, that as soon as death has deprived it of the body, it can turn upon the living as an evil and ruthless spirit. The soul of a good and peaceable man may suddenly turn into an evil spirit. There is therefore much intricate taboo associated with death, as the precepts will afterwards show. For the present, it will suffice to state as follows:

When a person dies, the body must be placed in its grave as speedily as possible. If the sun is still in the sky, when death occurs, then it is done at once, but if death occurs after sunset, then the body, if that of a man, must remain in the house or tent for three days, if that of a woman, for four days, or in some places, five. The body is tied up in the caribou skin which was used by the sick person to sleep on, and is set up in a crouching position. This work must be carried out by an old woman, who may have a little girl to help her. The dead body must never be carried out through the ordinary entrance to the dwelling. In the case of a snow hut, it is dragged out through a hole cut in the back wall; in the case of a tent, the skin that forms the tent is lifted up behind the sleeping place, and the body removed that way. In the winter it is generally dragged to the grave, in summer it is carried. The bodies of men and boys are laid in the grave with the face towards the east; women, on the other hand, must face south.

After death, there are two different places to which one may pass, either up into heaven to the Udlormiut, or People of Day; their land lies in the direction of dawn, and is the same as the Land of the Moon Spirit. The other place to which the dead may come lies down under the sea. It is a narrow strip of land, with sea on either side; and the inhabitants are therefore called Qimiujârmiut: "the dwellers in the narrow land." The immigrant Netsilingmiut call them Atlêt: "those lowest down", for they live in a world below the world in which we live.

Here also dwells the great Sea Spirit Takánakapsâluk.

As already mentioned, persons dying by violence, whether through no fault of their own or by their own hand, pass to Udlormiut; those dying a natural death, by disease, go to Qimiujârmiut. Life in the Land of the Dead is described later under Shamans. It is pleasant both in the Land of Day and in the Narrow Land. In the former, hunting is mainly confined to land animals, in the latter, the denizens of the sea. It appears however, from the stories, that the dead up in heaven can procure marine animals by the aid of the moon, and similarly, the dwellers in the underworld can obtain caribou meat.

Some hold that all dead persons, whatever the manner of their death, go first to Takánakapsâluk, who then alone determines where they are to dwell; those who have lived a good life without breach of taboo are sent on at once to the Land of Day, whereas those who have failed to observe the ancient rules of life are detained in her house to expiate their misdeeds, before being allowed to proceed to the Narrow Land. The dead suffer no hardship, wherever they may go, but most prefer nevertheless to dwell in the Land of Day, where the pleasures appear to be without limit. Here, they are constantly playing ball, the Eskimos' favourite game, laughing and singing, and the ball they play with is the skull of a walrus. The object is to kick the skull in such a manner that is always falls with the tusks downwards, and thus sticks fast in the ground. It is this ball game of the departed souls that appears as the aurora borealis, and is heard as a whistling, rustling, crackling sound. The noise is made by the souls as they run across the frost-hardened snow of the heavens. If one happens to be out alone at night when the aurora borealis is visible, and hears this whistling sound, one has only to whistle in return and the lights will come nearer, out of curiosity.

Shamans often visit the Udlormiut, not only for pleasure, but also in order to obtain a kind of "blessing", for it brings luck to all the village if one of its shamans makes this aerial journey, and such a shaman is said to be "pavuŋnᴀrtɔq": "he rises to paʏuŋa", or that which is highest of all.

Anyone having relatives among the Udlormiut and wishing to join them after death, can avoid being sent to the Qimiujârmiut; the survivors must then lay the body out on the ice instead of burying it on land. Blocks of snow are then set out round the body, not stones, as on land. Often indeed, a small snow hut is built up over the body as it lies. But it is not everyone who can reckon on their surviving relatives' or neighbours' taking all this trouble, and in order to make sure of coming to the Udlormiut, the best way is to arrange one's death oneself. This was done not long since by an old woman named Inuguk, of Iglulik. Her son had perished while out in his kayak, and as she did not live in the same village herself, the news did not reach her until the winter was well advanced. She was old and without other relatives, and could not be certain that others would comply with her wishes when once she was dead; she therefore cut a hole for herself in the ice of a big lake and drowned herself there in order to join her son.

Another example is likewise recorded from Iglulik: an old woman was frozen to death during a severe winter with scarcity of food. When her son learned the news, he went out one cold winter's night and lay down naked in the snow and was frozen to death himself. This he did because he was very fond of his mother, and wished to live with her in the Land of the Dead.

These suicides, however, had some special reason for taking their own lives. The Eskimos' fearlessness of death is more powerfully illustrated in the case of the many old men and women who ended their lives by hanging themselves. This is done probably not only because the Moon Spirit says that the whole thing is but a moment's dizziness, but possibly also because of an ancient belief that death by violence has a purifying effect. During our first winter in these regions, no fewer than three suicides took place among the few people we knew; two by hanging, the third by cutting the throat. Jacob Olsen was once staying in a village where an old woman committed suicide, and he gives the following account of the matter:

"During my stay at Chesterfield Inlet, I was once up inland hunting caribou with Pilakapsak and his wife Hauna, and in the course of our hunting we came down to a village called Paunat. Here there lived a man named Uhughuanajôq. There were seven others living in the same house with him, among them his mother-in-law, whose name was Aungêq; she was consumptive, and was spitting blood, but not very seriously ill. I often visited this house and talked with the old woman. One evening I went there as usual, and came in through the passage without noticing anything remarkable; the people were sitting about on the bench as they generally did; only I thought they seemed uncommonly silent. It was not the custom here to invite a visitor to sit down, and therefore, having emerged from the narrow entrance hole, I straightened myself up and went across at once to the spot where the sick woman used to lie. On coming nearer, I nearly cried out aloud: I found myself looking into a face that was perfectly blue, with a pair of great eyes projecting right out from the head, and the mouth wide open. I stood there a little to pull myself together, and now perceived a line fastened round the old woman's neck and from there to the roof of the hut. When I was able to speak once more, I asked those in the house what this meant. It was a long time before anyone answered. At last the son-in-law spoke up, and said: 'She felt that she was old, and having begun to spit up blood, she wished to die quickly, and I agreed. I only made the line fast to the roof, the rest she did herself.'

"I could not bear to look at the horrible corpse, which lay stretched out stark naked on the bench, and therefore asked who was going to cover her up for burial. At the same moment there came a widow and a little girl from one of the houses near by. These two gathered all the dead woman's belongings together and laid them on a caribou skin, which they then tied up; next, they began tying up the body itself in another skin, and I stepped forward to help, for there was no one else in the place who dared touch it. Then the woman and the little girl went out, having first armed themselves with their knives, and the rest of the household lay down to sleep. Both men and women laid their knives ready to hand; this they explained was

Scenes from the qulumᴇrtut games. The two upper pictures represent the trial of strength between the two teams, one of which is singing, the other waving their arms. The two iklɔrᴇ·k embracing each other before the contest begins. The lower picture shows the women going over to the team that won the archery contest. Drawing by the Eskimo woman Pakak.

Scenes from the qulumertut games, representing the archery contest. The posts are the targets. The lower picture shows the women's round-dance about the victorious team. Drawing by Pakak.

done lest the dead woman's soul should come back and frighten them.

"Early next morning all the sledges were set on edge outside the huts; this was to warn any visitors arriving that there was a dead body in the place.

"For five days the body was kept in the hut; none of the inmates went out, and no work was done. At last, on the fifth day, a hole was cut in the inner wall of the hut, and through this the body and all its belongings were dragged out by means of a long line, right away to the place where the grave was to be. The entire household followed, chatting and laughing as if nothing serious were the matter. A little way from the village, the body was covered up with snow blocks, and hardly was this done when all broke out into violent and uncontrolled lamentation; it was not weeping, but shouting and screaming. Then all went home. But for five days in succession, the grave was visited at the same hour of the day, and always with the same deafening cries. During all that time, no hunting was allowed to be done, and the members of the bereaved household were only allowed to eat food brought them from other houses.

"At last the snow hut was evacuated, a new one built, and life resumed its normal course."

— — —

I myself came in to Chesterfield somewhat later, immediately after an old man named Qalaseq had hanged himself. Both Qalaseq and his wife Qalalâq belonged to the local Catholic Mission, and since the missionary had often impressed on them that human life is God's and that it was therefore unlawful for us human beings to kill ourselves, Qalalâq was now very eager to explain to me that her husband had not died of hanging. He had been ill for a year, and since there was no prospect of his recovery, he had grown tired of life, and had asked his wife to lend death a helping hand, but in such a fashion that he should not die during the hanging itself, but should be released from the hide thong that was to strangle him before he finally expired. Qulalâq accordingly assured me most earnestly that she had strangled him with the thong, but before he was quite dead, she had removed it, and at the same time held up before him a little crucifix, which had been given them by the missionary. Therefore, according to her view, Qalaseq had really died a natural death; they had only "hurried death up a little, as it is apt to be so very slow at times".

Those whose offences against taboo are not wiped out by a violent death, and who have therefore to go to the Sea Spirit for purification before they can pass to the company of the "blessed" in the Narrow

Land, have then to pass through a period of purgatory, under the guardianship of Isarrataitsoq, the length of time varying, according to the magnitude of the offences, from one to two years, or even several years. Exceptionally good people may, however, get off with less than a year.

Those who passed to the Land of Day and had thus no need of purification were, however, according to some of the angákut, exposed to one great danger. This was Ululiarnâq. If she could get them to smile before they had quite reached the Land of the Blessed, and thus gain the right to tear out their entrails, they would have to live ever after with that same Ululiarnâq, pale, shrunken creatures with no strength to take part in the others' feasting and games.

The worst offence against taboo which any woman can commit is concealment of menstruation or abortion. Women during the menstrual period are especially unclean in relation to all animals hunted, and may thus expose the entire community to the greatest danger and disaster if they endeavour to conceal their impurity.

In the case of men, unnatural and perverse sex indulgence is regarded as the worst offence. By this is understood coition with animals, especially caribou and seals, which they have just killed, or with live dogs. There were also men who sought to satisfy their lust with the "sacred" earth itself, by making hollows in hummocks of earth and committing onanism there. Such offences are very severely condemned, but do not appear to have been, or even now to be, uncommon. It was possible, however, to palliate one's sins by confessing them to one's neighbours, and it was therefore not difficult to obtain information regarding such cases as soon as one got on the track. The shaman Anarqâq, for instance, whom I have often mentioned, and who spent a great part of the winter with us, had indulged in intercourse with caribou and seals; Qûvik, a young man from Repulse Bay, had made use of the earth, and Inûjaq, our adopted son, had used his dogs. These names are given merely to furnish examples from among those with whom we were personally acquainted.

This method of satisfying sex instinct however, was regarded as punishable, and the place where such souls have to undergo purification before they are suffered to live on in the eternal hunting grounds among the Qimiujârmiut, was in the house of Takánakapsâluk. Here they were laid up on the sleeping place under the same skin as the Sea Spirit's aged father, who tormented them and struck them on the genitals continually for a whole year or more, as long as he was not asleep. As a rule, a year from the date of death was considered sufficient for purification by suffering.

I did not meet anyone among the original inhabitants of the Aivilik or Iglulik who could tell me anything about life after death beyond what has already been stated. Inugpasugjuk however, an immigrant, was able to refer to certain old stories. When I asked him how it was possible to know anything at all about life after death, he referred to a well-known Netsilik shaman named Ánaituarjuk.

Life in the Land of the Dead under the sea.

It is related that a shaman named Ánaituarjuk was wont to visit the Land of the Dead under the sea. Once when he was down there, he stopped at a big tent. He entered the tent from behind, through a small opening by which a puppy that was tied up there was accustomed to enter. He chose this way because he must not go in the same way as the dead. He came in and found an old couple inside. The old man was making a shaft for a salmon spear, and was saying how dissatisfied he was with his work. He was looking at it critically, when suddenly he glanced up and caught sight of a stranger, and at once entered into conversation with him and said:

"You have come to a rich land and rich people. Outside the tent lie great slabs of fat suet from the caribou. We simply keep it in case our son should ever happen to be away longer than usual at his hunting."

Dead people live on just in the same way as while on earth, and store up food for the winter as they did when alive.

The old man further related as follows:

"There are many salmon up in a lake called Nutiplertôq", and he invited the stranger to settle at Ibjorshivik, as there were many caribou there. At Hiorarshivik there were many seals.

And the old dead man went on:

"In times long past, when I was out hunting at the blowholes one day, I fell through the ice and was drowned. When I came to myself, I was down at the bottom of the sea. Here I saw all round smooth ice free from snow. I looked about and caught sight of two dogs. I caught hold of them and drove off with them. A great stone lay ahead, and my two dogs went one to either side of the stone. and though the traces whereby they were harnessed to my sledge were invisible, they broke all the same, and I lost the dogs, which ran away from me. I then went on without them, on foot, and every time I passed a deserted camp of snow huts, I looked about for something that might be useful to me. At last one day I found a 'feeler' (this is an implement made of bent caribou antler, used to ascertain the shape and course of a blowhole below the surface) that someone had forgotten, and also a harpoon, and with these I began hunting at the blowholes".

Thus Ánaituarjuk told of life after death.

Told by
Inugpasugjuk.
(immigrant Netsilingmio).

— — —

Inugpasugjuk also stated that Nuliajuk, which was his name for the Sea Spirit, would sometimes carry off human beings, either because they had themselves committed some breach of taboo, or because some near relative of the victim had done so. She did not always punish the one actually guilty, and that was the cruel part of it; for when anyone had done anything wrong, there was no knowing which of his dear ones might suffer for it. Instances were known where Nuliajuk, having carried off a human being, did not kill, but turned the victim into some creature of the sea, so that the man or woman in question would have to live on as a seal or walrus or one of the animals that belonged to her. Only the so-called aŋᴇrlᴀrtukxiᴀq could in such case return to life, with the aid of a shaman. An aŋᴇrlᴀrtukxiᴀq was a human being who had by means of magic words been given the power to come to life again even after having in some way perished by drowning or having been murdered by an enemy.

Those who sought to wrest from Nuliajuk the human beings she had stolen away, must be shamans of such power that they were not afraid to threaten her. If she did not consent of her own free will, they must thrash or beat or otherwise ill-treat her until she gave up the person she had taken. It was to be understood that the soul of the stolen person lived on in the animal, while the body or bones remained with Nuliajuk. An old account of one such case is given in the following story:

Anarte, who perished at sea and came to life again, and afterwards fetched his dead brothers home from the Sea Spirit.

Anarte was out in his kayak when it capsized. He himself perished, and was for long a dead man. One day a great shaman was out in a kayak in the same waters. Suddenly he found he could make no progress; it seemed as if he were being held back by something, and when he turned round, he saw behind him Anarte. Then he thought:

"Perhaps Anarte wants to upset my kayak".

But Anarte answered: "I have no thought of upsetting your kayak; I am only here because I have become a sea animal."

Anarte begged the shaman to take him in to shore, and here he became a human being once more. Anarte thanked the shaman for his help, and then asked: "I know that my brother is also dead. When did he die?"

The shaman answered: "It is long since he died."

"At what season of the year did he die?"

"In winter. No human being did him any harm; the Sea Spirit alone was the cause of his death."

The shaman then took the dead Anarte with him to his village, and thus he returned to life. But it was not long before Anarte began making a staff out of straight pieces of caribou antler, and this staff he armed with sharp spikes made of the same material. With this staff he went off one day, when it was calm, down to the edge of the ice. Here he began to look about, to see whether the shining sea was smooth, and he ran on the shining sea as if it were smooth ice, gliding over it. Now and again he threw himself flat and looked down just as if he were looking through a blowhole on smooth ice. He was a good way out at sea when suddenly he disappeared down under water. In this manner he passed down to the Sea Spirit Nuliajuk. Here he entered the house of Nuliajuk and asked:

"Where has my brother gone?"

But Nuliajuk did not know. Anarte questioned her eagerly, but kept his horn staff with the sharp spikes still hidden. Now her father Isarrataitsoq began to take part in the talk, and mentioned various breaches of taboo which Anarte's little brother had committed. Then Nuliajuk lifted up the skin hangings and took out a lot of human bones, and putting the bones together, tried to make the skeleton stand up, but the skeleton fell down. Some of the bones were missing, and these she looked for, and setting them into the skeleton with the rest, tried again to make it stand up, but again it fell down. She could not find the missing bones, she said, but now Anarte brought out his stick, and Nuliajuk at once went very red in the face and found some more bones, and now the skeleton could stand up: it was Anarte's brother. If Nuliajuk had not brought out the missing bones, Anarte would have beaten her with his stick. Anarte then went out, letting his brother go first. Then they came up to the surface of the sea, and went on together, in to shore, and people saw them coming, Anarte and his brother, both of whom had been dead for a long time. They now mixed with the people of the village and went about as if they had never been dead, and took part at once in the sports of the young folk, just as they had done before.

Their parents, who were very old, lived a little distance from the village, at a place where they were wont to snare eiderduck; and they knew nothing of all this. A homeless girl was sent to tell them of their sons' return. At first she was afraid to go, but at last she was obliged to all the same. When she came into the old folk's house, one of them at once said: "Come and catch my lice." The girl did so, but she was afraid of the old people, and told a lie in order to have an excuse for running away. Not until she had reached the entrance did she give the message she had been asked to give: "Your sons have come back to the village; they are taking part in the sports with the young people over there." And then she ran back to the village as hard as she could.

"Hi, what's that you say?" Anarte's mother called after her.

"I was told to tell you that your sons are alive and have come back to the village, and they are now taking part in the sports with the young people there".

"Hi, you there" cried the old woman, delighted, "come back and take this little gift".

The girl was afraid they would kill her, and at first she did not dare to go back, and again the old mother called after her: "I won't hurt you. I only want to give you this". And the old woman gave the girl a fine knife by way of thanks, and they went off all three together to the village.

Afterwards the girl was married to one of the two young men who had returned to life, and the old parents lived happily to the end of their days with their two sons.

Told by
Inugpasugjuk.
(immigrant Netsilingmio).

— — —

With reference to this story, Inugpasugjuk stated that it was always a very dangerous thing to take another's life. People must have no secrets. All the evil deeds one tried to conceal grew and became dangerous, living evil. If one took the life of another human being, this must likewise not be kept secret from the neighbours, even though it were certain that the relatives of the person slain would have the blood of the slayer in revenge. It was therefore always great, strong, skilful and highly respected folk who dared to kill others. People of the ordinary middle class type took care to mind their own business, and rarely exposed themselves to danger.

The slayer who, for any reason, sought to conceal what he had done, always ran the risk of exposing himself to a danger which might be even greater than that which threatened him from those seeking vengeance. Evil deeds might always recoil upon the evildoer, and the slain persons could, after the expiration of the death taboo, either return as evil spirits frightening all about them to death, or, if it happened to be an aŋErlArtukxiAq, come to life again. When this happened, the man who had concealed the fact of his killing would always in some mysterious manner fall a victim to precisely the same death he had intended for his comrade. This is described in the story of Serêraut, or

The man who returned from the Land of the Dead.

There was once a man named Serêraut, who was out hunting seal with a companion. The other man had a wife, whom Serêraut wished to have, and when it now chanced that the other caught a bearded seal, Serêraut killed him and sent him to the bottom together with the seal he had caught.

It was summer and winter came. The dead man's wife lived with her mother, who was now old, and as Serêraut had not married her after all when he had killed her husband, they lived in great poverty. But their neighbours assembled in the dancing house and held a feast together.

One evening when they were having a song festival, Serêraut stood at the back of the feasting house looking on. Suddenly the man whom Serêraut had sent to the bottom of the sea stood there, together with the bearded seal, in the midst of the assembly, shooting up through the floor, and bearing in his body the harpoon head and line with which Serêraut had harpooned him. And now he, whom all knew to be dead, stood there and cried aloud: "Serêraut killed me, tied me to a bearded seal I had caught, and sent me to the bottom af the sea." Having uttered these words, he disappeared. The ghost disappeared again through the floor, and when the last little piece of the harpoon line had vanished, there stood Serêraut, his face red as blood, in the background of the assembly.

There was only a moment's pause, and then the dead man again shot up through the floor and cried aloud:

"Serêraut killed me, and sent me to the bottom of the sea with the bearded seal I had caught."

This time he was closer to Serêraut than before, and when he disappeared, Serêraut was even more red in the face than he had been the first time. All now turned to look at him, for it was plain to them that he had lied when he came home and said that a bearded seal had dragged his comrade down into the water and drowned him.

The next time the ghost came up through the floor it was right in front of Serêraut, and again it cried to those in the feasting house:

"Serêraut killed me and sent me to the bottom of the sea with the bearded seal I had caught."

This time, when he disappeared, and the last end of the line he carried with him was just vanishing through the floor of the snow hut, Serêraut himself disappeared through the same hole in the floor, and thus suffered the same fate as he had dealt out to his comrade. But a moment later, the man whom Serêraut had killed came into the feasting house, and this time he had no longer the line fastened to his body with which he had been sent to the bottom of the sea. His mother was sent for at once, and told that her son had returned from the Land of the Dead, and as soon as the old mother heard this, she exclaimed:

"This magic was spoken over my son, that he shall return to life if he dies", and she put on her boots and ran into the feasting house. The old mother came in with her head bowed down towards the floor, and not until she had grasped her son by the feet did she look up and holding him fast, told him that he had been so long coming back to life that she had begun to feel anxious, though she knew that he would always come back even if killed by some enemy. Not until then did she venture to clasp her son's head, and she looked into his face and pressed his head close to her and gave him her breast to suck.

Thus the young hunter returned to life and to his village, but Serêraut disappeared for ever. He had kept his misdeed a secret and therefore could not come to life again.

Told by
Inugpasugjuk.
(immigrant Netsilingmio).

— — —

Inugpasugjuk further stated that death did not find all beings equally easy to deal with. People who lived passionately, and were dangerous to their surroundings, and treated the precepts of their forefathers with scorn, were as a rule those whom death found most difficult to catch. If therefore, one had an enemy whom it was necessary to get rid of, care must always be taken to cut out the dead man's heart and see it eaten by dogs. When this was done, no magic spell on earth could bring the man to life again, even if he were an aŋᴇrlᴀrtukxiᴀq. This is related of a man named Saugalik.

Saugalik, who could not die.

Saugalik's brother harpooned a bearded seal, but was dragged down by it and drowned. From that day onwards, Saugalik sought only for bearded seals with a harpoon line fixed in their bodies. One day he saw a bearded seal with a harpoon line, and set himself to wait until it should fall asleep. When at last it had fallen asleep, he crept up to it and carried it to an island near by. Here he hung it up by the harpoon line, which was none other than his brother's, and began throwing stones at the creature until it was dead. Though Saugalik had thus killed the bearded seal which has dragged his brother to death, he still felt his revenge was not enough; for he was very fond of his brother.

Despite his sorrow, he took part nevertheless in all song contests, when people assembled in the feasting house. One day, when Saugalik was going out hunting at the blowholes, his daughter said: "What can it be, I wonder, that Saugalik mourns for so deeply? One moment he bursts out crying and sheds tears, the next he is taking part in song contests when everyone is most joyful."

Saugalik heard these words, but took no notice. One day he went out to fetch meat from a store pit, and when he returned, he sent for his daughter and her husband, to entertain them with the meat he had brought home. The daughter and her husband ate as much as they could, and when they could eat no more they had as much meat to take home with them as they could carry.

Saugalik had his bow and arrows hidden on the sleeping place, and only covered with a skin, and now, when his daughter's husband bent down to go out through the passage, he took his bow and arrow and shot him. Nobody approved of this action on the part of Saugalik, and the men of the village therefore killed him. After the three days had passed, during which there is strict taboo for a dead man, Saugalik came back again. He came back to life. And then they killed him a second time. But this time it was the same as before. When the three days of strict taboo had passed after his death, he came back alive and well as ever. Then they cut off his head, but when the usual three days had passed, he returned once more with his eyes in his chest. Then they killed him for the fourth time, but this time they cut out his heart and threw it to the dogs, and the dogs ate it. And thus at last they managed to kill him, and he never returned again to his village.

Told by
Inugpasugjuk.
(immigrant Netsilingmio).

It is necessary to be careful when speaking about death. Death must not be offended, and that is why people are loth to mention the names of deceased relatives. Some indeed are even afraid to utter the name of Nuliajuk, and simply say Takána, "the one down there".

There is a story told of how careful one should be in speaking of death. One must never say anything about death in fun, for in such case, that which was not meant in earnest, or at any rate meant only as a threat, may very often become reality. Thus it happened with Sautlorasuaq, who had once in a passion threatened to come again as a ghost.

Sautlorasuaq, who became a ghost.

Sautlorasuaq went out one day with his family on a journey to visit his cousin Utsugpatlak. On arriving at the village, they built a snow hut. As soon as they had finished building their snow hut, they went over to Utsugpatlak's house to eat, taking meat of their own in with them. When Utsugpatlak saw that his cousin had brought his own food, he was angry, and leapt towards him. He tore off a piece of the meat with his teeth, snatched it from Sautlorasuaq, and threw it to the dogs. For he took it as a sign that his cousin did not think he had food in the house, since he thus brought food of his own in with him, although he was a guest.

But Sautlorasuaq was angry, and said:

"When I die, I will come and haunt you, and you can do the same to me if you die first."

Many years after, Sautlorasuaq died. When he was on the point of death, he said:

"When I die, my soul will arise again in the shape of a bear. Therefore do not hurt the bear when you see it."

He died, and after the days of taboo for a dead man were over, true enough, there came a bear out of the house where Sautlorasuaq lay dead. The neighbours went after the bear, but the bear ran away. One of the men who was pursuing the bear said:

"It looked as if that might be Sautlorasuaq".

At these words, most of the men who were pursuing the bear turned back, but there were still some that kept on in chase. The swiftest of them got the bear and brought the dead bear home to his dwelling. But now it came to pass that the man who had killed the bear died shortly after, his windpipe burst. And all those who had eaten of the bear died likewise.

Thus Sautlorasuaq sought to avenge himself on his cousin by appearing to him in the guise of a bear. Afterwards, he was also seen in the form of a fox, and Utsugpatlak went about in deadly fear of what his cousin might hit upon next. At last he fell ill, while out on a journey, and while those with him were building a snow hut, he lay there close by waiting for the house to be finished. While he lay there, he heard the voice of Sautlorasuaq beside him, and the voice said:

"I have endeavoured to get at you in many different ways. But since it was always a failure, I will now leave you in peace."

That night Utsugpatlak slept in peace, and as he thereafter obtained the rest he needed, he got well again.

Told by
Inugpasugjuk.
(immigrant Netsilingmio).

— — —

Where a village strictly observes the taboo prescribed in case of death, and otherwise holds by the ancient precepts, no one ever need go in fear of the dead, once their breathing has been severed (kipisimalᴇrpän). But should anyone take it into his head to make a noise about the place where the soul has not yet left the body, or should work, or drive a sledge, go out hunting or arrange a song contest, then the dead man will return as an evil spirit. There are, however, never any definite rules for anything, for it may also happen that a deceased person may in some mysterious manner attack surviving relatives or friends whom he loves, even when they have done nothing wrong. Inugpasugjuk can give no explanation of this beyond suggesting that the dead perhaps do this out of longing for those whose companionship they lack in the Land of the Dead; and by frightening them to death or otherwise causing them to perish so that they die they would then be united at once in the hunting grounds of the dead, and the whole family could live on together. Often a ghost will appear in the form of a lethal fire, and in this, Inugpasugjuk's traditions agree entirely with what is known from of old in Greenland. It is stated there that a bright flame often shoots up from old graves, because the dead person has turned to fire.

As an instance of the manner in which a deceased father fetched his wife and son up to his hunting grounds in the Land of the Dead, we have the following story:

The ghost that came out of its grave as a fire and tickled wife and child to death.

There was once a woman who lost her husband. When a year had passed since his death, the woman drove out with her two sons, a half-grown youth and a little boy, to visit her husband's grave. It was evening by the time they reached the grave, and therefore they built a snow hut close by. While the woman was building, with her elder son, they had laid the little boy down among some skins, and now they perceived that the child lay there laughing all the time. Then the woman spoke, and said:

"It is the child's father, trying to tickle him to death. He will also try to tickle us to death. Make haste therefore and harness your dogs and let us hurry away."

The young man did so, and the ghost came as a fire, as a flame, out of the grave, and when it had tickled the little child to death, it fell upon the woman also and killed her in the same way. After that, it set off as a flaming fire in chase of the son who was driving away, and appeared suddenly on the sledge, flaming like a torch. But the young man struck at the fire with the shaft of his whip, and every time he did so, the flame drew back a little. All the way home he fought with the flame, until he reached his dwelling unharmed. All the neighbours were just then assembled in the feasting house, and he dashed in there and told them what had happened, and that his father's ghost pursued him in the shape of a fire. But there was a shaman present, and he charmed the fire away, he destroyed it, and thus saved the young man's life.

Told by
Inugpasugjuk.
(immigrant Netsilingmio).

— — —

Human beings are thus helpless in face of all the dangerous and uncanny things that may happen in connection with death and the dead. It is not sufficient to observe all taboo or live entirely according to the precepts of the ancients. An act for which one is not personally responsible may prove disastrous, and one may die without the least idea of it. And even though one may not fear to pass to the eternal hunting grounds, there is nevertheless the natural tendency of all living things to cling to life on earth. But whether the misfortune come from the Sea Spirit, from the weather, or from the deceased, ordinary human beings can do nothing to affect their fate. The only ones who can intervene and penetrate into all that is hidden from ordinary mortals are the angákut (aŋak˙ut), the shamans.

V.

The Angákut or Shamans.

The functions of shamans at the present day are many and various. The most important are as follows:

They must be physicians, curing the sick.

Meteorologists, not only able to forecast the weather, but also able to ensure fine weather. This is effected by travelling up to Sila.

They must be able to go down to Takánakapsâluk to fetch game, a power which they themselves explain thus: nak·aivaglune nErʒutinik manisaidlune, meaning literally: "they must be able to fall down (to the bottom of the sea) in order to bring to light the animals hunted."

They must be able to visit the Land of the Dead under the sea or up in the sky in order to look for lost or stolen souls. Sometimes the dead will wish to have a dear relative who is still alive, brought up to them in the Land of the Dead; the person in question then falls ill, and it is the business of the shaman to make the dead release such souls.

Finally, every great shaman must, when asked, and when a number of people are present, exercise his art in miraculous fashion in order to astonish the people and convince them of the sacred and inexplicable powers of a shaman.

Human beings have not always possessed the power of entering into communication with supernatural forces; they have only attained to the level of their present shamans' capacity through the experiments and experience of many generations.

The material here dealt with concerning the angákut, their training and their powers, I obtained from conversations with Aua and his relative Ivalo; in both cases, based on Iglulik traditions. I have however, also learned much that is valuable in this connection through Angutingmarik, a respected shaman of the Aivilik tribe, from Padloq, and from Inugpasugjuk, an immigrant Netsilingmio in whose house I lived for some time at Pikiuleq (Depot Island) near Chesterfield.

How shamans first arose.

In the very earliest times, men lived in the dark and had no animals to hunt. They were poor, ignorant people, far inferior to those living nowadays. They travelled about in search of food, they lived on journeys as we do now, but in a very different way. When they halted and camped, they worked at the soil with picks of a kind we no longer know. They got their food from the earth, they lived on the soil. They knew nothing of all the game we now have, and had therefore no need to be ever on guard against all those perils which arise from the fact that we, hunting animals as we do, live by slaying other souls. Therefore they had no shamans, but they knew sickness, and it was fear of sickness and suffering that led to the coming of the first shamans. The ancients relate as follows concerning this:

"Human beings have always been afraid of sickness, and far back in the very earliest times there arose wise men who tried to find out about all the things none could understand. There were no shamans in those days, and men were ignorant of all those rules of life which have since taught them to be on their guard against danger and wickedness. The first amulet that ever existed was the shell portion of a sea-urchin. It has a hole through it, and is hence called itEq (anus) and the fact of its being made the first amulet was due to its being associated with a particular power of healing. When a man fell ill, one would go and sit by him, and, pointing to the diseased part, break wind behind. Then one went outside, while another held one hand hollowed over the diseased part, breathing at the same time out over the palm of his other hand in a direction away from the person to be cured. It was then believed that wind and breath together combined all the power emanating from within the human body, a power so mysterious and strong that it was able to cure disease.

"In that way everyone was a physician, and there was no need of any shamans. But then it happened that a time of hardship and famine set in around Iglulik. Many died of starvation, and all were greatly perplexed, not knowing what to do. Then one day when a number of people were assembled in a house, a man demanded to be allowed to go behind the skin hangings at the back of the sleeping place, no one knew why. He said he was going to travel down to the Mother of the Sea Beasts. No one in the house understood him, and no one believed in him. He had his way, and passed in behind the hangings. Here he declared that he would exercise an art which should afterwards prove of great value to mankind; but no one must look at him. It was not long, however, before the unbelieving and inquisitive drew aside the hangings, and to their astonishment perceived that he was diving down into the earth; he had already got so far down that only the soles of his feet could be seen. How the man ever hit on this idea no one knows; he himself said that it was the spirits that had helped him; spirits he had entered into contact with out in the great solitude. Thus the first shaman appeared among men. He went down to the Mother of the Sea Beasts and brought back game to men, and the famine gave place to plenty, and all were happy and joyful once more.

"Afterwards, the shamans extended their knowledge of hidden things, and helped mankind in various ways. They also developed their sacred language, which was only used for communicating with the spirits and not in everyday speech."

— — —

When a young man or woman wishes to become a shaman, the first thing to do is to make a present to the shaman under whom one wishes to study. Sometimes two such instructors may be employed at the same time. The present given in the first place must be something valuable, an item from among one's own possessions which has cost the owner some trouble to obtain. Among the Iglulingmiut, wood was the most expensive of all, and it was therefore customary here to pay one's instructor with a tent pole. The wing of a gull was fastened to the pole as a sign or symbol indicating that the pupil should in time acquire the power of travelling through the air to the Land of the Dead up in heaven, or down through the sea to the abode of Takánakapsâluk. The young aspirant, when applying to a shaman should always use the following formula:

"takujumagama": "I come to you because I desire to see."

The gift would then be placed outside the tent, or the house, according as it was summer or winter, and would remain there for some time as a present to the helping spirits that would in time be at the pupil's command. The shaman could have the use of the tent pole afterwards himself, there was no difficulty about that, for the spirits are creatures of air and have no use for wood; they would have the ownership of it all the same, since it had once been given them by a human being, and that was enough for the spirits.

The evening after a shaman has received and set out a gift of this nature, he must do what is called sakavɔq: that is, invoke and interrogate his helping spirits in order to "remove all obstacles" (padzizaiᴀ·rniᴀrlugit) that is, to eliminate from the pupil's body and mind all that might hinder him from becoming a good shaman. Then the pupil and his parents, if he have any, must confess any breach of taboo or other offence they have committed, and purify themselves by confession in face of the spirits.

While all this is going on, the shaman remains on the bench behind a skin so hung as to conceal him on the innermost part of the principal seat. The pupil afterwards climbs up and sits down beside him, but not until he has purified himself by confession.

The period of instruction among the Iglulingmiut and Aivilingmiut is not particularly long, especially in the case of men. Some can make do with five days. It is understood, however, that the young shaman, after having been initiated by his experienced tutor, must continue his training on his own account, far from the dwellings of men, in the solitary parts where he can be alone with nature.

During the actual period of instruction he is constantly receiving tuition from one or two shamans, this taking place on the hidden part of the bench behind the curtain. But the shamans are not obliged to remain with the pupil the whole time, as they have special hours for tuition: in the morning, in the middle of the day, in the evening and at night. The pupil must, during the time he is here, never sit on the ordinary coverings spread over the bench, but have a pair of man's breeches laid out under him. He is only allowed to sit on these, and must not leave his place on any account, during the days his instruction lasts. Nor is he, throughout that time, ever allowed to eat his fill, but must eat as little as possible.

While a shaman has a pupil under instruction, he is not allowed to undertake any kind of hunting, and members of the pupil's household are likewise debarred from such occupation.

The first thing a shaman has to do when he has called up his helping spirits is to withdraw the soul from his pupil's eyes, brain and entrails. This is effected in a manner which cannot be explained, but every capable instructor must have the power of liberating the soul of eyes, brain and entrails from the pupil's body and handing it over to those helping spirits which will be at the disposal of the pupil himself when fully trained. Thus the helping spirits in question become familiarised with what is highest and noblest in the shaman-to-be; they get used to the sight of him, and will not be afraid when he afterwards invokes them himself.

The next thing an old shaman has to do for his pupil is to procure him an aŋak·ua by which is meant his "angákoq" i. e. the altogether special and particular element which makes this man an angákoq. It is also called his qaumanᴇq, his "lighting" or "enlightenment", for aŋak·ua consists of a mysterious light which the shaman suddenly feels in his body, inside his head, within the brain, an inexplicable searchlight, a luminous fire, which enables him to see in the dark, both literally and metaphorically speaking, for he can now, even with closed eyes, see through darkness and perceive things and coming

Scenes from the qulumᴇrtut games. Above: The men challenging each other to arm-pulling contests. Middle: Football. Below: pivlᴇrtᴀrtut, consisting in two and two bobbing up and down with bent knees while singing a song.
Drawn by Pakak.

tiklo·tut or the men who surprise a man asleep and force him to give a song-feast.

tivajo·k or the wife-changing game. The women wait in the snow house, the men stand outside ready to choose, whilst the mask-dancers stand beside the lamp block, singing. Drawn by Pakak.

events which are hidden from others; thus they look into the future and into the secrets of others.

The first time a young shaman experiences this light, while sitting up on the bench invoking his helping spirits, it is as if the house in which he is suddenly rises; he sees far ahead of him, through mountains, exactly as if the earth were one great plain, and his eyes could reach to the end of the earth. Nothing is hidden from him any longer; not only can he see things far, far away, but he can also discover souls, stolen souls, which are either kept concealed in far, strange lands or have been taken up or down to the Land of the Dead.

An aŋak·ua or qaumanᴇq is a faculty which the old shamans procure for their pupils from the Spirit of the Moon. There are also some who obtain it through the medium of some deceased person among the Udlormiut who is particularly fond of the pupil in question. Or again, it can be obtained through bears which appear in human form; bears in human form are the shamans' best helpers. And finally, it can also be obtained from the Mother of the Caribou, who lives far up inland, and is here called Pakitsumánga.

In addition to the bear, there is also another animal possessing qualities which may be of importance to the shamans. This is the lemming. It is said that the white lemmings fell down from heaven. They therefore possess an altogether peculiar knowledge of the diseases of mankind, and the causes of death. An aŋak·ua derived from the lemmings is therefore considered specially valuable.

But it is not enough for a shaman to be able to escape both from himself and from his surroundings. It is not enough that, having the soul removed from his eyes, brain and entrails, he is able also to withdraw the spirit from his body and thus undertake the great "spirit flights" through space and through the sea; nor is it enough that by means of his qaumanᴇq he abolishes all distance, and can see all things, however far away. For he will be incapable of maintaining these faculties unless he have the support of helping and answering spirits. The Eskimo term for these is: tɔ·ʳŋʳᴀq, pl. tɔ·ʳŋʳät, properly, spirit, also called apᴇrʃᴀq, pl. apᴇrʃät, one that exists to be questioned, an answering spirit. It is these which enable him to continue the work along the lines of instruction imparted by the old shamans. But he must procure these helping spirits for himself; he must meet them in person, and they should preferably be animals appearing in human form. He cannot even choose for himself what sort he will have. They come to him of their own accord, strong and powerful, if the young man shows promise. Fox, owl, bear, dog, shark and all manner of mountain spirits, especially iʲᴇrqät, are reckoned as powerful and effective helpers.

But before a shaman attains the stage at which any helping spirit would think it worth while to come to him, he must, by struggle and toil and concentration of thought, acquire for himself yet another great and inexplicable power: *he must be able to see himself as a skeleton.* Though no shaman can explain to himself how and why, he can, by the power his brain derives from the supernatural, as it were by thought alone, divest his body of its flesh and blood, so that nothing remains but his bones. And he must then name all the parts of his body, mention every single bone by name; and in so doing, he must not use ordinary human speech, but only the special and sacred shaman's language which he has learned from his instructor. By thus seeing himself naked, altogether freed from the perishable and transient flesh and blood, he consecrates himself, in the sacred tongue of the shamans, to his great task, through that part of his body which will longest withstand the action of sun, wind and weather, after he is dead.

As soon as a young man has become a shaman, he must have a special shaman's belt as a sign of his dignity. This consists of a strip of hide to which are attached many fringes of caribou skin, and these are fastened on by all the people he knows, as many as he can get; to the fringes are added small carvings, human figures made of bone, fishes, harpoons; all these must be gifts, and the givers then believe that the shaman's helping spirits will always be able to recognise them by their gifts, and will never do them any harm.

A man who has just become a shaman must for a whole year refrain from the following:

He must not eat the marrow, breast, entrails, head or tongue of any beasts; the meat he eats must be raw, clean flesh. Women during the first year are subject to even further restrictions, but the most important of all is that they are not allowed to sew a single stitch throughout that year.

The last thing a shaman learns of all the knowledge he is obliged to acquire, is the recitation of magic prayers or the murmuring of magic songs, which can heal the sick, bring good weather or good hunting. One can practise magic words simply by walking up and down the floor of one's house and talking to oneself. But the best magic words are those which come to one in an inexplicable manner when one is alone out among the mountains. These are always the most powerful in their effects. The power of solitude is great and beyond understanding. Here is a method of learning an effective magic prayer:

When one sees a raven fly past, one must follow it and keep on pursuing until one has caught it. If one shoots it with bow and arrow, one must run up to it the moment it falls to the ground, and standing over the bird as it flutters about in pain and fear, say out loud all that one intends to do, and mention everything that occupies the mind. The dying raven gives power to words and thoughts. The following magic words, which had great vitalising power, were obtained by Angutingmarik in the manner above stated:

nunamasuk
nunᴀrzuamasuk
uƀva mak·ua —
saunᴇrʒuit silᴀrʒu·p
qᴀqitɔrai -
pᴀrqitɔrai —
he — he —he.

tɔ·rɳrᴀ·rzuk
tɔ·rɳrᴀ·rzuk
udludlo
avatiɳnut
audlᴀrit
patqᴇrnagit
uʷai — uʷai — uʷai!

Translation:

Earth, earth,
Great earth,
Round about on earth
There are bones, bones, bones,
which are bleached by the great Sila
By the weather, the sun, the air,
So that all the flesh disappears,
He — he —he.

Spirit, spirit, spirit,
And the day, the day,
Go to my limbs
without drying them up,
Without turning them to bones
Uvai, uvai, uvai.

Aua is consecrated to the spirits.

Every good shaman can teach others of his knowledge, and help his pupils over the initial difficulties. Some, however, maintain that the best shamans are those who have never studied under others, but went out at once into the great solitude. This again is denied by those who hold that a good preliminary instruction is a necessary qualification, without which the shaman cannot obtain any benefit from his solitude in the wilds. It is a long schooling that is required before one can honestly undertake all the tasks which unfortunate fellow-creatures may put before one. So seriously are all preparations considered, that some parents, even before the birth of the shaman-to-be, set all things in order for him beforehand by laying upon themselves a specially strict and onerous taboo. Such a child was Aua, and here is his own story:

"I was yet but a tiny unborn infant in my mother's womb when anxious folk began to enquire sympathetically about me; all the children my mother had had before had lain crosswise and been still-born. As soon as my mother now perceived that she was with child, the child that one day was to be me, she spoke thus to her house-fellows:

"'Now I have again that within me which will turn out no real human being.'

"All were very sorry for her and a woman named Ârdjuaq, who was a shaman herself, called up her spirits that same evening to help my mother. And the very next morning it could be felt that I had grown, but it did me no good at the time, for Ârdjuaq had forgotten that she must do no work the day after a spirit-calling, and had mended a hole in a mitten. This breach of taboo at once had its effect upon me; my mother felt the birth-pangs coming on before the time, and I kicked and struggled as if trying to work my way out through her side. A new spirit-calling then took place, and as all precepts were duly observed this time, it helped both my mother and myself.

"But then one day it happened that my father, who was going out on a journey to hunt, was angry and impatient, and in order to calm him, my mother went to help him harness the dogs to the sledge.. She forgot that in her condition, all work was taboo. And so, hardly had she picked up the traces and lifted one dog's paw before I began again kicking and struggling and trying to get out through her navel; and again we had to have a shaman to help us.

"Old people now assured my mother that my great sensitiveness to any breach of taboo was a sign that I should live to become a great shaman; but at the same time, many dangers and misfortunes would pursue me before I was born.

"My father had got a walrus with its unborn young one, and when he began cutting it out, without reflecting that my mother was with child, I again fell to struggling within the womb, and this time in earnest. But the moment I was born, all life left me, and I lay there dead as a stone. The cord was twisted round my neck and had strangled me. Ârdjuaq, who lived in another village, was at once sent for, and a special hut was built for my mother. When Ârdjuaq came and saw me with my eyes sticking right out of my head, she wiped my mother's blood from my body with the skin of a raven, and made a little jacket for me of the same skin.

"'He is born to die, but he shall live,' she said.

"And so Ârdjuaq stayed with my mother, until I showed signs of life. Mother was put on very strict diet, and had to observe difficult rules of taboo. If she had eaten part of a walrus, for instance, then that walrus was taboo to all others; the same with seal and caribou. She had to have special pots, from which no one else was allowed to eat. No woman was allowed to visit her, but men might do so. My clothes were made after a particular fashion; the hair of the skins must never lie pointing upwards or down, but fall athwart the body. Thus I lived in the birth-hut, unconscious of all the care that was being taken with me.

"For a whole year my mother and I had to live entirely alone, only visited now and again by my father. He was a great hunter, and always out after game, but in spite of this he was never allowed to sharpen his own knives; as soon as he did so, his hand began to swell and I fell ill. A year after my birth, we were allowed to have another person in the house with us; it was a woman, and she had to be very careful herself; whenever she went out she must throw her hood over her head, wear boots without stockings, and hold the tail of her fur coat lifted high in one hand.

"I was already a big boy when my mother was first allowed to go visiting; all were anxious to be kind, and she was invited to all the other families. But she stayed out too long; the spirits do not like women with little children to stay too long away from their house, and they took vengeance in this wise: the skin of her head peeled of, and I, who had no understanding of anything at that time, beat her about the body with my little fists as she went home, and made water down her back.

"No one who is to become a skilful hunter or a good shaman must remain out too long when visiting strange houses; and the same holds good for a woman with a child in her amaut.

"At last I was big enough to go out with the grown up men to the blowholes after seal. The day I harpooned my first seal, my father had to lie down on the ice with the upper part of his body naked, and the seal I had caught was dragged across his back while it was still alive. Only men were allowed to eat of my first catch, and nothing must be left. The skin and the head were set out on the ice, in order that I might be able later on to catch the same seal again. For three days and nights, none of the men who had eaten of it might go out hunting or do any kind of work.

"The next animal I killed was a caribou. I was strictly forbidden to use a gun, and had to kill it with bow and arrows; this animal also only men were allowed to eat; no woman might touch it.

"Some time passed, and I grew up and was strong enough to go out hunting walrus. The day I harpooned my first walrus my father shouted at the top of his voice the names of all the villages he knew, and cried: 'Now there is food for all!'

"The walrus was towed in to land, while it was still alive, and not until we reached the shore was it finally killed. My mother, who was to cut it up, had the harpoon line made fast to her body before the harpoon head was withdrawn. After having killed this walrus, I was allowed to eat all those delicacies which had formerly been forbidden, yes, even entrails, and women were now allowed to eat of my catch, as long as they were not with child or recently delivered. Only my own mother had still to observe great caution, and whenever she had any sewing to do, a special hut had to be built for her. I had been named after a little spirit, Aua, and it was said that it was in order to avoid offending this spirit that my mother had to be so particular about everything she did. It was my guardian spirit, and took great care that I should not do anthing that was forbidden. I was never allowed, for instance, to remain in a snow hut where young women were undressing for the night; nor might any woman comb her hair while I was present."

"Even after I had been married a long time, my catch was still subject to strict taboo. If there but lived women with infants near us, my own wife was only allowed to eat meat of my killing, and no other woman was allowed to satisfy her hunger with the meat of any animal of which my wife had eaten. Any walrus I killed was further subject to the rule that no woman might eat of its entrails, which are reckoned a great delicacy, and this prohibition was maintained until I had four children of my own. And it is really only since I have grown old that the obligations laid on me by Ârdjuaq in order that I might live have ceased to be needful.

"Everything was thus made ready for me beforehand, even from the time when I was yet unborn; nevertheless, I endeavoured to become a shaman by the help of others; but in this I did not succeed. I visited many famous shamans, and gave them great gifts, which they at once gave away to others; for if they had kept the things for themselves, they or their children would have died. This they believed because my own life had been so threatened from birth. Then I sought solitude, and here I soon became very melancholy. I would sometimes fall to weeping, and feel unhappy without knowing why. Then, for no reason, all would suddenly be changed, and I felt a great, inexplicable joy, a joy so powerful that I could not restrain it, but had to break into song, a mighty song, with only room for the one word: joy, joy! And I had to use the full strength of my voice. And then in the midst of such a fit of mysterious and overwhelming delight I became a shaman, not knowing myself how it came about. But I was a shaman. I could see and hear in a totally different way. I had gained my qaumanEq, my enlightenment, the shaman-light of brain and body, and this in such a manner that it was not only I who could see through the darkness of life, but the same light also shone out from me, imperceptible to human beings, but visible to all the spirits of earth and sky and sea, and these now came to me and became my helping spirits.

"My first helping spirit was my namesake, a little aua. When it came to me, it was as if the passage and roof of the house were lifted up, and I felt such a power of vision, that I could see right through the house, in through the earth and up into the sky; it was the little Aua that brought me all this inward light, hovering over me as long as I was singing. Then it placed itself in a corner of the passage, invisible to others, but always ready if I should call it.

"An aua is a little spirit, a woman, that lives down by the sea shore. There are many of these shore spirits, who run about with a pointed skin hood on their heads; their breeches are queerly short, and made of bearskin; they wear long boots with a black pattern, and coats of sealskin. Their feet are twisted upward, and they seem to walk only on their heels. They hold their hands in such a fashion that the thumb is always bent in over the palm; their arms are held raised up on high with the hands together, and incessantly stroking the head. They are bright and cheerful when one calls them, and resemble most of all sweet little live dolls; they are no taller than the length of a man's arm.

"My second helping spirit was a shark. One day when I was out in my kayak, it came swimming up to me, lay alongside quite silently and whispered my name. I was greatly astonished, for I had never seen a shark before; they are very rare in these waters. Afterwards it helped me with my hunting, and was always near me when I had need of it. These two, the shore spirit and the shark, were my principal helpers, and they could aid me in everything I wished. The song I generally sang when calling them was of few words, as follows:

Joy, joy,
Joy, joy!
I see a little shore spirit,
A little aua,
I myself am also aua,
The shore spirit's namesake,
Joy, joy!

"These words I would keep on repeating, until I burst into tears, overwhelmed by a great dread; then I would tremble all over, crying only: "Ah-a-a-a-a, joy, joy! Now I will go home, joy, joy!'

"Once I lost a son, and felt that I could never again leave the spot where I had laid his body. I was like a mountain spirit, afraid of human kind. We stayed for a long time up inland, and my helping spirits forsook me, for they do not like live human beings to dwell upon any sorrow. But one day the song about joy came to me all of itself and quite unexpectedly. I felt once more a longing for my fellow-men, my helping spirits returned to me, and I was myself once more".

The spirits call for Niviatsian.

Niviatsian, aua's cousin, was out hunting walrus with a number of other men near Iglulik; some were in front of him and others behind. Suddenly a great walrus came up through the ice close beside him, grasped him with his huge fore-flippers, just as a mother picks up her little child, and carried him off with it down into the deep. The other men ran up, and looking down through the hole in the ice where the walrus had disappeared, they could see it still holding him fast and trying to pierce him with its tusks. After a little while it let him go, and rose to the surface, a great distance off, to breathe. But Niviatsian, who had been dragged away from the hole through which he had first been pulled down, struggled with arms and legs to come up again. The men could follow his movements, and cut a hole about where they expected him to come up, and here my father actually did manage to pull him up. There was a gaping wound over his collarbone, and he was breathing through it; the gash had penetrated to the lung. Some of his ribs were broken, and the broken ends had caught in one of his lungs, so that he could not stand upright.

Niviatsian lay for a long time unconscious. When he came to himself, however, he was able to get on his feet without help. The wound over the collarbone was the only serious one; there were traces of the walrus's tusks both on his head and in different parts of his body, but it seemed as if the animal had been unable to wound him there. Old folk said that this walrus had been sent by the Mother of the Sea Beasts, who was angry because Niviatsian's wife had had a miscarriage and concealed the fact in order to avoid the taboo.

Niviatsian then went with his companions in towards land, but he had to walk a little way apart from them, on ice free from foot-marks. Close to land, a small snow hut was built, and he was shut in there, laid down on a sealskin with all his wet clothes on. There he remained for three days and three nights without food or drink, this he was obliged to do in order to be allowed to live, for if he had gone up at once to the unclean dwellings of men after the ill-treatment he had received, he would have died.

All the time Niviatsian was in the little snow hut, the shaman up at the village was occupied incessantly in purifying his wife and his old mother, who were obliged to confess in the presence of others all their breaches of taboo, in order to appease the powers that ruled over life and death. And after three days, Niviatsian recovered, and had now become a great shaman. The walrus, which had failed to kill him, became his first helping spirit.--That was the beginning.

Another time he was out hunting, it was on a caribou hunt up in land, he ran right up against a wolverine's lair. The animal had young ones, and attacked him furiously. It "wrestled" with him all day and night and did not leave hold of him until the sun was in the same place as when it had begun. But in spite of the animal's sharp teeth and claws, there was not a single wound on his body, only a few abrasions. Thus the wolverine also became his helping spirit.

His third helping spirit was Amajorjuk, the ogress with the great amaut on her back, in which she puts the human beings she carries off. She attacked him so suddenly, that he was in the bag already before he could think of doing. The bag closed over him at once, and he was shut in. But he had his knife round his neck, and with this he stabbed the woman in the back, just behind the shoulderblade, and she died. The amaut was as thick as walrus hide, and it took him a long time to cut his way out and escape. But now he discovered that he was altogether naked; he had no idea when he had been stripped of his clothes, nor did he know where he now was, save that it must be far, far inland. Not until he came down close to the sea did he find his clothes, and then he got safely home. But there was a horrible smell of rotten seaweed all over his body, and the smell hung about his house so obstinately that it was half a year before it went away. This ogress also became his helping spirit, and he was now regarded as the greatest of shamans among mankind.

— — —

The methods of attaining magic power here indicated lay particular stress on the inexplicable terror that is felt when one is attacked by a helping spirit, and the peril of death which often attends initiation. Most helping spirits make their first appearance by attacking the person concerned in some violent and mysterious manner. Most dreaded of all helping spirits was im'ap tᴇria', the sea ermine. This creature is fashioned like the land ermine, but is more slender, lithe and swift, and able to dash up out of the sea so suddenly that defence is out of the question. It has dark, smooth skin, and no hair save a little at the tip of the tail and on the lobes of the ears. When a man was out at sea in his kayak, it would shoot up swiftly as lightning from the depths and slip into his sleeve, and then, running over his naked body, fill him with such a shuddering horror that he almost lost consciousness.

The shaman Niviatsian before mentioned inherited his special qualifications from his mother, Uvavnuk, who obtained her aŋak·ua in a manner hitherto unknown:

Uvavnuk is struck by a ball of fire.

Uvavnuk had gone outside the hut one winter evening to make water. It was particularly dark that evening, as the moon was not visible. Then suddenly there appeared a glowing ball of fire in the sky, and it came rushing down to earth straight towards her. She would have got up and fled, but before she could pull up her breeches, the ball of fire struck her and entered into her. At the same moment she perceived that all within her grew light, and she lost consciousness. But from that moment also she became a great shaman. She had never before concerned herself with the invocation of spirits, but now iŋnᴇru·jäp inua, the spirit of the meteor, had entered into her and made her a shaman. She saw the spirit just before she fainted. It had two kinds of bodies, that rushed all glowing through space; one side was a bear, the other was like a human being; the head was that of a human being with the tusks of a bear.

Uvavṅuk had fallen down and lost consciousness, but she got up again, and without knowing what she was doing, came running into the house; she came into the house singing: naluʃa·ruƀlune tamaisalo patsisaialᴇrlugit: there was nothing that was hidden from her now, and she began to reveal all the offences that had been committed by those in the house. Thus she purified them all.

Every shaman has his own particular song, which he sings when calling up his helping spirits; they must sing when the helping spirits enter into their bodies, and speak with the voice of the helping spirits themselves. The song which Uvavṅuk generally sang, and which she sang quite suddenly the first evening, without knowing why, after the meteor had struck her, was as follows:

"imᴀrju·ƀle im·na
aulᴀrjᴀ·rmaŋa
iŋᴇʀajᴀ·rmaŋa
ᴀqajagin·ᴀrmaŋa.

nᴀ·rʒugʒu·p im·na
aulᴀrjᴀ·rmaŋa
iŋᴇʀajᴀ·rmaŋa
aulagᴀrinᴀrmaŋa".

Translation:

"The great sea
Has sent me adrift,
It moves me as the weed in a great river,
Earth and the great weather
Move me,
Have carried me away
And move my inward parts with joy."

These two verses she repeated incessantly, aliaŋnᴀr^{d}lune i. e. intoxiated with joy, so that all in the house felt the same intoxication of delight, alianaigusulᴇrlutik, and without being asked, began to state all their misdeeds, as well as those of others, and those who felt themselves accused and admitted their offences obtained release from these by lifting their arms and making as if tò fling away all evil; all that was false and wicked was thrown away. It was blown away as one blows a speck of dust from the hand:

"taiva·luk, taiva·luk: away with it, away with it!"

But there was this remarkable thing about Uvavnuk, that as soon as she came out of her trance, she no longer felt like a shaman; the light left her body and she was once more quite an ordinary person with no special powers. Only when the spirit of the meteor lit up the spirit light within her could she see and hear and know everything, and became at once a mighty magician. Shortly before her death she held a grand séance, and declared it was her wish that mankind should not suffer want, and she "manivai", i. e. brought forth from the interior of the earth all manner of game which she had obtained from Takánakapsâluk. This she declared, and after her death, the people of her village had a year of greater abundance in whale, walrus, seal and caribou than any had ever experienced before.

A shaman's journey to the sea spirit Takánakapsâluk.

The girl who was thrown into the sea by her own father, and had her finger joints so cruelly cut off as she clung in terror to the side of the boat has in a strange fashion made herself the stern goddess of fate among the Eskimos. From her comes all the most indispensable of human food, the flesh of the sea beasts; from her comes the blubber that warms the cold snow huts and gives light in the lamps when the long arctic night broods over the land. From her come also the skins of the great seal which are likewise indispensable for clothes and boot soles, if the hunters are to be able to move over the frozen sea all seasons of the year. But while Takánakapsâluk gives mankind all these good things, created out of her own finger-joints, it is she also who sends nearly all the misfortunes which are regarded by the dwellers on earth as the worst and direst. In her anger at men's failing to live as they should, she calls up storms that prevent the men from hunting, or she keeps the animals they seek hidden away in a pool she has at the bottom of the sea, or she will steal away the souls of human beings and send sickness among the people. It is not strange therefore, that it is regarded as one of a shaman's greatest feats to visit her where she lives at the bottom of the sea, and so tame and conciliate her that human beings can live once more untroubled on earth.

When a shaman wishes to visit Takánakapsâluk, he sits on the inner part of the sleeping place behind a curtain, and must wear nothing but his kamiks and mittens. A shaman about to make this journey is said to be nak·a·ʒɔq: one who drops down to the bottom of the sea. This remarkable expression is due perhaps in some degree to the fact that no one can rightly explain how the journey is made. Some assert that it is only his soul or his spirit which makes the journey; others declare that it is the shaman himself who actually, in the flesh, drops down into the underworld.

The journey may be undertaken at the instance of a single individual, who pays the shaman for his trouble, either because there is sickness in his household which appears incurable, or because he has been particularly unsuccessful in his hunting. But it may also be made on behalf of a whole village threatened by famine and death owing to the scarcity of game. As soon as such occasion arises, all the adult members of the community assemble in the house from which the shaman is to start, and when he has taken up his position — if it is winter, and in a snow hut, on the bare snow, if in summer, on the bare ground — the men and women present must loosen all tight fastenings in their clothes, the lacings of their footgear, the waistbands of their breeches, and then sit down and remain still with closed eyes, all lamps being put out, or allowed to burn only with so faint a flame that it is practically dark inside the house.

The shaman sits for a while in silence, breathing deeply, and then, after some time has elapsed, he begins to call upon his helping spirits, repeating over and over again: "tagva ᴀrqutin·ilᴇrpɔq — tagva nᴇruvtulᴇrpɔq": "the way is made ready for me; the way opens before me!"

Whereat all present must answer in chorus: "taimaililᴇr^{d}le": "let it be so!"

And when the helping spirits have arrived, the earth opens under the shaman, but often only to close up again; he has to struggle for a long time with hidden forces, ere he can cry at last:

"Now the way is open".

And then all present must answer: "Let the way be open before him; let there be way for him".

And now one hears, at first under the sleeping place: "Halala — he — he — he, halala — he — he — he!" and afterwards under the passage, below the ground, the same cry: "Halele — he!" And the sound can be distinctly heard to recede farther and farther until it is lost altogether. Then all know that he is on his way to the ruler of the sea beasts.

Meanwhile, the members of the household pass the time by singing spirit songs in chorus, and here it may happen that the clothes which the shaman has discarded come alive and fly about round the house, above the heads of the singers, who are sitting with closed eyes. And one may hear deep sighs and the breathing of persons long since dead; these are the souls of the shaman's namesakes, who have come to help. But as soon as one calls them by name, the sighs cease, and all is silent in the house until another dead person begins to sigh.

In the darkened house one hears only sighing and groaning from the dead who lived many generations earlier. This sighing and puffing sounds as if the spirits were down under water, in the sea, as marine animals, and in between all the noises one hears the blowing and splashing of creatures coming up to breathe. There is one song especially which must be constantly repeated; it is only to be sung by the oldest members of the tribe, and is as follows:

"aŋᴇrsɔrte·kpik
qalume· kanaŋ·a
nuitᴇrtuŋa
supiktertuŋa
aŋnᴇrsɔrte·kpik
in·ᴀrtᴇrtuŋa
qiluje·kpik"

The text, like all magic texts, is not clear; qiluje·kpik is the same as qiluniᴀrpa^{v}kit: I will pull you up by the hands. aŋᴇrsɔrte·k-pik i. e. nᴇqᴇqaŋ·ilᴇrmät: "because we are without food", qalume· is the term for the hollow on the left of the entrance hole, a hollow in the floor of the house, where water often collects. supiktᴇrtuŋa i. e. wriggle, bore a way up. Orulo translated it as follows:

We reach out our hands
to help you up;
we are without food,
we are without game.
From the hollow by the entrance
you shall open,
you shall bore your way up.
We are without food,
and we lay ourselves down
holding out hands
to help you up!

An ordinary shaman will, even though skilful, encounter many dangers in his flight down to the bottom of the sea; the most dreaded are three large rolling stones which he meets as soon as he has reached the sea floor. There is no way round; he has to pass between them, and take great care not to be crushed by these stones, which churn about, hardly leaving room for a human being to pass. Once he has passed beyond them, he comes to a broad, trodden path, the shamans' path; he follows a coastline resembling that which he knows from on earth, and entering a bay, finds himself on a great plain, and here lies the house of Takánakapsâluk, built of stone, with a short passage way, just like the houses of the tunit. Outside the house one can hear the animals puffing and blowing, but he does not see them; in the passage leading to the house lies Takánakapsâluk's dog stretched across the passage taking up all the room; it lies there gnawing at a bone and snarling. It is dangerous to all who fear it, and only the courageous shaman can pass by it, stepping straight over it as it lies; the dog then knows that the bold visitor is a great shaman, and does him no harm.

These difficulties and dangers attend the journey of an ordinary shaman. But for the very greatest, a way opens right from the house whence they invoke their helping spirits; a road down through the earth, if they are in a tent on shore, or down through the sea, if it is in a snow hut on the sea ice, and by this route the shaman is led down without encountering any obstacle. He almost glides as if falling through a tube so fitted to his body that he can check his progress by pressing against the sides, and need not actually fall down with a rush. This tube is kept open for him by all the souls of his namesakes, until he returns on his way back to earth.

Should a great shelter wall be built outside the house of Takánakapsâluk, it means that she is very angry and implacable in her feelings towards mankind, but the shaman must fling himself upon the wall, kick it down and level it to the ground. There are some who declare that her house has no roof, and is open at the top, so that she can better watch, from her place by the lamp, the doings of mankind. All the different kinds of game: seal, bearded seal, walrus and whale, are collected in a great pool on the right of her lamp, and there they lie puffing and blowing. When the shaman enters the house, he at once sees Takánakapsâluk, who, as a sign of anger, is sitting with her back to the lamp and with her back to all the animals in the pool. Her hair hangs down loose all over one side of her face, a tangled, untidy mass hiding her eyes, so that she cannot see. It is the misdeeds and offences committed by men which gather in dirt and impurity over her body. All the foul emanations from the sins of mankind nearly suffocate her. As the shaman moves towards her, Isarrataitsoq, her father, tries to grasp hold of him. He think it is a dead person come to expiate offences before passing on to the Land of the Dead, but the shaman must then at once cry out: "I am flesh and blood" and then he will not be hurt. And he must now grasp Takánakapsâluk by one shoulder and turn her face towards the lamp and towards the animals, and stroke her hair, the hair she has been unable to comb out herself, because she has no fingers; and he must smooth it and comb it, and as soon as she is calmer, he must say:

"pik'ua qilusinEq ajulErmata": "those up above can no longer help the seals up by grasping their foreflippers".

Then Takánakapsâluk answers in the spirit language: "The secret miscarriages of the women and breaches of taboo in eating boiled meat bar the way for the animals".

The shaman must now use all his efforts to appease her anger, and at last, when she is in a kindlier mood, she takes the animals one by one and drops them on the floor, and then it is as if a whirlpool arose in the passage, the water pours out from the pool and the animals disappear in the sea. This means rich hunting and abundance for mankind.

It is then time for the shaman to return to his fellows up above, who are waiting for him. They can hear him coming a long way off; the rush of his passage through the tube kept open for him by the spirits comes nearer and nearer, and with a mighty "Plu — a — he — he" he shoots up into his place behind the curtain: "Plu-plu", like some creature of the sea, shooting up from the deep to take breath under the pressure of mighty lungs.

Then there is silence for a moment. No one may break this silence until the shaman says: "I have something to say".

Then all present answer: "Let us hear, let us hear".

And the shaman goes on, in the solemn spirit language: "Words will arise".

And then all in the house must confess any breaches of taboo they have committed.

"It is my fault, perhaps", they cry, all at once, women and men together, in fear of famine and starvation, and all begin telling of the wrong things they have done. All the names of those in the house are mentioned, and all must confess, and thus much comes to light which no one had ever dreamed of; every one learns his neighbours' secrets. But despite all the sins confessed, the shaman may go on talking as one who is unhappy at having made a mistake, and again and again break out into such expressions as this:

"I seek my grounds in things which have not happened; I speak as one who knows nothing".

There are still secrets barring the way for full solution of the trouble, and so the women in the house begin to go through all the names, one after another; nearly all women's names; for it was always their breaches of taboo which were most dangerous. Now and again when a name is mentioned, the shaman exclaims in relief:

"taina, taina!"

It may happen that the woman in question is not present, and in such case, she is sent for. Often it would be quite young girls or young wives, and when they came in crying and miserable, it was always a sign that they were good women, good penitent women. And as soon as they showed themselves, shamefaced and weeping, the shaman would break out again into his cries of self-reproach:

"pitᴀqaŋ'icumik, piʃuŋa pitᴀqaŋ'icumik, piʃuŋa pitᴀqᴀrpät ɔqᴀrniᴀrtutit": "I seek, and I strike where nothing is to be found! I seek, and I strike where nothing is to be found! If there is anything, you must say so!"

And the woman who has been led in, and whom the shaman has marked out as one who has broken her taboo, now confesses:

"qalipsulᴀ'rama ɔqᴀrädlaŋ'in'ama kap'iasukluŋa iglume pigama": "I had a miscarriage, but I said nothing, because I was afraid, and because it took place in a house where there were many".

She thus admits that she has had a miscarriage, but did not venture to say so at the time because of the consequences involved, affecting her numerous house-mates; for the rules provide that as soon as a woman has had a miscarriage in a house, all those living in the same house, men and women alike, must throw away all the house contains of qituptɔq: soft things, i. e. all the skins on the sleeping place, all the clothes, in a word all soft skins, thus including also ilupᴇrɔq: the sealskin covering used to line the whole interior of a snow hut as used among the Iglulingmiut. This was so serious a matter for the household that women sometimes dared not report

Above and below: Various situations from the gymnastic exercises on stretched seal-skin thongs at the qulumᴇrtut games. — Centre: Singing in festival house, the women's chorus on the platform. Drawn by Pakak.

Apak, a young wife, daughter of the shaman Aua, was visionary without being a shaman, and has here attempted to reproduce one of her visions, a four-legged mountain spirit whom she saw outside the snow houses one dark evening when she went out. She strictly observed all taboo and firmly believed in the avenging effect of all violation of taboo. She herself, shortly before her confinement, had eaten from a cooking pot that was used by all in the house, though her father had preremptorily ordered her to have one of her own, from which no one else had to eat. She gave birth to a boy — the highest desire of both her and her husband — but immediately after the boy was born he was turned into a girl. This happened while she was alone in the maternity house and before anyone had seen the child. Nobody for a moment thought of doubting her statement. The mountain sprite shown was seen by her not long before she was to have her child, and she took it as an omen that some evil would happen to her when her child came. Drawn by Apak.

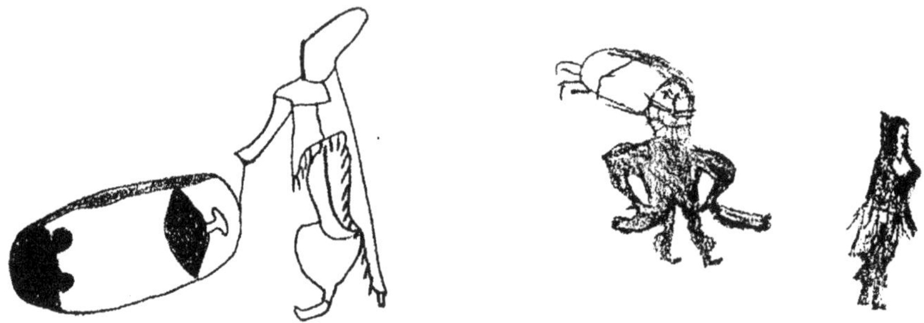

Two pictures of Ululiarnâq with the moon spirit as Orulo imagines her. On the extreme right is a shaman doing what he can in order not to laugh. Drawn by Orulo.

a miscarriage; moreover, in the case of quite young girls who had not yet given birth to any child, a miscarriage might accompany their menstruation without their knowing, and only when the shaman, in such a case as this, pointed out the girl as the origin of the trouble and the cause of Takánakapsâluk's anger, would she call to mind that there had once been, in her menstruation skin (the piece of thick-haired caribou skin which women place in their under-breeches during menstruation) something that looked like "thick blood". She had not thought at the time that it was anything particular, and had therefore said nothing about it, but now that she is pointed out by the shaman, it recurs to her mind. Thus at last the cause of Takánakapsâluk's anger is explained, and all are filled wih joy at having escaped disaster. They are now assured that there will be abundance of game on the following day. And in the end, there may be almost a feeling of thankfulness towards the delinquent. This then was what took place when shamans went down and propitiated the great Spirit of the Sea.

Aua's account of pavuŋnᴀrtut's journey to the Land of the Dead.

"The great shamans of our country often visit the People of Day for joy alone; we call them pavuŋnᴀrtut (those who rise up into heaven). The shaman who is about to make the journey seats himself, as in the case of nak·a·jɔq, at the back of the sleeping place in his house. But the man who travels to the Land of Day must be bound before he is laid down behind the curtain; his hands must be fastened behind his back, and his head lashed firmly to his knees; he also must wear only breeches, leaving legs and the upper part of the body naked. When this is done, the men who have bound him must take an ember from the lamp on the point of a knife, and pass it over his head, drawing rings in the air, and say: "niɔʀuniᴀrtɔq aifa·le": "Let him who is now going a-visiting be fetched away".

"Then all lamps are put out, and all visitors in the house close their eyes. They sit like that for a long while, and deep silence reigns throughout the house. But after a time, strange sounds are heard by the listening guests; they hear a whistling that seems to come far, far up in the air, humming and whistling sounds, and then suddenly the shaman calling out at the top of his voice:

'Halala — halalale, halala — halalale!'

"And at the same moment, all visitors in the house must cry: 'Ale — ale — ale!'; then there is a sort of rushing noise in the snow hut, and all know that an opening has been formed for the soul of the shaman, an opening like the blowhole of a seal, and through it the soul flies up to heaven, aided by all those stars which were once human beings. And all the souls now pass up and down the souls' road, in order to keep it open for the shaman; some rush down, others fly up, and the air is filled with a rushing, whistling sound:

"'Pfft — pfft — pfft!'

"That is the stars whistling for the soul of the shaman, and the guests in the house must then try to guess the human names of the stars, the names they bore while living down on earth; and when they succeed, one hears two short whistles: 'Pfft — pfft!' and afterwards a faint, shrill sound that fades away into space. That is the stars' answer, and their thanks for being still remembered.

"Often a shaman will remain away for a long time, and his guests will then entertain themselves by singing old songs, always with closed eyes. It is said that there is great joy in the Land of Day when a shaman comes on a visit. They do not perceive him at first, being occupied with their games and laughter and football. But then there is heard the cry: 'niɔʀᴜᴀrzuit, niɔʀᴜᴀrzuit!' ringing out over the ground: 'Visitors, visitors'. And at once people come running out of the houses. But the houses have no passage ways, no entrances or exits, and therefore the souls come out from all parts, wherever they fancy, through the wall or through the roof. They shoot right through the house, and though one can see them, they are nevertheless nothing, and there are no holes in the houses where they passed through. And they run towards the visitor, glad to greet him, glad to bid him welcome, for they believe it is the soul of a dead man, like themselves. But then when he says: 'pu^{d}la·liuvuŋa' 'I am still of flesh and blood', they turn away dissappointed.

"Up in the Land of Day, the thong with which the shaman was bound falls away of itself, and now the dead ones, who are always in high spirits, begin playing ball with it. Every time they kick it, the thing flies out into the air and seems to take the shape of all manner of beings, now a caribou, now a bear, now a human being. They are fashioned by a mass of little loops, which form of themselves at a mere kick from one of the dead.

"When the shaman has amused himself a while among all the happy dead, he returns to his old village. The guests, who are awaiting him with closed eyes, hear a loud bump at the back of the sleeping place, and then they hear the thong he was tied with come rushing down; this does not fall behind the curtain, but down among all the waiting members of the household. Then the shaman is breathless and tired, and only cries:

"'Pjuh — he — he — he!'

"Afterwards he tells of all that he has seen and heard."

— — —

The journey to the Land of the Dead in heaven is not always made, however, merely for pleasure. As long as a shaman is treating a sick person, he must devote himself entirely to this work, and at certain definite times of the day sakavɔq: i. e. he invokes his helping spirits. This is done as a rule four times during the twenty four hours: morning, noon, evening and night. Not until the patient is cured may the shaman resume his everyday business of hunting. Should the treatment fail, and the patient die, this is generally due to witchcraft; more will be said about this elsewhere. Should it be a shaman summoned from another village, however, who is treating the sick person, he may leave his patient before the cure is complete, when the disease lasts a very long time, but must then undertake to leave behind some of his helping spirits in charge. A shaman who has done this will say of himself that he "lacks something"; that he is "not altogether himself" for the helping spirits that remain behind to look after the patient are a part of himself. And as long as a shaman lacks some of his helping spirits, he will not, as a rule, go out hunting; he would feel the power of his senses impaired by the loss.

A séance among the Aivilingmiut of the present day.

As long as the shamans are telling of what happened in the olden days, their imagination is naturally borne up by all that distance has rendered great and wonderful. The old accounts gain colour, and again and again we are told that the generation in which we live is grown feeble and incapable. In the olden days — ah, there were real shamans then!. But now, all is mediocrity; the practice, the theories of all that one should know may still be remembered, but the great art, the dizzying flights to heaven and to the bottom of the sea, these are forgotten. And therefore I was never able to witness a spirit séance which was really impressive in its effect. There might be a certain atmosphere about them, but mostly in the scenes in which all took part, and in the faith and imagination evident among the audience; they might also be uncanny and thrilling as scenes of native life, and even fascinating. One saw terrified, unhappy human beings fighting against fate; one heard weeping and outcries in the dark night of life. But apart from the effect thus produced by the actors and their environment the manifestation of magic in itself was always more or less transparent, and among these tribes at least had nothing of the true spiritual uplift, which they themselves were able to impart to the old traditions. Nevertheless, the shamans were never humbugs or persons who did not believe in their own powers; and it was also extremely rare to meet with any scepticism among the listeners.

I once made the acquaintance of a highly respected shaman named Angutingmarik; when we discussed problems or theories, his answers often impressed me. Nor was he by any means lacking in self-appreciation. Here is his own estimate of his position:

"As to myself, I believe I am a better shaman than others among my countrymen. I will venture to say that I hardly ever make a mistake in the things I investigate and in what I predict. And I therefore consider myself a more perfect, a more fully-trained shaman than those of my countrymen who often make mistakes. My art is a power which can be inherited, and if I have a son, he shall be a shaman also, for I know that he will from birth be gifted with my own special powers."

This Angutingmarik once held a seance at which Jacob Olsen, who was present in company with Therkel Mathiassen, was able to write down all that was said, and I was myself subsequently enabled to test the accuracy of the account by going through it with Jacob Olsen and Angutingmarik together. The description of the proceedings given below is a literal translation. This method of invocation, a very common one among the Aivilingmiut, is an intermediate form between the sakajut type, where the shaman sits behind a curtain of skins on the sleeping place, and the qilajut, of which examples will be given later on. No tricks of any sort are here employed, everything being left to the answering spirits invoked, who give the shaman his cue, whereby he is enabled throughout to make suggestions furnishing occasion for the confessions made. It must of course be borne in mind that in a little Eskimo village, everyone nearly always knows all about everybody else, despite all efforts on the part of any individual to keep anything secret, and however firm his conviction that nobody knows. But should the shaman have nothing definite to go upon, he will keep to matters of ordinary everyday life in which he can be sure that all the women offend against taboo. And he can nevertheless confidently reckon on astonishing all with his knowledge. In the course of his questioning he must always appear to be accusing himself: "Is it my fault?" For he knows that if he does not succeed in ascertaining the cause of the disease, then he is either a poor shaman who cannot, or a black magician who will not cure, and is using his art in the service of evil. It is therefore essential for him to have the listeners' repeated assurance that it is not he who is responsible for the sickness. The listeners on their part must help him to the utmost of their power in eliciting confessions of all offences, for should any such be definitively concealed, it might mean disaster to the whole community. Hence the highly dramatic dialogue which always takes place between the shaman, the audience and the sick person. And all, shaman and audience alike must do what they can to furnish excuses for the offences committed, for such indulgence on the part of human beings tends to appease the anger of the Sea Spirit.

Angutingmarik purifies a sick person.

A woman named Nanoraq, the wife of Mákik, lay very ill, with pains all over her body. The patient, who was so ill that she could hardly stand upright, was placed on the bench. All the inhabitants of the village were summoned, and Angutingmarik enquired of his spirits as to the cause of the disease. The shaman walked slowly up and down the floor for a long time, swinging his arms backwards and forwards with mittens on, talking in groans and sighs, in varying tones, sometimes breathing deeply as if under extreme pressure. He says:

"It is you, you are Aksharquarnilik, I ask you, my helping spirit, whence comes the sickness from which this person is suffering? Is it due to something I have eaten in defiance of taboo, lately or long since? Or is it due to the one who is wont to lie beside me, to my wife? Or is it brought about by the sick woman herself? Is she herself the cause of the disease?"

The patient answers:

"The sickness is due to my own fault. I have but ill fulfilled my duties. My thoughts have been bad and my actions evil."

The shaman interrupts her, and continues:

"It looks like peat, and yet is not really peat. It is that which is behind the ear, something that looks like the cartilage of the ear? There is something that gleams white. It is the edge of a pipe, or what can it be?"

The listeners cry all at once:

"She has smoked a pipe that she ought not to have smoked. But never mind. We will not take any notice of that. Let her be foregiven. tauva!

The shaman:

"That is not all. There are yet further offences, which have brought about this disease. Is it due to me, or to the sick person herself?"

The patient answers:

"It is due to myself alone. There was something the matter with my abdomen, with my inside."

The shaman:

"I espy something dark beside the house. Is it perhaps a piece of a marrow-bone, or just a bit of boiled meat, standing upright, or is it something that has been split with a chisel? That is the cause. She has split a meat bone which she ought not to have touched."

The audience:

"Let her be released from her offence! tauva!".

The shaman:

"She is not released from her evil. It is dangerous. It is matter for anxiety. Helping spirit, say what it is that plagues her. Is it due to me or to herself?"

Angutingmarik listens, in breathless silence, and then speaking as if he had with difficulty elicited the information from his helping spirit, he says:

"She has eaten a piece of raw, frozen caribou steak at a time when that was taboo for her."

Listeners:

"It is such a slight offence, and means so little, when her life is at stake. Let her be released from this burden, from this cause, from this source of illness. tauva!"

The shaman:

"She is not yet released. I see a woman over in your direction, towards my audience, a woman who seems to be asking for something. A light shines out in front of her. It is as if she was asking for something with her eyes, and in front of her is something that looks like a hollow. What is it? What is it? Is it that, I wonder, which causes her to fall over on her face, stumble right into sickness, into peril of death? Can it indeed be something which will not be taken from her? Will she not be released from it? I still see before me a woman with entreating eyes, with sorrowful eyes, and she has with her a walrus tusk in which grooves have been cut."

Listeners:

"Oh, is that all? It is a harpoon head that she has worked at, cutting grooves in it at a time when she ought not to touch anything made from parts of an animal. If that is all, let her be released. Let it be. tauva!"

Shaman:

"Now this evil is removed, but in its place there appears something else; hair combings and sinew thread."

The patient:

"Oh, I did comb my hair once when after giving birth to a child I ought not to have combed my hair; and I hid away the combings that none might see."

Listeners:

"Let her be released from that. Oh, such a trifling thing; let her be released. tauva!"

Shaman:

"We have not yet come to the end of her offences, of the causes of her sickness. Here is a caribou breast come to light, a raw caribou breast."

Listeners:

"Yes, we know! Last summer, at a time when she was not allowed to eat the breast of a caribou she ate some all the same. But let her be released from that offence. Let it be taken from her. tauva!"

Shaman:

"She is not yet free. A seal comes forth; plain to be seen. It is wet. One can see how the skin has been scraped on the blubber side; it is all plain as could be."

The patient:

"I did scrape the skin of a seal which my son Qasagâq had killed at a time when I ought not to have touched seal skins."

Shaman:

"It is not yet removed. It has shifted a little way back. Something very like it, something of the same sort, is visible near by."

Listeners:

"Oh that was last summer, when her husband cut out the tusk from a walrus skull, and that was shortly after he had been ill, when he was not yet allowed to touch any kind of game. Let her be released from that. Do let it be taken from her! tauva!"

Shaman:

"There is more to come. There are yet cases of work, of occupations which were forbidden; something that happened in the spring, after we had moved over to this place."

The patient:

"Oh, I gave my daughter a waistbelt made of skin that had been used for my husband's quiver."

Listeners:

"Let this be taken away. Let her be released from it. tauva!"

Shaman:

"It is not yet taken away. She is not released from it as yet. Perhaps it has something to do with the caribou. Perhaps she has prepared caribou skins at a time when she ought not to have touched them."

Listeners:

"She has prepared caribou skins. She helped to stretch out the skins at a time when she was living in the same house with a woman who had her menses. Let her be released from that tauva!"

Shaman:

"She is not freed from guilt even yet. It seems now as if the earth beneath our feet were beginning to move."

Patient:

"I have picked moss at a time when I ought not to have touched earth at all, moss to melt lead with for my husbands rifle bullets."

Shaman:

"There is more yet, more forbidden work that has been done. The patient has not only melted lead for her husband when it was taboo, but she did it while still wearing clothes of old caribou skin, she did it before she had yet put on the garments made from the new autumn skins."

Listeners:

"Oh these are such little things. A woman must not be suffered to die for these. Do let her be released."

Shaman:

"She is not released. It may perhaps prove impossible to release her from these burdens. What is that I begin to see now? It must be blood, unless it is human filth. But it is outside the house, on the ground. It looks like blood. It is frozen, and covered with loose snow. Someone has tried to hide it."

Patient:

"Yes, that was in the autumn. I had a miscarriage, and tried to conceal it, I tried to keep it secret to avoid the taboo."

Listeners:

"This is certainly a great and serious offence. But let her be released nevertheless. Let her be released. tauva!"

Shaman:

"We wish her to get well again. Let all these obstacles be removed. Let her get well! And yet I see, and yet I espy things done which were forbidden. What do I see? It looks as if it were a caribou antler. It looks like that part of the antler nearest the head."

Patient:

"Oh that was a caribou head I once stole in order to eat it, though it was forbidden food for me at the time."

Listeners:

"That was very wrong, but all the same, let her be released, let her be released from that. tauva!"

Shaman:

"There is still something more I seem to see; something that as it were comes and disappears just as I am about to grap it. What is it? Can it be the man Amarualik, I wonder? It looks like him. I think it must be he. His face is bright, but he is blushing also. He is as bright as a living being. It looks as if he wanted to show me something. And yet another person. Who is that? The patient must have no secrets. Let her tell us herself. Let her speak to us herself. Or can it be my cousin Qumangâpik? Yes, it is he. It is Qumangâpik. The size is right, and he has a big nose."

Patient:

"Alas, yes, it is true. Those men have I lain with at a time when I ought not to have lain with any man, at a time when I was unclean."

Listeners:

"It is a very serious offence for a woman to lie with men when she is unclean. But never mind all that. Let her be released, let her get well."

Shaman:

"But there is more yet to come." And turning to his spirit, he says:

"Release her from it all. Release her, so that she may get well. There is still something hereabout, something I can faintly perceive, but cannot yet grasp entirely."

The patient:

"Before the snow came, and before we were allowed to work on the skins of newly captured caribou, I cut up some caribou skin for soles and sewed them on to our boots."

Shaman:

"That is there still! There is more yet. The sources of disease are doubtless all in the patient herself, or can it be that any are in me? Can it be my fault, or that of my helping spirits? Or can those here present as listeners be guilty in any way? Can they have any part in the disease? (This was a reference to Therkel Mathiassen and Jacob Olsen, who had been digging among the ruins. It is considered sacrilege to touch the houses of the dead.) What can be the cause of that which still torments her? Can it be forbidden work or forbidden food, something eatable, something eaten of that which was forbidden, and nothing said? Could it be a tongue?

Patient:

"Alas, yes, I ate a tongue when it was forbidden me to eat caribou tongue."

Listeners:

"tauva, let her be released from this burden, from this offence."

Shaman:

"She is not yet released. There is more yet about forbidden food."

Patient:

"Can it be because I once stole some salmon and ate it a time when salmon was forbidden me?"

Listeners:

"Let her foolishness, let her misdeeds be taken from her. Let her get well."

Shaman:

"She is not yet released. There is more yet; forbidden occupations, forbidden food, stealing. Can it be that she is trying to hide something from us? Is she trying to conceal something, I wonder?"

Listeners:

"Even if she is trying to keep something concealed, let her be released from that, let her get well."

Shaman:

"There are still offences, evil thoughts, that rise up like a heavy mass, and she was only just beginning to get clean. The confessions were beginning to help her."

Listeners:

"Let all evil thoughts disappear. Take away all evil thoughts."

Shaman:

"Many confessions has the patient made, and yet it seems difficult! Can it be that she is beyond cure? But let her get well, quite well. Raise her up. But you cannot. You are not able to relieve her of her illness, though many of the causes have now been removed. It is terrible, it is dangerous, and you, my helping spirit, you whom I believe to be here with us, why do you not raise her up and relieve her of her pain, of her sickness? Raise her up, hold her up. Now once more something appears before my eyes, forbidden food and sinews of caribou."

Listeners.

"Once more she has combed her hair although she was unclean. Let her be released from that; let it be taken away from her. Let her get well. tauva!"

Shaman:

"Yet again I catch a glimpse of forbidden occupations carried on in secret. They appear before my eyes, I can just perceive them."

Listeners:

"While she was lying on a caribou skin from an animal killed when shedding its coat in the spring, she had a miscarriage, and she kept it secret, and her husband, all unwitting, lay down on the same skin where that had taken place, and so rendered himself unclean for his hunting!"

Shaman:

"Even for so hardened a conscience there is release. But she is not yet freed. Before her I see green flowers of sorrel and the fruits of sorrel."

Listeners:

"Before the spring was come, and the snow melted and the earth grew living, she once, wearing unclean garments, shovelled the snow away and ate of the earth, ate sorrel and berries, but let her be released from that, let her get well, tauva!"

Shaman:

"She is not yet released. I see plants of seaweed, and something that looks like fuel. It stands in the way of her recovery. Explain what it can be."

Listeners:

"She has burned seaweed and used blubber to light it with, although it is forbidden to use blubber for sea plants. But let her be released from that, let her get well. tauva!"

Shaman:

"Ha, if the patient remains obstinate and will not confess her own misdeeds, then the sickness will gain the upper hand, and she will not get well. The sickness is yet in her body, and the offences still plague her. Let her speak for herself, let her speak out. It is her own fault."

Patient:

"I happened to touch a dead body without afterwards observing the taboo prescribed for those who touch dead bodies. But I kept it secret."

Shaman:

"She is not yet released. The sickness is yet in her body. I see snow whereon something has been spilt, and I hear something being poured out. What is it, what is it?"

Patient:

"We were out after salmon, and I happened to spill something from the cooking pot on the snow floor". (When salmon are being sought for, care must be taken never to spill anything from a cooking pot either in the snow, in a snow hut, or on the ground in a tent).

Shaman:

"There are more sins yet. There is more to come. She grows cleaner with every confession, but there is more to come. There is yet something which I have been gazing at for a long time, something I have long had in view ..."

Listeners:

"We do not wish that anything shall be dangerous. We do not wish anything to plague her and weigh heavily upon her. She is better now, it is better now. Let her get well altogether."

Shaman:

"Here you are, helping spirit, dog Púngo. Tell me what you know.

Explain youself. Tell me, name to me, the thing she has taken. Was it the feet of an eiderduck?"

Patient:

"Oh, I ate the craw of a goose at a time when I was not allowed to eat such meat."

Listeners:

"Never mind that. Let her be released from that, let her get well."

Shaman:

"But she is not yet released. There is more yet. I can still see a hollow that has been visible to me all the time, ever since I began taking counsel of my helping spirits this evening. I see it, I perceive it. I see something which is half naked, something with wings, I do not understand what this can mean."

Patient:

"Oh, perhaps a little sparrow, which my daughter brought into the tent at a time when I was unclean, when it was forbidden me to come into contact with the animals of nature."

Listeners:

"Oh, let it pass. Let her be excused. Let her get well."

Shaman:

"She is not yet released. Ah, I fear it may not succeed. She still droops, falling forward, she is ill even yet. I see a fur garment. It looks as if it belonged to some sick person. I suppose it cannot be anyone else who has used it, who has borrowed it?"

Listeners:

"Oh, yes, it is true, she lent a fur coat to someone at a time when she was unclean."

Shaman:

"I can still see a piece of sole leather chewed through and through, a piece of sole leather being softened."

Patient:

"The spotted seal from the skin of which I removed the hair, and the meat of which I ate, though it was taboo."

Listeners:

"Let it pass. Let her be released from that. Let her get well."

Shaman:

"Return to life, I see you now returning in good health among the living, and you, being yourself a shaman, have your helping spirits in attendance. Name but one more instance of forbidden food, all the men you have lain with though you were unclean, all the food you have swallowed, old and new offences, forbidden occupations exercised, or was it a lamp that you borrowed?"

Patient:

"Alas yes, I did borrow the lamp of one dead. I have used a lamp that had belonged to a dead person."

Listeners:

"Even though it be so, let it be removed. Let all evils be driven far away, that she may get well."

Here the shaman ended his exorcisms, which had taken place early in the morning, and were now to be repeated at noon and later, when evening had come. The patient was by that time so exhansted that she could hardly sit upright, and the listeners left the house believing that all the sins and offences now confessed had taken the sting out of her illness, so that she would now soon be well again.

qilanɛq.

The simplest method of consulting the spirits is called qilanɛq, and to exercise this art it is not always necessary to be a shaman: it is therefore used as a rule only in cases of slight illness. qilajɔq, pl. qilajut, the one who is to consult the spirits, lays a person down on the floor, or on the sleeping place, face upwards, the operator's waistbelt being often fastened round the subject's head. Various questions are now put to the qila·ŋa: the person through whose head the spirits are to answer. While asking the questions, the operator endeavours to raise the person's head by means of the belt, calling upon the spirit, which is supposed to enter on the scene immediately below the body of the qila·ŋa. When the latter's head grows heavy, so heavy that the operator, despite all his efforts, cannot move it in the slightest degree, this means that the spirits are present and answer in the affirmative. If, on the other hand, the head is normal and easily moved, this constitutes a negative answer to the question put. This art can, as mentioned, be exercised by others besides shamans, as a rule by women, but certain conditions have then to be fulfilled. Thus for instance, Aua's wife Orulo could not practise qilanɛq if the qila·ŋa also bore the name of Orulo. In place of a human subject, one can also in certain cases use one's own leg, or a cushion of caribou skin. The line, or waistbelt, is then fastened to this instead of to a head. I once wrote down the proceedings in such a case of qilənɛ́q, with all that was said; the account is as follows:

The object was to ascertain the cause of a particular illness. The qilajɔq sat down beside the qila·ŋa and uttered the following words, tugging all the time at the strap, which was fastened to the head:

"kivfAqat·A·rtA·rlaŋa, kivfAqat·A·rtA·rlaŋa, kivfAqat·A·rta·lA·rlaŋa. tagva kivfAqat·A·riʷagit!": "Let me try to lift your head a little. Let me try to lift your head a little. Let me try to lift your head. Now I am lifting your head."

The head becomes heavy, the qilajɔq cannot lift it, the spirit is present, and the qilajɔq says:

"tagva taǵvun·Arputit aŋErʃu·ta·nik un·ErnialErputit": "Now you have arrived. Tell us now what is the cause of the patient's sufferings."

Then again:

"tauʷiniuʃutit?": "Are you a spirit that was once a human being?"

The head becomes heavy, the spirit answers yes. The qilajɔq asks again:

"aipatiminik?" This is shaman language, and means: "Is the illness due to forbidden food?"

The head grows lighter, the shaman lifts it with ease, and the listeners answer:

"a·k·agɔq": "No!"

"isArajaŋnik?": "Is the illness due to forbidden work?"

The spirit answers:

"Yes!"

The next question is:

"Is it because he has been working with iron?"

The spirit answers:

"Yes!"

The patient must now himself state on what occasion he has committed a breach of taboo by working with iron. As soon as he has confessed, all present must lift up their hands and say:

"taiva·luk": "Let it be; away with it."

Again the qilajɔq asks:

"aipatiminik?": "Has he worked with iron at a time when he was on a certain diet?'

The spirit answers:

"Yes!"

The qilajɔq asks:

"kaŋErʒugʃamik?': "Has he worked with iron at a time when he had also eaten the heads of animals killed?"

The spirit answers:

"Yes!"

People in the house cry aloud:

"taiva·luk, taiva·luk!": "Away with it! Let it be!"

If there is any suspicion that woman with a newly born child has patched her clothing immediately after the capture of a bearded seal, or, in the case of a man, if it be suspected that his wife has patched or used her needle to his footgear while she was unclean, the question put is:

"aŋ'nɔrsäŋnik?": "Is it clothing?"

Should the spirit answer yes, then it remains to investigate further, with constant pulls at the line, what breach of taboo has taken place and under what circumstances. So the questioning goes on, letting the spirit answer all the time, until the presumable cause of the sickness has been ascertained.

When the qilavɔq is at an end, the qilajɔq who has interrogated the spirits lifts up the qila'ŋa and says:

"kaxat'iŋ'ilagit, aka'jɔq kisiät!": "I have done this not in order to hurt your head, but only for good."

ilise·riʃᴀrnᴇq: The practice of witchcraft and black magic.

ilise'cut, that is, men or women who practise harmful magic, are persons easily angered (niŋ'aʃ'ᴇraicut). There are two kinds of such black magic or withcraft. Either one may bring misfortune upon another through the medium of an evil spirit, tupiläk, or it can be effected through an evil shaman. In Greenland, a tupiläk is a destructive monster, formed by magic power out of the bones of all manner of beasts. An evil man or woman makes a tupiläk that it may devour his or her enemy. In the Hudson's Bay district, the natives were aware that men had once possessed the power of making tupilait, but the art was now lost to them. tupiläk, pl. tupilait, was now merely the term for an evil spirit.

A man who has fallen ill owing to the effects of witchcraft is called a sujuktitᴀq. When he gets well, it is said that the shaman has "hit" him; it is believed that the forces utilised by evil spirits came into existence of themselves, and can only be controlled by great shamans.

If now a shaman desires to injure a person by magic, someone whom he does not like and of whom he has grown envious, he will first endeavour to obtain some object belonging to the person concerned; this he takes and speaks ill over it, and keeps on speaking ill over it, hoping thus to pass on the evil to the person he desires to hurt. And should he discover a powerful or destructive force, such as for instance that which may lie concealed in a grave, then he must rub the object he is speaking ill over into the grave. This may give rise to sickness, madness or enmity ending in homicide.

ilise'cut can also steal away the soul of a human being by supibluɳo: by "blowing it out", so that the soul rushes out of the body; care must be taken, however, that the persons to be injured have no idea that they have enemies; it is essential to maintain friendly relations with them in everyday life. When at last the object is so far attained that the soul has been driven out of the victim, helping spirits are called in to pursue and destroy it. And it will then not be long before the man who has lost his soul falls ill and dies. Should it be discovered that a shaman is given to the practice of stealing souls — and the suspicion may arise where a shaman is unfortunate with his patients — then he will be killed by his neighbours. Here also the recoil of evil deeds upon the evil-doer is well known: for when a soul is stolen away and the man dies, the stolen soul may return and slay the one who stole it.

Obsession by evil spirits.

It may happen that a village is haunted by evil spirits. Such are called **nunaluit** or **tupilait**. By evil spirits is understood not only fabulous beasts and the mountain spirits here referred to, which live out in the wilds, on earth, but also the ghosts of dead souls, which have become hostile to mankind, and dangerous, owing to failure to observe precisely the rules of taboo after their death. A shaman setting out to fight such beings and render them harmless must arm himself with a walrus knife, or that particular kind of snow knife which is made from walrus tusk with no iron edge inserted, and which is called **havu·jᴀq**.

These evil spirits may either be fashioned in mystic wise by the shamans, or may come into existence of themselves; when they appear in a village, all the game vanishes from the district, and unless the evil spirits are driven out, the people will starve. The evil spirits are very dangerous. If a person other than a shaman sees them, he will die of it. An evil spirit must never be attacked with the right hand or arm, but only with the left. They are also called tɔ·^{r}ɳ^{r}a·luit, in contradistinction to tɔ·^{r}ɳ^{r}ait, which are the helping spirits of the shaman. When a shaman strikes an evil spirit with his knife, he says: "tɔ·^{r}ɳ^{r}a·lukpuɳa": "I have caught a tɔ·^{r}ɳ^{r}a·luk".

I give here in translation, an account of a seance as recorded by Jacob Olsen:

"It was said that there were evil spirits in our village on Southampton Island. Everyone was afraid. No one dared to go out, and at last the shamans were requested to drive the evil spirits away. All the people of the village then assembled in the largest of the huts.

"A shaman often does not feel strong enough to set out against the

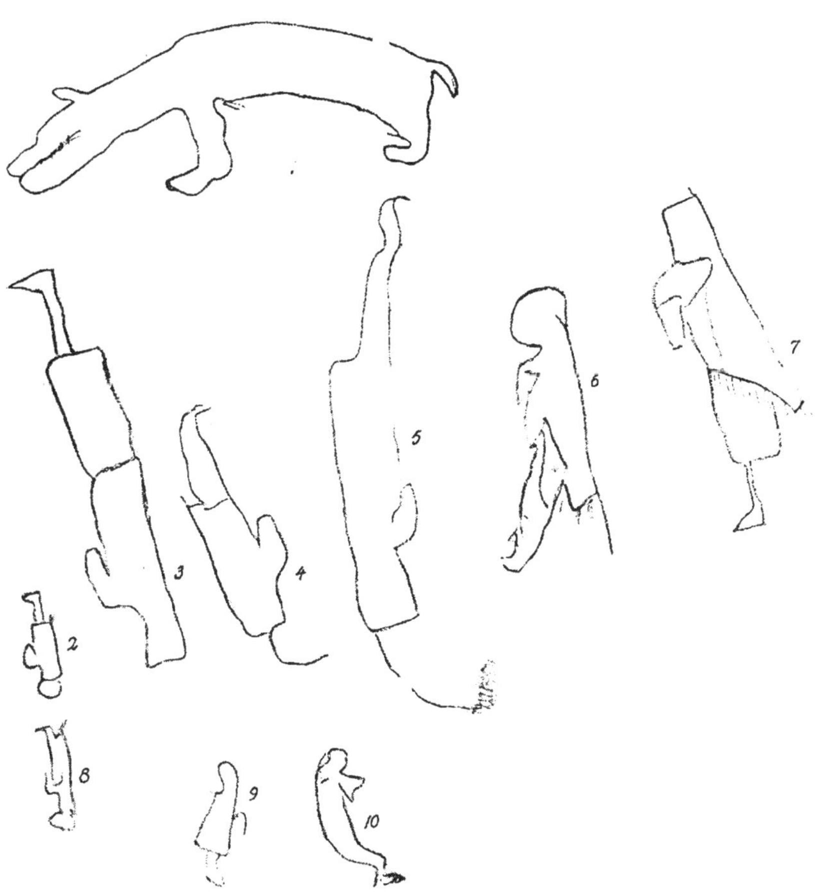

The helping spirits of the shaman Unaleq: 1) the spirit Tulorialik, 2) the Indian spirit Itqileq, 3) the ghost Alo. 4—5) Two spirits that are both called Norssutilik, because they have a nɔrʃut: a tassel on a flexible stick placed over the frock-hood, 6) the ghost Arnangnakluk, who was a woman, 7) Angusingâvnâ, who was once a man, 8) the Indian spirit Itqileq, 9) the female spirit Kavliliúkâq, 10) Kamingmâlik, the spirit of a woman of the tuneq people. Drawn by Unaleq.

Above: The encircled figure represents the mother of the sea animals, who sits on the bottom of the sea and broods over the fate of man. The other drawing is intended to be Putuliq, or "the spirit of the many holes"; while he was out fishing for salmon one day it came up to him from the bottom of a lake; it wanted to help a human being and became his helping spirit. Its speciality is: accoucheur, for all its holes have an encouraging effect upon the child, which more easily emerges from the womb when it sees the many holes. — Below, to left: One spring day near a village Anarqâq saw this being, which is called Qungiaruvlik. It was his father's helping spirit, here seen stealing a child which she is putting into her amaut. Anarqâq's mother's helping spirits, Puksinâ on the right and Navagioq on the left, killed Qungiaruvlik. Drawings by Anarqâq.

evil spirits by himself, and may then get another shaman to help him. So it was in this case. But first of all the spirits had to be invoked in the usual way. On such an occasion, it is the shaman alone who sings, and the one who began was Angutingmarik. He sang:

‘aunalikiᴀq aulasiƀlugo
aulasi^{d}lᴀrpit
asiᴀrmiune ma·ɴe.
aulasɨn·a^{d}lᴀrame
takunialᴇrsɔq
ᴇʀ·avᴇqaja·ŋ·icɔq ta$_{u}$pna
ajɔqutaunialᴇrame qai
saŋmiŋmᴀrit·ɔq
tipjᴀrse tipjᴀrse
qaklilᴇrit qaklilᴇrit
apᴇrʃᴀriwagit apᴇrʃᴀriwagit
tag^{v}a ma·n·a akiniᴀrtutit
hai u^{w}ai hai
ʃe — ʃe — ʃe!

‘What can it be that moves
which moves me
somewhere out over the earth, away from here,
which moves and will thus become visible,
something without entrails,
something that seeks to do evil,
something moving straight towards us.
Helping spirit Tipjarse, Tipjarse,
come, come to me,
I consult you and I interrogate you
And you must answer,
hai — u^{w}ai — hai,
ʃe — ʃe — ʃe.

When this song was sung, the shaman took his listeners one by one and made as if to pick out all the evil from them, the others meanwhile shouting in chorus: “taiman·aitɔra·luit u^{w}aŋ·at pᴇ·raululᴇrlit tauva!’: ‘Let all that kind of evil be driven out of them.’

“And then as usual all have to confess their various offences and breaches of taboo, the shamans taking it in turn to interrogate and let their helping spirits point out the culprits.

“A shaman driving out any form of evil must stand with his head towards the sky, his eyes closed, and his hands together. He must wear mittens. He must cough with every word he speaks, and frequently change his voice; whenever he does so, the listeners must cry: ‘ade·-ade·’: ‘keep on, keep on!’ As soon as all confessions have been made, — and this may occupy the greater part of the night — the shamans must go outside two and two. Then after a little while one of them comes in and says that a number of evil spirits have now appeared out in the village. The exorcism and confessional are then resumed, with the result that many more evil spirits become visible outside. Now the people begin to feel terrified in earnest, and beg and entreat the shamans to help them. So they go out again, and at once all those inside must cry all together: 'tipjᴀrse tipjᴀrse, tauva!' The helping spirit Tipjarse must help them. This time, when the shamans come in, one man spreads out a pair of men's breeches before them, and on these they must now seat themselves, side by side, up on the bench. The lamps are extinguished, and all present close their eyes. No one is allowed to sit with open eyes while the lamps are out; to do so would mean blindness. The shamans now call up their spirits by song, and here is the song which was sung:

'ipnaivna· taⁱpʃumane
pigilᴀ·rtᴀra nukigilᴀ·rtᴀra
ᴇrqasukpəsuk·aluᴀrtuŋa uvaŋa
aŋnikiᵈliᵈlᴀrpāp·uŋa ma·ne
quksaliᵈlᴀrpāp·uŋa ta·unut
tak·ut·ukʃᴀq ipnaivna piʷalᴇriga
mitliᴀra atajulilᴇrpäŋmăt
halala halala halala
tautuŋnᴀrziŋmät ipnaivna
itluᴀrilᴇrpäk·iga ipnaivna
akiuktukʃatut aulasin·ᴀrmät
sukatᴀrsimaʃutut ᴇrʒäsimaʃutut
ipnaivna taupna piʷalᴇrtlugo
numalɔruluit qai piᴀrniᴀrai.
aklᴇru·latᴇrivuŋa ma·ne
halala halala halala uʷai
ʃe — ʃe — ʃe!'

'Once long ago
There was a spirit of mine
A spirit I had deprived of strength, and made weak,
hai, uʷai, hai.
Often I took much trouble
often I pondered on matters hidden,
hai, uʷai, hai.
But nevertheless I feel myself small,
nevertheless I tremble at the judgment of men.
I call upon the one that shall come,
It is as if the afterbirth stuck in my throat,
I am suffocating,
halala — halala.
But when the heavens became visible
I was filled with joy,
And I moved as one resisting,
as one who can put strain on the muscles set together,
as one who can clench his teeth.
I will now exterminate evil spirits,

I and my helping spirit together!
The spirit that long ago
I rendered powerless and weak.
But the first time I saw it
I trembled
So that my teeth chattered with fear.
Halala — halala — halala — u^{w}ai
ʃe — ʃe — ʃe.'

"The shamans now alter their voices, speaking in such a way as to be unrecognisable, and breathe deeply, and then they ask someone to light the lamps. As soon as it is light, they declare that their helping spirits have, during the singing, driven all the evil spirits away from the village. The moment they rise from their seat, a man must come running up to remove the breeches on which they had been sitting while they sang.

"At times, however, the shamans will not be content with merely singing. They go out themselves to do battle with the evil spirits, and when they return, their hands and arms are bloody from the fight, and their clothing in rags.

— — —

"During our stay at Southampton Island, I was witness to such a case, where a shaman named Saraq went out to fight against evil spirits, but I discovered that he had taken some caribou blood with him beforehand, and rubbed himself with this, without being discovered by anyone else. When he came in, he stated that the shaman who had been out with him had been unable to hold the evil spirit, but he, Saraq, had grasped it and stabbed it, inflicting a deep wound. It had then made its escape, but the wound was so deep that he could not conceive the possibility of its surviving. All believed his report, all believed that he had driven away the evil spirit which had been troubling the village, and no one was afraid any longer. But when the audience dispersed after the ceremony to go to their own dwellings, they fired off a gun in the air."

On the day after evil spirits have been driven off, no one is allowed to go out hunting. Early next morning, all must repair to the house where the ceremony took place, and this must be done before any food is taken. When all are assembled, the shamans must proceed a second time to drive out the evil from the hearts of those present, and once more all breaches of taboo must be mentioned. As soon as the shamans have finished, and left the house, all the men must go after them, and they must now walk three times round the house. When they re-enter, they lead one of the shamans with them in a dog's harness, dragging him in by the trace. The shaman behaves like a madman as long as he is thus harnessed, lashing out on every side.

Not until the harness is taken off does he return to his normal manner, and concludes with the singing of a spirit song. And now at last the entire community assembles for a grand feast, a banquet composed of all the best food there is. After the meal, a kind of market is held, each person laying out all the objects of value he possesses on the floor, knives, skins, and other desirables. These are exchanged for others' possessions' without regard to the value of the article obtained in return. It must be done out of pure delight at having escaped the danger. The concluding item on the programme consists in taking a small piece of white skin, poking a stick of wood through it and placing it by the window. Another hole is made in the white skin, in the middle, and oil is smeared over it, when the following words are uttered, addressed to the skin: "Kisiät, kisiät": "only through there, only through there!" This piece of skin so placed is called ije, or the eye. The eye is intended to keep watch for any evil spirits approaching the village, and frighten them away.

After the hunt for evil spirits, all are happy once more, and no longer afraid of anything. Everyone who has taken part must take a small piece of wick, twist a sinew thread round it and lay it outside or on top of his snow hut. This is a sacrifice to the spirits, the good spirits who aided in destroying the evil.

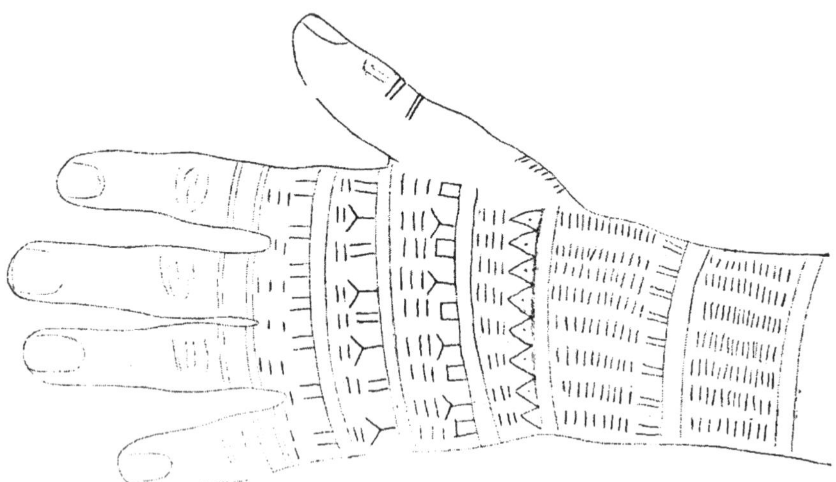

Tattooed female hand by Pakak. Great significance was attached to tattooing. especially in former days; for the woman who had handsome tattooing always got on well with Nuliajuk when, after life on earth, she passed her house on the way to the land of the dead.

VI.

Amulets.

But the powers even of the most skilful shamans have their limits. They may intervene and change ill fortune to good, alleviate disaster, but they cannot directly support the destiny of the individual, still less be ominipresent when an evil fate reaches out towards its victim. They are, of course, quite ordinary persons in everyday life. Everyone must therefore have his own personal and particular talisman, which is ever with him, and such individual protection is found in the amulets, which are worn on the person, and in such magic words as each may know.

An amulet is called ᴀ·ʳɳʳuᴀq, pl. ᴀ·ʳɳʳuʃ·ät; or one may also say: pit·ɔrqut, pl. pit·ɔrqutit.

Every individual has, it is true, a natural helper in his soul namesake, as already mentioned. This is expressed as follows: "atᴇrput ikajɔrtigᴀ·rput iluɳᴇrsualulᴇra·ɳapta", which means: "we obtain aid from our namesakes when we strive with all our strength against any peril". By this is understood dangerous weather, ill-luck in hunting, peril at sea or in a blizzard.

'ativut atiᵛtalo atiɳe qaniktume·p·ut" means "Our namesakes and the namesakes of our namesakes are near us". All the dead who bear the same names as we ourselves are near us all, so that the one after whom I myself am named is nearest to me, and he again nearest to his namesake, and so on throughout the series. But all this is no more than one is born with; something further is needed to cope with extraordinary circumstances, and it is for this purpose amulets are worn.

The Iglulingmiut, in contrast to the Netsilingmiut, use very few amulets, but their view of the manner in which they render service is the same. As a matter of fact, they are worn without any further thought of the magic power which radiates from them, and it was therefore not an easy matter to arrive at the wearers' own estimate of the properties they possessed. The following account is the result of numerous conversations on the subject.

It is not the amulet itself, but the soul of the animal from which it is taken which has the effective helping power. But it is not a matter of indifference what part of the animal one takes for the purpose; on the contrary, it is essential that certain particular parts shall be used. A woman in childbirth for instance must use a raven's claw as toggle in the strap which fastens her amaut (carrying bag for a child) at the bottom. It is afterwards given to the child as an amulet, and brings vitality and success in hunting. But even though these powers of good luck do not emanate from the claw itself, but from the soul of the raven, an amulet made from another part of the raven's body would be of no avail.

The amulet acts by magic, and it is therefore not absolutely and exclusively confined in its effects to the actual wearer. It may be given away to another person, but the magic power can only be conveyed to the new owner if he gives something in return. Unless this is done, the power of the amulet is not transferred to the new owner, even though he may carry it about on his person. Hence it is quite possible to lose an amulet and yet retain its virtue. Among the Caribou Eskimos, amulets had to be obtained from people dwelling at a distance; here, it was quite legitimate to procure them from one's fellow-villagers, as long as some payment was given. It is also a common thing to obtain the head of a harpoon from an old man who is no longer able to hunt; the luck which had previously attended the former user in hunting will then be transferred to the new possessor of the implements. Certain implements have this peculiar property: that seals do not mind being killed by them, and it is this which gives success in hunting. Even articles of clothing may bring luck. At Iglulik, sleeve linings were purchased from a decrepit old man who had formerly been an expert at hunting caribou, to give to a boy whose father had always been unfortunate in that branch of the chase; he had, indeed, never once succeeded in getting a caribou, as these animals refused to let him kill them. His son now had the sleeve linings of the good hunter sewn into his sleeves, and every time he had a new tunic made, the old, worn and greasy linings were put into it. And he became a mighty caribou hunter.

The natives have a strong and firm belief in the effect of amulets and the power which they can exert in time of peril on behalf of the wearer. But here again we find something of the same thing that I have already noted in regard to belief in shamans: the cases are mostly found in stories and myths, rarely in real life. This does not, however, do away with the faith that a miracle may after all perhaps once take place in one's own case, and so men still trustingly wear their amulets. The most famous of amulets are the skin and skull of the strong little ermine, or a lemming, the dried skin of which is worn inside the hood. The wearer of such an amulet can, when attacked by any superior force, breathe life into it, and the ermine or lemming will then, small and inconsiderable as it is in outward seeming, dash in unnoticed among the hostile party, but with such force as to drive right through the bodies of the enemies, as a rule up through the anus and out at the mouth, exterminating a whole party in a moment. This form of amulet is known throughout the whole of Canada, as well as in Greenland and Alaska. Among the Iglulik tribe, it is best known through the following variant of the story of Kâgjagjuk:

The powerful ermine amulet saves Kâgjagjuk and his brother.

There were once three homeless children, two brothers and a sister. The elder brother was grown up, the other two were still but little children. The younger brother was named Kâgjagjuk. One spring, the elder brother, who was married, had been out hunting seal on the ice. He had crawled up to a seal and harpooned it, and when he came home, he asked his little brother and sister to go out and fetch it.

The two did as their brother had said, and went far out on the ice to get the seal. While they were far out at sea, the ice broke away, and they drifted over to Southampton Island. Here they met with people, but they were not good people, they ill-treated and starved the children, and gave them the roughest and most wearisome tasks. The girl was obliged to plait sinew threads all the time, and Kâgjagjuk had to empty urine vessels, and every time the boy had been outside with one, and was coming in through the passage again, they would lift him up by taking hold of his nostrils with the fangs of a bear. (This is precisely as in the Greenland version, where he is also lifted up by the nostrils).

Sometimes Kâgjagjuk would say: "Do not be so cruel to me. You had better not go too far, for my brother is a great shaman".

Summer came, and the elder brother decided to set out in search of his brother and sister. And he came to Southampton Island and found them. The people of the village there were pleased at having visitors, and made preparations for singing and dancing in the feasting house (qaɢ·e). They set the little brother to work beating out blubber, the hardest piece of blubber they could find, from a bearded seal.

As soon as the elder brother arrived, and caught sight of the younger one, he said:

"Be sure not to tell these people who I am. Let me see how they treat you". And now, when he saw they had given him a piece of blubber to beat, he said:

"Hadn't I better do that?" And so he began beating out the blubber to make oil for the lamps in the feasting house. Then he filled the lamps, and when they were filled, he threw the rest of the oil in the faces of the people near. The lamps were lit, and the song contest was held and lasted all night. In order not to lose any of the singing, any who wanted to make water did so in pots, instead of going outside, and gave the vessels as usual to Kâgjagjuk to empty.

Once again the elder brother said:

"Perhaps I had better do that". And then he took the urine vessel from his little brother and threw the contents out on the floor. This caused great confusion among those present, and they began leaving the house. Hardly had they got outside when they began piling up snow before the entrance, so that the brothers could not get out. But now the brother called out and begged them, before covering up the entrance, to give them the skin he used for sitting on in his kayak. They gave it to him, and in that skin was fastened an ermine. This was his amulet, and at once he began to soften the skin, making water over it to render it thoroughly soft. At last he was able to breathe life into it, and then he said to the ermine, as soon as it was alive:

"Go out and eat up all these people." Then the ermine slipped out, and hardly had it got outside when one heard people crying:

"Look, an ermine, an ermine!"

And they began to hunt it about. But the little ermine flung itself upon them, ran right through them and killed them in that way, one by one. There was great confusion, and when it was discovered that it must be an amulet belonging to the man in the house which was killing them all, they opened the house again and cried.

"We do not wish to harm you any more".

The elder brother went out, and the people being now so throughly frightened, were amiable, and so he did not harm them, but let the rest go. Then he made ready for the journey. He had quite forgotten about his little sister. He had just started off when he remembered and turned back at once to fetch her, but it was too late. They had already killed her, by hanging her up on a drying frame. When he saw this, he turned back at once to return to his village, but took with him now two women, the two women who had been wont to lift Kâgjagjuk up by the nostrils in the passage. These were now to be wives for Kâgjagjuk.

On returning home, the elder brother began to look after the younger one and teach him things. He dried the skin of a bearded seal and made it as hard as wood, and trained Kâgjagjuk to be a strong man by beating him with the hard skin. So he grew and became big, but only in the upper part of the body, where his brother was wont to beat him; his legs were small and short. And when he was grown up, he had the two women for his wives.

Kâgjagjuk obtained two ear ornaments of walrus tusk. They hung down from his ears, so that when he lay down, they knocked against each other; and the moment the two pieces knocked together, his wives had to come and lie down beside him; if they were not there on the instant, he would be furious, and beat them till they wept. So harsh and cruel was Kâgjagjuk towards his wives that one had her shoulder dislocated, and the other lost one eye. No wonder then, that the two women often mourned over their fate and were sorrowful, but then Kâgjagjuk would sing to them, thus:

"Dear little wife, dear little wife,
Weep not, cease longing for your home,
Cease longing for your home,
You will be given suet to eat,
Delicious suet,
And eyes, luscious eyes,
All this you will be given,
And tender juicy shoulder pieces
Given you as gifts,
Tender juicy shoulder meat."

And then, when he had finished singing that song, he would beat them again before they lay down to sleep. Thus he repaid their wickedness. And that is the end of the story.

Told by
Ivaluardjuk.

No one can altogether dispense with amulets, and this is apparent especially in the fact that a man may sometimes become incapable of all that is required in a hunter and head of a family, living thenceforward only as an object of scorn to his fellows. The reason is that his amulets are worthless, having been given to him by one who had no power of entering into communication with the supernatural. This explanation shows that it is not enough that the amulet in itself shall have magic power, but the giver, the one who makes an amulet out of the common object whatever it may be, must likewise possess such power. If now the passive amulets can somehow get their force renewed, a change at once takes place in the owner, who from being the meanest of unskilful hunters now suddenly appears as surpassing even the best. As an instance of how a useless amulet can be rendered effective once more, we have the following story of an unsuccessful hunter, who was aided by the naked magic bear:

Netsersuitsuarshuk, whose amulets were given new power.

Netsersuitsuarshuk could not kill seals. It was utterly impossible for him ever to catch a seal. He went out with the other men of the village, and watched at the blowholes as they did, but never managed to get a seal himself. Sometimes he would remain behind after the others had gone home, and stay for some time, but always without success, and when he got home, his wife would abuse him and show her contempt by refusing to give him water to drink. And often he had to go begging for water to other houses, when he was thirsty.

But one day, when he was out at the blowholes, and as usual had remained behind after the others had gone home, he heard a creaking in the snow behind him, and turning round, perceived a bear approaching; a naked bear without any skin. The bear spoke to him, and asked, if he had not a lemming for an amulet.

"Yes", answered Netsersuitsuarshuk, "I have a lemming for an amulet."

The bear then asked for it, and Netsersuitsuarshuk gave up the amulet. The bear blew out the skin of the lemming, and endeavoured to put it on, but failing in this, it blew a second time, and now the little lemming's skin stretched out to such a size that the bear was able to put it on. And at the same moment, the bear sprang upon Netsersuitsuarshuk and began fighting with him, and after they had wrestled for a long time, the bear said:

"When you get home, ask for water as usual. If your wife should refuse to give you any, then get up on the sleeping place and lie down with your head turned inward, lie there quite quietly and ask me to come. But do not say it out loud. Just wish me there, and I will come and show myself at the window."

Netsersuitsuarshuk then went home, and the bear left him, after giving him back the amulet.

Netsersuitsuarshuk came home, and as usual, asked his wife for a drop of water to drink. But not only his wife refused him water to drink; his wife's father and mother likewise would give him none. Then he got up on the sleeping place and lay down and wished for the bear. At once a bear appeared outside the window and thrust its head in, and the wife and her mother and father were so frightened, that they gave Netsersuitsuarshuk water to drink. And the moment he had drunk the water, the bear disappeared, and all in the house lay down to sleep.

Next day, the men went out hunting, and this time, it was not long before Netsersuitsuarshuk got a seal. On the following day they went out hunting again, and this time he got two seals, and so it went on. He caught them so quickly that he could bring home his catch in the morning, and his wife and her parents, who had formerly despised him, lived now in abundance on his hunting.

Told by
Inugpasugjuk.

Among amulets particularly characteristic of the Iglulingmiut and Aivilingmiut may be mentioned the excrement of a newly born ermine, placed in a stocking so as to touch the skin of the foot; this makes one a good walker, and is a protection against any pains in the feet.

On the shoulders of the inner jacket white strips of hide from the belly of the caribou are sewn; these are called "warmers". Whoever wears them will never feel cold.

A dried navel-string, sewn into the inner jacket, is a protection against evil spirits.

The milt of a fox, sewn into the instep of a boy's stocking, will keep him from falling through thin ice.

The udder of a hare, smoked over a slow fire and sewn into the breast of a woman's inner jacket, gives rich and abundant milk.

The outer integument of a caribou antler, sewn into the hood, gives long hair. Long hair means a strong soul. Whoever cuts his hair cuts away part of this soul.

The skin of a snipe may be placed in the fore-end of a kayak; this renders the craft seaworthy, and the man in it will not upset in a heavy sea.

A small doll, made from the extreme hard point of bone in the penis of a walrus, skilfully carved with arms and legs, is sewn into a boy's inner jacket, and he will then, when out alone after caribou, never encounter the dangerous mountain spirits called i^JErqät.

Waste oil from the lamp, sprinkled in the passage and round about the house, is a protection against evil spirits.

The magic power inherent in amulets can also be used to drive out sickness from the body. The sick person is beaten with his amulets, which are as a rule sewn into his inner jacket.

Jacob gave me an account of one such beating scene, which he witnessed at Tíkerârjualâq, the native name for Eskimo Point, which is the southernmost Eskimo settlement on the west coast of Hudson's Bay, now inhabited by the Caribou Eskimos, who here call themselves Pâdlimiut:

"One day I perceived that all the people of the village had gathered in a large group in a circle round their tents, and as I could not understand what they were about I went over to look. There was at this time a great deal of sickness in the village, spring colds for the most part, which it was supposed must be due to evil spirits. Just as I came up, a little girl, the daughter of Qunâq, came out of their tent, carrying under her arm her inner jacket, which had amulets sewn on all over it. All the men stood drawn up in a great circle, and the girl slipped in between them; once inside the circle, she walked round, following the direction of the sun, beating all the men and women one by one with her amulets. Every time anyone was hit, the others cried: 'iluaɽ'iut ahivakᴀr[d]le!': 'Let the cause of the sickness hasten away from here!'. As soon as the girl had made the round of the party, she returned to the tent, still carrying her inner jacket under her arm.

"Afterwards, all who had been beaten with the amulets gave the child handsome gifts, and there was no one but was convinced that her amulets had cleansed them from all disease. And there was great joy in the village, the fear of the evil spirits had disappeared, and in the evening a great song feast was held in the tent of the little girl's father. The joy of the people in their festival was supposed to strengthen the good spirits of the amulets."

VII.

Erinaliu·tit or magic words.

Of all sources of power, magic words are the most difficult to get hold of. But they are also the strongest of all, for it was a word — a magic word — which in the olden days, when mankind lived in the dark, gave them light; and it was by means of a magic word that death was brought into life at the time when human beings were beginning to overcrowd the earth.

Magic words, magic songs or magic prayers are fragments of old songs, handed down from earlier generations. They can be bought, at a high price, or communicated as a legacy by one who is dying; but no other person save the one who is to use them may hear them, otherwise they would lose their force. They are called **Erinali^{u}·t, pl. Erinaliu·tit.**

Erinaliu·tit may also be apparently meaningless sentences heard once in the days when the animals could talk, and remembered ever since through being handed down from one generation to another. Sometimes also a seemingly senseless jumble of words may derive force by a mystic inspiration which first gave them utterance. On the day when a man seeks aid in magic words, he must not eat of the entrails of any beast, and a man when uttering such words must have his head covered with his hood; a woman must have the whole spread of the hood behind thrown forward over her face.

Reference is constantly made to the inconceivable and wonderful effect of magic words in the stories, but the words themselves are not to be ascertained from such sources, being invariably omitted. The person who once knew them has kept them as a private source of power for his own use, and the story-teller has therefore to content himself with describing the effects. These particular stories in which magic words alter men's destiny or change their lives, turning men into animals and *vice versa,* are mostly told to children in order to give them an idea of how mighty a power lies hidden in words. Best known is the story of the old grandmother, who, in order to find food for her grandchild, changed herself into a young man by means of magic words. This story is also known throughout the whole of Greenland, and is invariably given as a remarkable instance of what words could do in the olden days. But the drastic manner in which the grandmother was changed into a man must not be regarded as in any way indecent in its conception; it must be borne in mind that obscenity was unknown among the Eskimos, and all parts of the body equally decent. Whenever I heard this story told it was always as an admiring expression of the power of human beings to help themselves out of difficulties, and though one might perhaps laugh heartily at the means employed, these were nevertheless only taken as an outcome of imagination:

Magic words that changed the old woman to a young man.

Once people left their village and went off on a hunting expedition, leaving an old woman and her grandchild behind all by themselves. The grandchild was a girl, and old enough to be married, but there was no husband to be found for her. The old woman was in despair at their loneliness, and had no idea what to do for food. So she decided to turn herself into a man. She knew about magic words, and sang over her body. The stick which she used for trimming the moss wick of her lamp she made into a penis, testicles she made out of her drinking bowl, and her own genitals she removed and turned into a sledge. So great was the power of her words, that when she was out at the call of nature, she made dogs out of the bits of snow she had used to wipe herself behind with. She made a harpoon and a kayak out of her meat skewer. And thus she became a man; a young man, moreover, with all a man's hunting implements. And now she went out hunting and got all manner of game. On her return home, she would stand her sledge up outside the house. But one day when she was out hunting on foot, there came a man to the house. The girl asked him in, and when he came in, he enquired whose sledge it was standing up outside.

"It is my grandmother's" said the girl.

"Then whose dogs are those outside, and whose is that kayak?"

"All my grandmother's" answered the girl.

"And who has been a husband to you, seeing that you are plainly great with child?"

"My grandmother!"

The man was still there when the grandmother came home, and

he heard her moving about outside, shouting orders to the dogs and now and then striking them. At last she came into the passage, but on catching sight of a stranger, she felt so ashamed, that she suddenly grew old again, and became her former self, an old woman such as she had been before the magic words had changed her into a young man. And stooping with age as she stood by the passage, speaking in the voice of an aged woman, she said:

"Dear little grandchild, come and help me."

And the grandchild went to help her, for she was now so exhausted that she could not get in without help.

Thus the old woman became her former self once more for shame at being surprised by a stranger. And here ends this story.

Told by
Naukutjik.

The communism which necessarily prevails in Eskimo society in order that all can manage to exist renders it a duty for the family to care for all helpless persons; among such are reckoned fatherless children, widows or old men and women who on account of age are no longer able to keep up with the rest on the constant hunting expeditions. In the absence of immediate relatives, the village as a whole is charged with the care of those who are unable to provide for themselves. But although such might often be inconceivably modest in their demands, they might sometimes be left to their fate. This applies more especially to old women, who could no longer render any useful service. Often pure heartlessness was the cause, but it might just as often be the severity of the struggle to make ends meet, which forced the head of a household to restrict the number of mouths to be fed, in times of scarcity, when despite all efforts he could not even procure food enough for those nearest of kin. Orphan children were blocked up in snow huts and left there, buried alive. They were called "mato·ruʃ·ät": "those who have been covered up". Old and worn-out folk would be left behind on the road when unable to keep up with the rest on a journey; one day the old creature would lag behind, and be left, in the track of the sledges, no one troubling to fetch the laggard in to camp when the snow huts were built. These were called "qimatät": "those who were left behind". Sometimes also, the party would simply neglect to take them along when first setting out from the old site, and they might then freeze or starve to death — often a lingering death, unless they chose to hang themselves rather than suffer so long. — But though the severe conditions of life were responsible for these cruel customs, it was nevertheless always reckoned a shameful thing to be guilty of such heartlessness. And the stories, which have always a moral touch, and point very clearly the difference between right and wrong, generally provide some miraculous form of rescue for such unfortunates, with a cruel and ignominious death for those who abandoned them. Here again the miraculous element is introduced by magic words, as the following stories will show. Some tribes, for instance, have a tradition that thunder and lightning were two poor children, sisters, whom no one cared about, or troubled to help. And one day when their fellow-villagers moved away to another place, the two were mato'ruʃ'ät: they were buried alive in a house. And the evil that had been done them gave their tongues force; they wished to become fire and roaring in the heavens, in order to take vengeance on their heartless neighbours, and their words had power; they became thunder and lightning, and frightened all their former fellow-villagers to death, Sila helping them to take vengeance upon those who had wished them to perish. Among the Iglulingmiut, however, there is another variant of this story of the two thunder sisters, and this is therefore given in another place. As an instance of how magic words could help those who were cast out by their fellows may here be given the following:

The old woman who enticed the animals to her house.

There was once an old woman, with her little grandchild, whom the neighbours had left behind at a village. All the others went away to new hunting grounds, and none would take these two with them. So they remained behind among all the empty snow huts, and had nothing to eat, and only worn-out clothing, and no sinew thread to mend their poor rags. The old woman did not know what to do, and thought she must die of hunger together with her little grandchild. But one day she suddenly remembered that she knew a magic song which was good for calling animals to a village. The words were old and powerful, good for calling up game, and she set herself down on the sleeping place and began to recite the magic words. And when she had finished, she told her grandchild, a little girl, to go outside and see if there were animals in sight. The little girl went out and came rushing in a moment after and said that she could see a host of little animals trotting along over the snow, all small creatures, the lemmings in front and after them the ermine. And when the old grandmother heard that, she said to her grandchild: "These creatures are too small. Go out and say to them: 'My grandmother says you must pass on'." And the little girl did so, and all the lemmings and

While hunting caribou Anarqâq met this spirit which is called Nârtôq (the pregnant, or the one with the big stomach). It looked horrible: its nose was on its forehead and the lower jaw ran into its breast. It rushed threateningly at him, but disappeared when he prepared to defend himself. Later on it appeared to him again, but this time it was calm, and said that its name was Nârtôq. The cause of its hot-headedness was that Anarqâq himself was too easily angered. In future he need never be afraid of it, if only he changed his disposition and abandoned his short temper. It became one of his best helping spirits. Drawn by Anarqâq.

Igtuk, or the boomer. When booming is heard in the mountains, it is Igtuk that makes the noise. No one knows where he stays; he is made otherwise than all other living things; his legs and arms are on the back of his body, his great eye is just level with his arms, whilst his nose is hidden in his mouth; on the chin is a tuft of thick hair and below it, on a line with his eye, are his ears. The mouth opens and discloses a dark abyss, and when the jaws move one can hear booming out in the country. Drawn by Anarqâq.

the ermine passed by the house. Then came the other animals, one after another, bigger and bigger ones came, even wolves and bears; these they were afraid of, and always the little girl went out and said: "My grandmother says you must pass on." And so they passed by, and after the dangerous animals came others. There came great hosts of hares, but these also the little girl told to pass on. Then there came a herd of caribou, and to these at last the old grandmother said: "You are to come inside; come right into the house!" And the caribou came trotting up to the passage and tried to get in, but it was too small, and there was no room for them to get in. At last they too had to pass by. Then there came a huge band of foxes, and again the old grandmother said to her grandchild: "Tell them I ask them to come in!" And the foxes jumped in through the passage, and kept on pouring in, and so many were they that soon there was no room for any more, and again the old grandmother said to her grandchild: "Go out and say the rest are to pass on.". Now the house was full of foxes, and the grandmother and her little grandchild began killing them, but there were so many that the ones underneath were suffocated already before they could get at them. Afterwards they skinned all those foxes, and laid up great stores of meat, and made clothes and sleeping skins and rugs of the skins, but the long sinews of the tails they used for sewing thread.

Thus they escaped with their lives, because the old grandmother knew a magic song which had power to entice the animals.

Told by
Ivaluardjuk.

Magic words can be of such power that they will create life out of dead things; they can make old clothes come to life. This is related in the story of:

Igimarajughugjuaq.

Itimarajughugjuaq lived far from the dwellings of men, far from his relatives, alone with his wife and children. Once when they were short of food, he killed his children and ate them. His wife cooked the children for him, and when their little hands suddenly clenched while they were cooking, she would always burst out crying. Thus Igimarajughugjuaq ate his children, and now that only his wife was left, he felt he would like to eat her as well. His wife, who was a shaman, grew suspicious, and one day when her husband was out, she stuffed out her clothes with odd bits of skins, laid out the whole on the sleeping place and called the thing to life, by reciting magic words over the garments, which gave them life and the power of speech.

"When he stabs you, be sure to cry out Ow, Ow," said the woman when she had finished the bundles.

Igimarajughuggjuaq came home, and stabbed his wife all in a moment as he came leaping in through the passage. "Ow, Ow!" cried the bundle of skins, and fell down on the floor. Then said Igimarajughugjuaq: "One might think it was a human being, since it said 'Ow, ow'." Then he sat down to consult his spirit, for he also was a shaman. His wife had hidden herself in a room at the side of the house where they kept skins and meat, and when the spirit informed him of this, Igimarajughugjuaq tried to stab his wife in the little side room, stabbing about in all directions. He just grazed her little finger, and that was all.

Next morning, when Igimarajughugjuaq had gone out, his wife fled away home to her parents.

Her husband came home, saw her footmarks and went off in chase. When he came up with her, she placed herself with her back to a precipice, and as he tried to grasp her she threw herself out over the precipice, uttering a magic word as she did so. Then there was soft snow down below, and she fell without hurt. Her husband looked down after her over the precipice, but as he could not see her anywhere he turned back and went home. The woman continued her flight and got safely home to her parents. They hid her away at once; and it was not long before her husband appeared in the village. His father-in-law took a side of walrus meat into the house to thaw, for he intended to behave as if nothing were the matter, and entertain his son-in-law with food, and so a feast were made ready, and the father-in-law said: "It is said that Igimarajughugjuaq eats his children."

"Who said that, who said that?" asked Igimarajughugjuaq.

"Your wife!"

"Where is she?"

"She went off in an umiAq that came by here."

Igimarajughugjuaq then ate nearly the whole of that side of walrus meat. After the meal, they fastened straps across the ceiling of the house, and began doing exercises with them. Igimarajughugjuaq would not join in at first, but his brother-in-law kept urging him to do so, and after a time he took part in the game. But hardly had he caught hold of the straps when the others rushed at him as he hung there, bound him, and killed him. This vengeance was taken upon the evil brother-in-law, and his wife saved her life by magic words.

Told by
Naukatjik.

Powerful words could not only give life to dead things and save human life, but could also transform or kill or annihilate as in the following story:

Powerful words close up a ravine and change a man to frost.

Once a band of children were playing near a ravine close to Naujan. A little distance from land, out on the ice, stood a man by a blowhole, watching for seal. Again and again the cries of the children disturbed him, and at last he grew angry, and so cried out, turning towards the land:

"May the ravine close over them!"

Hardly had he uttered those words when the ravine closed over the children.

The parents could not understand what had become of the children, and when they went out to look for them, they discovered that the ravine had closed over them. In vain they tried to break an opening in the closed ravine; the rocks were not to be hammered asunder. Then suddenly they caught sight of a man out on the ice, listening at a blowhole for seal, and realising that it was he who was the cause of the disaster, they were furious, and cried:

„May you be changed into frost!"

His wife waited a long time for her husband, who was out after seal, but when he did not come, she went out to look for him. She found him completely covered with rime, and so she set to work to brush it off. She kept on brushing it off, but as she did so, the man grew smaller and smaller, and at last there was nothing left of him at all. He had been altogether changed into frost. And rime frost turns to nothing when it is brushed away.

But the bereaved parents constantly returned to their children who were shut up in the ravine. All they could hear was the sound of the children weeping. They could also hear a song from a girl with a child in her amaut:

"Do not weep, little one,
Your mother will fetch you,
Mother is coming for you
As soon as she has finished
Her new kamiks.

Do not weep, little one,
Your father will fetch you,
Father is coming as soon as he has made
His new harpoon head,
Do not weep, little one,
Do not weep!"

The children kept on crying, but as they did so, they were suddenly changed into guillemots, which came flying out through crevices in the rocks.

And that is how guillemots were first made. And that is why they always keep to narrow crevices in the rocks.

Told by
Ivaluardjuk.

How the snow bunting and the ptarmigan were made.

There was once an old grandmother who was left alone with her grandchild in a double house. And they lived each in one part of the double house when their village was deserted.

One evening the little girl said to her grandmother:

"Oh, grandmother, do tell me something."

But her grandmother answered:

"I have nothing to tell you. You just keep quiet. You just go to sleep."

But the grandchild went on:

„Dear grandmother, tell me, do tell me a story."

And as the child would not be quiet, the grandmother at last began:

„Look, out from the cave there come many little naked lemmings; they are coming towards us, they are such horrible things, it makes one shiver all over. Tju, tju, tju."

The grandchild was so frightened that she leapt out through the passage of the snow hut, and that so quickly that her grandmother could not stop her. The little girl turned into a snow bunting out of sheer fright, and now her grandmother sat there in despair at not having been able to catch her. And she sat there alone on the sleeping place and kept on saying:

"Oh, my dear little grandchild, oh, my dear little grandchild." And she sat there weeping, and kept on wiping her eyes. At last her eyes were all red and bloodshot. Then she took her sewing bag and fastened it round her neck, and put the needles into her kamiks, and then suddenly she fell to cackling and became a ptarmigan. Then she spread her wings and flew away. And from her come all the ptarmigan.

Told by

Ivaluardjuk.

As will be seen, in all these stories, only the actual happenings are recorded; not in a single instance are the magic words given; for they would lose their power in a moment if repeated.

Obviously, it is almost impossible to elicit any ᴇrinaliu·tit from people who themselves believe in the miraculous power of the words. Those who possess the words will not part with them, or if they do, it is at a price which would soon ruin an expedition. A gun with an ample supply of ammunition was regarded, for instance, as a very natural price for a few meaningless words. One can, however, instead of buying, sometimes obtain ᴇrinaliu·tit by barter, and I availed myself of this, giving magic words from Angmagssalik, in East Greenland, in exchange for others from Iglulik. In this manner I obtained the following magic words from Aua, who had learned them from an old woman named Qiqertáinaq. She was very old, and her family had handed down the words from generation to generation, right from the time of the first human beings. It was essential to remember them in the right order otherwise they had no value. In return for this valuable information, Aua had provided Qiqertáinaq with food and clothing for the rest of her life. Every time he wished to make use of the magic words, he had first to utter her name; for only through her had the words any power. The words were to be muttered in jerks and repeated in a whisper, as secrets entrusted to Sila. Aua's method of referring to Qiqertáinaq when using her magic words was, in his own language, as follows: "aivaluŋniᴀrama" (a shaman's word for ᴇrinaliɔriᴀrama, meaning: "because I wish to utter an ᴇrinaliu·t") qɪqᴇrtain·aup qanianik qaŋᴇrluŋa": "using as my mouth the mouth of Qiqertáinaq".

Words which make heavy things light.

To be uttered beside a heavily laden sledge. The speaker stands at the fore end of the sledge, speaking in the direction of the traces. Also used when setting out on a long journey, and wishing to be light-footed and untiring:

ɔqiglisaut:
"nɔʀaligᴀ·rʃup
sivorᴀr^{d}lugutainik
sivorᴀr^{d}luguseʀluŋa
pisukpäŋniᴀrtuŋa.
ukaliᴀrʃu·p
sivorᴀr^{d}lugutainik
sivorᴀr^{d}luguseʀluŋa
pisukpäŋniᴀrtuŋa.
tᴀʀup mikʃa·nut
au^{d}lɔrtaililuŋa
uƀlup mikʃa·nut
au^{d}lɔrpäŋniᴀrtuŋa."

"I will walk with leg muscles
which are strong
as the sinews of the shins of the little caribou calf.
I will walk with leg muscles
which are strong
as the sinews of the shins of the little hare.
I will take care not to go towards the dark.
I will go towards the day."

Words to be used in the morning on getting up.

If there is sickness in a village, but not in one's own household, one may take the inner jacket of a child, put on one's own hood, thrust one's arms into the sleeves of the child's jacket, as if to put it on, and then recite the following, early in the morning, before anyone has been out on the floor.

makitᴇrut.
"iva· — va·
naujan·u·p
makitᴇruta·nik
makitᴇrusᴇr^{d}luŋa
makip·äŋniᴀrtuŋa
tᴀʀup mikʃa·nut
qiwiᴀrtailiƀluŋa
uƀlup mikʃa·nut
sa·p·aŋniᴀrtuŋa."

"I arise from my couch
With the morning song of the grey gull,
I arise from my couch
With the morning song to look towards the dark,
I turn my glance towards the day".

Words to a sick child.

nutARArsiut:
"nutArqāp
Arnavit
iwiaŋ·e·
iŋ·maglArpu·k
ama·magiArtɔrit
imEriArtɔrit
qAq·amit, qAqäp qa·ŋanit una
tauŋusiksiArsiɔriArtɔrit
pudlāʃArsiɔriArtɔrit."

"Little child! Your mother's breasts are full of milk.
Go and be nursed,
Go and drink!
Go up to the mountain!
From the summit of the moutain you shall seek health,
You shall draw life."

Words to stop bleeding:

auksiut:
"qupanuArʃu·p man·a
aŋajɔrqa·ŋata
aua man·a
saluŋmArsAru·k
qiju·k
aua man·a
saluŋmArsAru·k!"

"This is blood from the little sparrow's mother.
Wipe it away!
This is blood
That flowed from a piece of wood.
Wipe it away!"

Words to call up game.

qaŋnit:
"imasiArŋaut
ublɔrA·rsuk·ut maniArtɔrniArputit
nunasiArŋaut
ublA·rA·rsuk·ut maniArtɔrniArpu·tit."

"Beast of the Sea,
Come and offer yourself in the dear early morning!
Beast of the plain!
Come and offer yourself in the dear morning!"

These simple, heathen prayers, whispered out into the air from some spot in the snow where no foot has left its mark, were for the Eskimo sacred words, which in some mysterious way brought aid.

VIII.

Precepts or Rules of Life and Conduct for all Occasions.

From birth to death, human beings have to regulate their lives according to the powers that control human weal and woe, and whose anger can give rise to suffering and hardship, not only for the person who has offended, but for the whole village. Obligations towards the higher powers are thus not a private matter, but one affecting the entire community, and the individual must conform to the rules — numerous and irksome though they may be — which are held to be pleasing or conciliating to the divine powers.

This applies under all conditions of life, but more particularly at times when help is most needed, during pregnancy, at birth, and while the infant is yet a helpless creature in itself, at the time of transition from childhood to womanhood, during sickness and at the hour of death, and last but not least in hunting, where the sustenance of all is at stake.

Breaches of taboo can, however, be made good by confessing them, and one is even thanked for so doing.

The great majority of the following rules I obtained from Aua and his wife Orulo.

Pregnancy.

When a young woman in her first pregnancy feels the life of the child in her body, she must undo her plait and tie her hair at the back of the neck, so that it hangs down loose from the neckband. She must wear it thus for three days. This is called ikuŋainʼartɔq, and gives a speedy delivery.

A pregnant woman who wishes her child to be a boy must cut off the unfeathered mouth part of a naujavik: the great gull without black wings, the grey gull. This mouth portion must be cut away so as to form a ring, i. e. it must not be cut across, and the penis of a fox then sewn into it; this amulet is worn either on the woman's kinia (apron) or on the ako (the tail of her outer coat behind); the remainder of the bird's skin must be flayed off at the same time, but may be used for anything desired, e. g. as a cloth for wiping the fingers when greasy after eating.

A pregnant woman must make two small dolls from a sako·t (iron scraper for softening skins) which has belonged to someone since dead; these dolls are to be placed as amulets in her inner jacket, one under each armpit. Such amulets, which are called imnᴀrmiŋ (let it be an adult) render the foetus light for the mother to carry.

A pregnant woman must be quick to run out of the house or tent whenever she is called from outside; she will then have a speedy delivery.

If she is quick to help others, i. e. hurries to those making ready for a journey and makes herself useful to them (pᴀrnaktut tamaisa ɔrnilᴇrtɔqat·ᴀ·rlugit) then her child will turn out a helpful man or woman.

Pregnant women must not eat animals shot through the heart.

A pregnant woman must never go outside without her mittens on.

A live bee must be rolled over the back of a pregnant woman and afterwards kept; when she has given birth to her child, this bee will become an effective amulet; fastened on top of the head in a hair band, it gives long life.

Birth and conduct in the birth hut (ᴇrnivik).

When a woman feels the birthpangs coming on, then if it is winter, a snow hut must be built; if summer, a tent erected for her. This house or tent, which is quite small, and resembles a dog kennel, is called ᴇrnivik, or ᴇrnivialuk, and is used only for the actual birth.

As long as the woman is there, the house must not be added to or repaired, even in case of bad weather. Not until the child is born is a proper house, or a real tent, set up; this is then called kinᴇrvik.

When a women feels the birth pangs, all her belongings must at once be moved outside the house where she has been living, and may not be taken in again before she herself returns from the lying-in house.

Women in giving birth lie either half over to one side or with the back to the couch, the head pressed against the wall of the house and a small block of snow under each arm to rest the elbows. Sometimes also, delivery takes place in a kneeling position. In such case, a hollow is made in the ground below, and the child glides down into this as it emerges from the womb. The Iglulik women maintain that they as a rule have an easy and painless delivery; they use the expression: "sɔ·r^{d}lo anᴀrtɔq": "as easy as an evacuation". Where the birth takes a long time, a sealskin thong is tied round the waist and pulled tight to force the child out quickly. Women must effect their own delivery without help, and must be alone in the ᴇrnivik; even where the birth is difficult, no one is allowed to assist: "tᴇrigiʃanᴇrmut" is the expression used, i. e. "she is considered too impure for anyone to be near her". Anyone rendering aid would become impure in turn, and subject to the same troublesome, year-long taboo as the woman herself. The obligations involved interfere so seriously with domestic duties that the community will not allow any married woman, not even the patient's mother, to incur them. But more important than domestic considerations are those of religion; not even a solitary woman, without relatives to consider, may assist; for the powers, or the spirits would be angered at the inability of a woman to manage by herself; or the animals would be offended if a woman aiding another in childbirth should touch a newborn infant not of her own bearing. The only thing that can be done for a woman in cases of difficulty is to apply to a shaman, who may then either summon his helping spirits, and by their aid make matters easier, or utter a magic prayer or magic song, to ease the birth. A high price is paid to the shaman for this service. Among his dues are some of the best implements the woman's husband possesses, and his best dog into the bargain.

As a matter of fact, help is practically speaking never asked for. Every woman considers it a point of honour to bring forth her child unaided.

Prior to her delivery, the woman must have found either a flint, called kukikʃᴀq, or a piece of white quartzite, ɔrʃu^{w}iᴀq. This is sharpened, and used to cut the umbilical cord, which is first tied round half an inch from the navel; the knife must always be held in the left hand. After about three days, the stump of the cord generally falls off. If the child is a boy, he must have the stump, and the little flint knife used to cut it with, as amulets. They are sewn into his inner jacket on either side of the chest.

If the afterbirth will not come, the woman must make as if to vomit. Then when it has come, it is placed on a block of snow, high up, where the dogs cannot get at it. In summer, on a high stone.

A newly born infant is cleansed by being wiped all over with the skin of a sᴀrvᴀ·q, a small snipe; water must not be used.

After birth, the child must always be placed naked in the amaut; clothes for an infant must not be made until after it is born.

When the child is particularly welcome, and it is earnestly desired that it shall live, a magic formula or magic prayer is sung over it, before even it has been given the breast. This is called an anErnErsiut, or prayer for the spirit of life.

If a newly born infant be sung over while its body is being cleansed for the first time, then the child will make up many songs of its own when it grows up. All that is needed is to sing one of one's own songs without words, while cleansing the child. Petting songs, Aqautit, in the Greenland sense of the word, are unknown, but one can AqArpɔq a child. Orulo's Aqaut runs thus: "kakilisAq-a·; kakilisAq-a·": "you little stickleback, you little stickleback." When it was said to her, she had to stick out her little finger and jump on to her mother's lap.

In naming the child, some deceased person is invoked, whose name is then uttered by the child's mother. If a boy, for instance, is to be named Ujarak, then his mother will say: "Ujarak, qai-qai tamArpit": "Ujarak, come hither quickly, come hither quickly all of you" (i. e. with all that appertains to you).

This again is connected with the belief in namesake souls. A child cries for a name, and when the one whose name-soul is to take up its dwelling in the newly born infant is summoned, care must be taken that all the qualities that soul possessed are communicated to the child. Hence the word tamArpit.

If it is desired to render a boy invulnerable against animals and men, especially shamans and their attacks by means of witchcraft, if it is desired to prevent him from being bitten to death or otherwise killed by animals: walrus, bear, wolverine etc. and hinder shamans from causing him sickness of body by taking away his soul, then a shaman must be summoned as soon as the child is out of the womb and has had the mother's blood wiped from its little mouth; the shaman must be present before the afterbirth is taken, and his business is then to *take the soul out of the boy's body and lay it in under his mother's lamp.* The soul must then remain there as long as the boy lives. A person can thus live without a soul in its body, the soul being deposited elsewhere.

Children born backwards, i. e. feet foremost, must afterwards wear caps with the hair turned upward, not, as otherwise customary, with the hair pointing down. This applies to all the caps worn afterwards through life.

The Mother's Residence in the Lying-in House (kinErvik).

After the birth, the woman cleans herself all over, in winter with snow, in summer with water, and cuts away afterwards such portions of her clothing as may have become stained with blood. She is now ready to proceed to the kinErvik, and remains there for one or two months, or according to circumstances, sometimes three; if she has been unfortunate with her previous children for instance, her taboo will be more severe according to the number and nature of such earlier misfortunes.

A woman while in the kinErvik may receive visitors, but is strictly forbidden to go visiting herself, nor may she have intercourse with her husband during that period. She is regarded as so unclean, so dangerous to her surroundings that her impurity is supposed to issue forth in an actual, albeit invisible, smoke or vapour, which drives away all the game. Shamans who have been up to the moon have seen from there how these emanations arise from women in childbed and during menstruation. Should they during such times break their taboo, all this foul smoke or impurity collects in the form of filth in the hair of the Mother of the Sea Beasts, who in disgust, shuts up all the game in a house, leaving mankind to starve. A woman recently delivered must therefore always have her hood thrown over her head when she goes out, and must never look round after game.

In the kinErvik she must have her own wooden drinking vessel or wooden tray (pu'gutAq) from which to drink soup, and in which to place the meat she eats. She must also have her own cooking pot and her particular wooden ladle, which is used either for soup or for water, and these must always be placed in front of her, near the lamp, the wooden ladle in the wooden mug, and in that again a meat fork made of caribou horn or a piece of pointed marrow bone.

Every morning she has to melt ice or snow for drinking water. Every time she drinks, she must put a drop of water into the child's mouth with her middle finger. This must be done immediately after the child is born, and repeated every time the mother drinks. The finger in question is supposed to possess a peculiar power in regard to infants, so that the water thus dripping into the mouth will prevent the child from ever suffering from thirst. And the main idea is always of male children, as future hunters. Thirst is universally regarded as the worst of all sufferings, and far more dreaded than hunger.

Hanging beside her lamp, the mother must have a small skin bag, (miŋulErtEqutEqArfia). Whenever she is about to eat, she must cut off a small piece of meat, rub it on the child's mouth, and place it in the bag, before commencing her meal. This is called miŋulErtEriʒɔq, and is regarded as a sacred rite — a sacrifice in effigy to the spirits, the dead, and the holy meat. This act protects the child against hunger, and renders it skilful in hunting later on, bringing abundance of game. Another interpretation says that it is nutAra'lu'p atiŋe nErEr-qublugit: in order that the child's namesake soul may have something to eat.

The young mother is not allowed to cut up meat herself for boiling. This must be done either by young girls or older women. Not until it is cooked may she take it up herself from the pot and place it in her pu'gutᴀq. She must take great care never to spill any. Should a piece of meat fall outside the pu'gutᴀq, it must at once be picked up and thrown on the right of the lamp (kaŋia).

The miŋulᴇrtᴇrivɔq ceremony comes to an end when the stay in the kinᴇrvik is over, and the woman then takes the skin bag, filled with tiny fragments of meat, and carries it to the blowhole of a seal. Into this she throws all the scraps of meat, the first meat which has touched the boy's lips, and in a way served as his first flesh food. They are thus thrown back into the sea whence they came, and some people believe that by miŋulᴇrtᴇrinᴇq the separate pieces receive souls and become seals once more, which can be caught again by the boy when he grows up. If the child is a girl, the scraps of meat are merely thrown out on the edge of the beach at the expiration of the kinᴇrvik period. The empty skin bag is flung out on the ice.

While a woman remains in the kinᴇrvik she must always have the skin from the head of a seal spread over her lap while eating. This is called her aklᴇra, or apron. When the kinᴇrvik period is over, the aklᴇra is also laid out beside a seal's blowhole, if the child is a boy.

A woman in the kinᴇrvik must never eat meat of animals other than those killed by her own husband. At Iglulik, however, there is an exception to this rule, as at certain times of the year, three specially chosen men are sent out after walrus, which are supposed to yield the finest meat of all. Meat caught by these men may be freely eaten.

Women in the kinᴇrvik may not eat the meat of animals killed suddenly; seals for their eating must after being wounded have life enough left to come up at least once to the surface and breathe, i. e. they must not eat sa'muŋᴀ'rtɔq or one that dies immediately after sinking.

A woman in the kinᴇrvik eats twice a day if she has given birth to a boy, but must never eat her fill; she has three meals a day if the child is a girl. In the evening, after the last meal, a small piece of meat is placed in the dipper, also intended for the child's atᴇq, or name-soul.

If it is a boy, and the mother wishes him to be specially fortunate in hunting, she eats not twice, but three times a day, but never eating her fill; for the mother's hunger renders the child light, i. e. swift in hunting, and such a boy will make a capture when others are heavy and over slow at the work.

All these rules are observed for exactly as long as the woman remains in the kinᴇrvik.

The mother's homecoming. — Protection of the child.

At the end of the kinErvik period, the mother washes herself all over and throws away the clothing she had on at the time of the birth, for a woman must always have an inner jacket on when her child is born; she must never have the upper part of her body bare at the time. The same inner jacket is to be used all the time she is in the kinErvik, and only now that she is returning to her husband's house is she to put on new garments throughout.

In the olden days, it was the custom at Iglulik for a woman on discarding her clothes after leaving the kinErvik to give them to an old woman, who remade them so that the upper part became the lower. The old woman was then supposed to wear them.

At this time also the child must have new clothing, before being allowed to enter the father's house, but the old garments, i. e. the child's first clothes, are afterwards kept in the sErluAq, the small apartment where skins and furs are kept, and must remain there until an opportunity occurs to place them either in a raven's nest or in a gull's nest, or out on a small island in a stream.

When a woman lies with her husband for the first time after giving birth to a child, she must, if the child be a boy, smear the father's semen over the child's breast. This gives strong life.

When the kinErvik period is over, the woman must pay a visit to every house in the village, or if in summer, to every tent, and on these visits she must take with her the little mug with which she took soup or water from her pot; into this is placed, at each house, a small piece of raw meat, which she must take home and boil; not until this is done may she drink cold water; as previously mentioned all water for her drinking had previously to be lukewarm.

This custom of going out and receiving presents of meat from all the neighbours is called kiglilEruta·: that whereby a limit is set for her kinErvik period.

For a whole year after childbirth the woman may not eat raw meat, nor may she eat flesh of any animal wounded in the heart, stomach or foetus.

On the first occasion of eating raw meat after childbirth the woman must, if her child be a boy, ARisErpɔq, i. e. a piece of intestine about $1^1/_2$ metres long, and a piece of liver, are placed in her cooking pot, taken out again quickly, so as to be hardly more than dipped in the boiling water, and the woman must then swallow the intestine whole, without cutting it, and immediately after eat the liver, which must likewise not be masticated, but swallowed rapidly (she must not cut either one or the other).

On a newborn infant's first evacuation, the mother must wipe the child behind with her hair and afterwards rub the fæces into her hair; this will prevent her hair from falling out later on.

If it is desired to give a child long hair, the outer integument of a caribou antler is sewn into the hood.

When a boy begins to eat, he must first be given a little caribou fat, and afterwards lean meat; if this is done, he will, when he grows up and becomes a hunter, never get out of breath while running.

When an infant boy or girl has eaten, the body is stretched, the child being held by the middle finger of its left hand and the corresponding toe of the right foot, at the same time one must blow on the fingers and smack the tongue. The same is done with the other hand and opposite foot, this gives rapid growth.

When a boy's limbs have been stretched, he is taken on the lap, set upon the apron (the piece of skin from the head of a seal which a woman after childbirth wears over her lap in order not to spill on her clothes), which is folded, and a piece of meat is then placed on the pu·gutᴀq, or meat tray; the meat fork is then placed in the child's hands, and the hands guided so that the child harpoons the meat; at the same time, motions must be made as if the child were rowing in a kayak: pᴀrtiŋ·uᴀrlugo: he is made to go through the same movements as a man paddling in his kayak.

The ivutɔ·q on the head of a newly born child (the stuff that looks like dirt on the temples), must not be washed off, but allowed to wear off by itself.

When a woman has no more milk, or has not sufficient, the nipple of a hare is smoked over her lamp flame, and afterwards hung as an amulet over her breast, outside the inner jacket.

A very effective amulet for a woman is a fish called qukʃaunᴀq. (I have not been able to identify this fish, but it is described as very small, and living in salt water close to the beach; it is very swift in its movements, and when grasped, twines round the hand). If a qukʃaunᴀq be sewn into the tail (aka) of a girl's fur coat, she will give birth to a son in time, and may further be sure of a rapid and painless delivery.

A mother who has a son must boil the head of a dog, and then pretend that the dog's head is the child's iglɔq or "song-cousin" that is, the man one likes most of all to sing with, or have as partner in athletic sports, compete with and sometimes sing abusive songs about. The mother must then let the child's little hands strike the head of the dog, pretending that the dog's head represents the song-cousin's head. This is supposed to give the boy "a hard head against fisticuffs". Afterwards, the mother herself eats the dog's head.

Above: Two restless souls. The big one is called Nâlaqnaq; the listener; large mouth, two teeth, tongue protruding, shapeless hands with six fingers; moves at a run. The other is Púngoq, or the dog; long ears, two mouths, three legs, the rearmost shapeless. One night while sleeping in a stone shelter these evil spirits came over him and would have eaten him if the dogs had not kept them at a distance. — Below: Kigutilik, or the spirit with the giant's teeth. One spring he was out sealing, and this monster came up out of an opening in the ice; it was as big as a bear but higher; with long legs which had large bumps at the joints; two tails, one big ear that only seemed to be joined to a fold in the skin, and teeth as gross as a walrus's tusks. It was bare and only had hair in fringes. It emitted a mighty roar: "Ah — ah — ah!", and he became so frightened that he fled home without first securing it for a helping spirit. Drawn by Anarqâq.

To the left the spirit Nuvatqik, who can change himself into a dog and into a man. It has no belly and has three tusks in its mouth. It is a good soul-seeker, i. e. as a helping spirit it finds the stolen soul and therefore heals the sick. It has a hot temper: the first time Anarqâq saw it, it split open his brow; but once it is tamed, it is obedient and gentle. — Middle: Sangungajoq, a dead man from Iluileq (Adelaide Peninsula), who has now become a helping spirit. On the right: Uvliaq, whom Anarqâq has inherited from his mother's brother; it is bare, has no hair whatever, looks ugly but is otherwise not dangerous. It heals the sick too . . .

To left: Nasalik: the one with the cap. This cap is of wood, but out of the wood grows hair of musk oxen; its eyes are level with the corners of its mouth, and its long tongue hangs out between the eyes. The haunch of one hind leg hangs almost loose and wobbles when it walks. To right: the spirit Issitôq (the one with the big eyes). Originally it had been the helping spirit of a fox, but now Anarqâq had taken possession of it. It only consists of head and legs; its hair is of willow twigs. Drawings by Anarqâq.

A woman with a baby must always have water in her water vessel, which must always be placed on the left of her lamp, on the spot which is called kit'iane. This is in order that all who are thirsty may come in and obtain water. The seal thus learns that no one in the vicinity of this boy need ever be thirsty, and many seals will afterwards come to the boy and let him capture them. Thirst is the worst thing seals can suffer from.

If a small piece of the spleen of a fox be sewn into the instep of a boy's stocking, he will not fall through thin ice as a grown man.

Newly born male children are often given, as their first garments, a dress of raven's skin with the feathers outside. The ravens always manage to find something; this gives good hunting.

If it is desired that a little girl shall become a rapid and skilful needlewoman, then, as soon as she is old enough to begin sewing, a sewing ring is made for her from the muzzle of a caribou; this sewing ring may also be fastened to her inner jacket.

If a child loses a tooth, the tooth is wrapped in a piece of meat and given to a dog. Then the boy will soon grow a new tooth.

When a young virgin or mother combs her hair, all children in the house must pull down their hoods. If not, they will die.

Man and woman with children must closely observe their taboo. If they do not, the children may lose their wits, or they will die early.

A woman with young children must not eat any caribou meat save the flesh of the hind legs.

A woman who is still bearing children must never eat the flesh of a caribou cow with milk in the udder.

When a boy is out visiting, he must not remain too long in one house. If he does so, the seals he is to hunt will remain long under water, i. e. he will find it difficult to catch them.

Boys who have not yet caught bearded seal or walrus must not play cat's cradle (string figures). If they do, then they are liable to get their fingers entangled in the harpoon lines and be dragged out into the sea.

Boys and young men must never eat fat or suet from the upper part of a caribou breast; if they do, they will get out of breath when running.

Boys must never eat marrow from the forelegs of a caribou; to do so would render them slow in running.

A son who is never allowed to lie midway between his father and mother will be invisible to the animals he hunts, so that he can easily approach them. A bear may walk right past such a boy without seeing him.

Marriages are arranged while the parties are still little children.

The betrothal often takes place directly after birth, or even before; but where the woman in question lives at some distance from her intended husband, and arrives at marriageable age without his coming to fetch her, a man of her own village may move into the same house with her and live with her for the time being. When then the husband-to-be comes to fetch her, she is placed in the middle of the floor, and the two men try each to drag her to him. The stronger gets her.

Children are not allowed to address old people by name, but only by terms of relationship, or as it'ɔq: head of the household, in the case of an old man.

Adolescence: A boy's first capture; a girl's menstruation.

When a firstborn son gets his first seal, an old woman makes a bag out of the skin of the animal's head, and in this bag she must afterwards keep the moss which serves as wick for her lamp. This bag is called mᴀrŋun: moss wick ("bag" is understood), and must remain in the old woman's possession as long as she lives and be buried with her when she dies. This gives the seals which the boy catches good blubber for lamp oil. (There is a great difference in the quality of blubber in this respect. Some seals yield blubber which gives a poor light in the lamps, others good).

The extreme joints of the flippers of the first seal caught by a firstborn son are kept for a year and then placed in a grave. Then, when the young man later on becomes a great hunter, and some shaman or other grows envious, and endeavours to take away his catch by magic, i. e. steal the souls of the animals he gets, the attempt will prove fruitless. The shaman's helping spirits will be afraid of the outer part of the flippers placed in the grave, and will then protect the boy's catch against all evil.

When a boy get his first seal, he must take off his outer and inner jackets, lay them on the ice and throw himself down flat on them, and before the seal is yet dead, his father must drag it across his back; this will prevent the seals from being afraid of him. The first seal is cut up in the house, and eaten by the parents and as many others as they can. It is distributed among the houses and eaten as quickly as possible. The head may only be eaten by the father or mother. When the skin has been taken off, it must be shared out among as many men as possible for slippers, but all the bones of this firstcaught seal must be gathered together and dropped through a blowhole. When this is done, the soul returns to the bones, and the young man may keep on catching the same seal.

A young man must never eat the flesh of the first animal of any species he kills.

When a young man comes home after killing his first seal, he must not beat the snow from his chothes with the snow beater; for to do so would frighten away the seals he would otherwise catch later on.

If a young man kills any animal for the first time the heart of that particular animal must only be eaten in his house or tent, and nowhere else. Its blood must not be touched by any woman.

The first time a young man makes a kill, he must give away the skin of the animal killed.

Sometimes the first seal a boy kills is cut up by women alone; but there must be many women present in such case, and the mother must hold the seal by a line fastened round its head, pulling at the line occasionally and raising the head a little, for the head is to be her share.

All animals killed by a young man whom others are endeavouring to make a skilful hunter, by means of amulets or magic prayers, must be cut up with great care. None of the bones must be broken, and care must be taken always to divide at the joints. He himself must never break the bones of any animal caught or killed.

The marrow bones of animals killed by a firstborn son are never to be eaten with a knife, but must be crushed with stones.

A woman menstruating, or having a miscarriage, must at once inform others; all must know that she is unclean.

Woman during their menstruation must never come in to young men who have not killed one of every kind of game. The young man is called kiliŋajɔq.

Women during menstruation may not enter a house where it is the custom to have song festivals.

Among the Aivilingmiut near Repulse Bay, a woman during menstruation may not go out of the house, and must make water and evacuate indoors. This is in order that no animal hunted may see her while she is unclean.

Menstruating women may not cut raw meat or eat it; and the meat they eat must be cooked in a special pot, from which no one else may eat.

Women menstruating, or having a miscarriage, or in childbirth, may not prepare the skins from the legs of caribou; the skin of caribou legs is altogether regarded with quite particular respect. There are some hunters, for instance, whose own wives are not allowed to prepare the skins of caribou legs from animals killed by their husbands, this work having to be done by other women.

Menstruating or otherwise unclean women may not beat out blubber for lamps.

In the neighbourhood of Repulse Bay, a menstruating woman may not go out into the open without first washing herself in the urine of a child.

Rules for residence in a village under various circumstances of life.

Certain customs must be scrupulously observed in building the snow hut which is to protect one against storm and cold. No one can explain why it is that the work must be done in a particular fashion; all that is known is that the traditions are strict rules handed down from previous generations, and that it is dangerous to neglect them.

The first thing to be done in building a snow hut is to draw a line round where one stands indicating the shape and size desired for the iglo. The snow hut is built up in the form of a slightly oblong beehive of the domed type; the walls above the inner part of the sleeping place at the back and over the entrance hole in front are called the broad sides; the two others, above the lamp sites, are called long sides. As soon as the shape of the hut has been marked out in the snowdrift, one must always begin by cutting out the blocks to be used for the foundation of the long side, and not until these are done may the broad side blocks be cut. This brings luck. And finally, a man who has children must always, when proceeding to cut out the broad side blocks, use a saw for the first block, and not his knife. He will then have strong children. The blocks are now laid in place for the wall, the bases being so cut as to make them lean inwards and form the dome, but a particular cut is also given at the same time so as to make a slight inclination towards the next block, one supporting the other. In the shaping of each block, great care must now be taken to scrape or cut away the snow with an outward movement of the knife, never inward towards the interior of the hut. This is very important, for a movement of the sharp knife in the direction of the space to be occupied would destroy the luck of the household.

The keyblock, which finally closes the last space left in the domed roof, must always be so placed that its softer part lies uppermost. This gives luck. The soft part is that which formed the lower face as it was cut out from the snowdrift, the upper, exposed surface, acted on by the wind, being always harder. Finally, care must be taken to shape the snow blocks forming the entrance to the house, the "doorway" so to speak, with rounded edges, never with sharp.

Finally, it is important that the closing block fills up a large space. If the blocks have been carried in so fine a spiral that only a small gap is left for the last block, this gap must be enlarged before it is closed for good. When this is done, the women of the household will have easy delivery in childbirth.

The block of fresh-water ice which serves as a window in a snow hut must always be removed before leaving the hut on changing ground. Also, the snow block which is used to close the entrance from within at night, the so-called uk·uᴀq, which is generally kept inside the house, must be thrown out. This will make the sons of the house good hunters. Finally, before setting out, all gnawed skulls of seals caught from the site to be abandoned must be set out on the ice some little way from the house. The same is done with caribou recently shot. The heads must always face in the direction in which the party is setting out. The souls of the animals slain will then follow the same course, and good hunting will result.

If only a few remain behind when the rest leave a village, they must build new huts for themselves. Unless this is done, no further animals will be caught.

When a family leaves a snow hut and does not wish others using it after them to have good hunting, one of the party leaving must sweep all the caribou hairs which are always left behind on the sleeping platform, in towards the inner side. All game will then leave the immediate neighbourhood of that hut, and the new people will hunt in vain. This method of making a snow hut unlucky is called piŋ·usᴇrluinᴇq.

Stones which have been used for "kau^{w}ᴀrsikʃut": i. e. for hammering blubber so as to make the oil flow freely when placed in the lamp, or stones which have been used as hammers to crush marrow bones, must always be thrown outside when a house is abandoned.

When setting out from a coast other than one's native tract, one must shout out various things towards the land, as for instance: "I have left behind a stickleback!" "I have left behind luscious meat from a caribou breast!" "I have left a mussel!". This is to give the spirits of the alien land the impression that generous gifts have been set out for them on leaving.

On sleeping in a new snow hut for the first time, one must not sleep over long, or poor hunting will result. It is necessary to show the souls of the animals that one is eager to capture them. Very early in the morning one must go outside and walk three times round the house in the direction of the sun. This gives long life.

When snow is to be melted for water in a pot, it must never be placed behind the lamp, but always in front.

A childless couple may bring the skins for their sleeping place into a new snow hut through the entrance in the ordinary way. But those with children must cut a special hole in the wall above the sleeping place through which the caribou skins are drawn.

People living in a snow hut only built on the ice must not use last year's ice to melt for water, but only snow; if the fresh ice which was once sea ice be used for drinking water, then the young ice will break up, and the party be carried out to sea.

A man suffering want through ill success in hunting must, when coming to another village and sitting down to eat, never eat with a woman he has not seen before.

On Sentry Island, a woman out visiting must only eat boiled meat from her own pot if there is a woman in the village whom she has not seen before.

At the villages of Iglulik, Pingerqalik and Alangneq, no fuel grown from the earth must ever be used for cooking, but only bones and blubber, or the flame of the lamp.

Persons gathering eggs in places where they are not known (places with which they are not familiar?) must wait till they return home before eating the eggs, they must not eat any while gathering.

Travellers on reaching the last ravine of the Tununeq country before the ice begins, on the way from Iglulik to Ponds Inlet, must bend down, grasp their knees and turn somersaults, if driving this way for the first time.

Whoever cuts his hair cuts away a part of his soul. It is customary therefore to wear the hair in sulup·a·tit, or plaits rolled into a knot over the ears; this keeps hold of the soul.

If a man's hair is cut, the cuttings must never be thrown away, but must be burned in the house or tent.

On sneezing, or breaking wind behind, one must say, "qᴀ·ᵓq", in order to live, or to have a long life. This, however, only applies to women. Only men who have committed a murder are required to do the same. If it is a little child who does either, the mother must smack her lips, uttering the same whistling sound used in calling a dog.

When old clothing is thrown away, it must first be torn into pieces. Unless this is done, the owner will have to wear it in the Land of the Dead.

A whip with a handle made from the penis of a bear is good for frightening away evil spirits.

Waste oil from the reservoir of a lamp, poured out in the passage and further sprinkled in drops round about the house keeps away evil spirits.

During a thunderstorm, a small piece of white-bleached skin and a firestone and a small kamik sole are laid out as an amulet; this is a sacrifice to the souls of the "thunder girls".

When a piece of soapstone has been broken off to make a lamp, some small object must first be made from a fragment of the same block that is to be used for lamp or cooking pot, as for instance a miniature lamp or pot; this will prevent the actual object when in use from being easily broken.

Mud intended for shoeing the runners of sledges must only be cut in winter, after the snow has fallen, never cut in summer and kept till winter.

At times when the sea ice is breaking up owing to storms, only men with powerful amulets may cut turves for their sledge runners.

Cat's cradle is only to be made in the time when the sun cannot be seen; when the sun once more rises above the horizon, ajagᴀrpɔq, a ring-and-pin game, must be used instead.

Anyone dreaming of another person, a dream of ill omen, must receive gifts from the nearest relatives of the man for whom the dream prophesied ill luck, and a shaman should, to make sure, call up his helping spirits. When all this is done, then the helping spirits belonging to the man who had the dream will protect the man threatened by the dream.

If a man born on a rainy day falls into the water, it will rain on that day; if a man born on a stormy day falls into the water, there will be a storm.

The first time the sun appears after the period of darkness, children must run into the snow huts and put out the lamps, so that they can be lighted anew; this is called suvʃɔraiʃut: those who blow out. The new sun must be attended everywhere by new light in the lamps.

When two namesakes meet, they must exchange gifts. This strengthens their souls and pleases all their deceased "name-cousins".

Taboo and hunting customs from Iglulik and Aivilik.

The sea spirit Takánâluk demands taboo for all sea animals because they were made from her fingers. But also the land animals have to be considered. There are numerous and complicated rules for what must and what must not be done in connection with capture of the different animals. It is essential to make an altogether definite distinction between the different kinds of game, especially between those of the sea and those of the land, which must not be allowed to come into contact one with the other save when special precautions are taken. Certain rules and customs must be observed in hunting, to prevent the souls of the animals slain from harming the man who deprived them of their bodies.

Fundamental rules are the following:

When a whale, a bearded seal or a bear is killed, no man's or woman's work must be done for three days. It is also strictly forbidden during these three days to cut turf or gather fuel from the earth. Clothing may, however, be mended; and distinction is here to be observed between ordinary needlework and actual mending.

If a man comes home with an animal which he has killed out at the edge of the ice, he must not enter the house on his return until he has removed his outer clothing.

Seal.

When a seal is brought into a house, no woman in the house may sew or do any other work until the seal has been cut up. This applies, however, only to winter hunting, in snow huts, not in tents during summer.

As long as a newly captured seal has not been cut up, the following things are taboo:

Rime must not be wiped from the window pane.

Skins from the sleeping place must not be shaken out over the floor.

The mats of plaited willow twigs must not be straightened or rearranged.

No oil must be spilled from the lamp.

No work must be done with stone, wood or iron.

Women must not comb their hair, wash their faces or dry any footwear.

When a bearded seal has been captured, no scraping of hair from skins must be done for three days.

When seal are caught, it is not allowed to shift camp the next day, but not until two days after the first catch; this is because the seals would be offended if the hunters were not grateful for the catch they had got.

When a seal is brought into a snow hut, a lump of snow is dipped into the water bucket, and allowed to drip into the seal's mouth; it is the soul of the seal that drinks. In summer, it does not require water.

Persons hunting seal from a snow hut on sea ice may not work with soapstone.

All bearded seals caught require a special sacrifice. The Mother of the Sea Beasts is particularly fond of bearded seals, and they know it, and when they have been killed by human hands, they go to her and complain; therefore special precautions are observed when a bearded seal has been killed.

As soon as it is heard that a bearded seal has been caught; ugjuktɔqᴀrpɔrɔ˙q, the sleeping rugs must be made ready without delay, as this must not be done for three days after the capture of bearded seal. During these three days it is likewise forbidden to shift camp.

If a seal is brought into a house and there is a widow of not more than a year's standing present, she must at once pull up her hood, and she may not express her pleasure at the capture.

Young girls present in a house where a seal is being cut up must take off their kamiks and remain barefooted as long as the work is in progress.

Men may cut up their catch on the ice-edge if food is to be eaten out there, but a seal brought home must not be cut up except by the women.

When the seal has been cut up and lies in pieces on the floor, a lump of fresh snow is laid on the spot where its head was, and trodden down there. The Sea Spirit does not like women to tread on the spot where the seal's head has lain.

As long as näcᴇq: a fjord seal, remains on the floor and has not yet been cut up, the sleeping rugs must not be touched, i. e. arranged, set in place, or shaken.

The soul of a seal resides in the naulᴀq: the harpoon head, for one night after the seal has been killed. Hence the harpoon head, with line and shaft, must be taken into the house and placed beside the lamp when the hunter comes home after killing a seal. This is done in order that the soul may be warm throughout the night it remains in the harpoon which killed the animal.

When a seal is caught in Tasiujaq, the great lake at Pingerqalik, near Iglulik, the same sacrifice must be made as in the case of a man who has lost his brother. The severity here is due to the fact that it is a fresh-water lake, and the seal is thus not in its proper element. Perhaps the soul of the seal regards the lake as a sanctuary, and this has therefore to be specially considered. The rule to be observed is that the hunter concerned must not sanäʃ˙ᴀrpɔq: work with hunting implements, fashion hunting implements and the like. He must also cook all his food in a special pot until a year has elapsed from the time of the capture. — There was once a man who caught a seal in this lake without observing the prescribed taboo. He fell down dead shortly after, without any previous illness.

If a seal or bearded seal is captured, all the women of the village must touch the meat of it with their first fingers. Before the seal is cut up, the woman's husband must sprinkle water on its face.

Women must never make sinews of a seal. Any one trying to sew with sinews of an ordinary fjord seal will die of it, for the sinews of the seal are so short that the animal is ashamed of them, and its soul will kill anyone trying to use them.

Walrus.

Meat of seal or walrus must never be brought into a house immediately after the animal is killed, but not until the day after. Otherwise, the neighbourhood will suffer from a scarcity of game.

When people are living in a snow hut on the ice, and hunting walrus from there, the wicks used in the lamps must be made exclusively of shavings from walrus tusk crushed to powder. Moss wicks must never be used.

During winter, work must only be done with old walrus tusks, i. e. those of last year's catch; tusks from the last winter may not be worked on until the seals have young. When the dark season is over, and the sun is high in the heavens, in March-April, the taboo is not so strict.

The wing of a gull is dipped in waste oil from the lamp and thrust into the harpoon line between the harpoon head; then when the hunter arrives at the blowhole of walrus, he sucks the feather and spits out the oil over the blowhole; the walrus will then have no fear and will not notice the presence of men.

A naked — i. e. newly born and dried — lemming, i. e. one so small that it has no hair as yet, is placed inside the hunting float; the walrus will then not turn against the float and destroy it when harpooned.

If a woman is unfaithful to her husband, while he is out hunting walrus, especially on drift ice, the man will dislocate his hip and have severe pains in the sinews.

At Iglulik, no marrowbones may be cracked in the walrus season. At Usuarssuk on the other hand, there is no objection to this, but the man who has captured a walrus may only eat marrow from the hind legs and only when the bone has been cracked by someone else. At Iglulik, all the marrow bones are stored away until the spring, when they may be eaten freely.

If a walrus is killed at that period in autumn when the women are busy sewing their garments of caribou skin, all needlework must be stopped for a month.

Customs in connection with whaling (Repulse Bay).

If a woman sees a whale, she must point to it with her middle finger.

In the olden days, the whales used to move along the coast quite close in to shore, so the men always had their hunting implements ready on the beach, with the harpoon line fastened to a big stone and the harpoon close by. But one night when two men were going to change wives, and their wives, while all were asleep, went to the men they were to lie with, they saw a whale coming along by the shore, quite close to the beach; and in their eagerness, they ran to a harpoon and harpooned the whale. They got it, but since then the whales never move along close inshore, as they feel degraded at one of their number having been harpooned by a woman.

When a whale has been harpooned, all the women must lie down on the sleeping place with limbs relaxed, and loosen all tight fastenings in their clothes, laces of kamiks, waistband: tᴇqiʃ·iut. Unless this is done, the whales will run the boat far out to sea, dragging it by the line that is made fast to the harpoon head. All this applies to young women and wives. Old women on the other hand may look on freely at the whaling.

As soon as a whale is harpooned, the boys must be tied up together, in pairs, one's left leg to the other's right, and thus bound, they must hobble off inland until out of sight of the sea. If the boys are an odd number, so that one is left over, then it is his business to push the bound pairs and make them tumble over; for the more they do so, the better. It is supposed that the difficulty experienced by the boys in their progress is communicated to the whale, so that after being harpooned, it finds it hard to swim away. Old women may also be lashed together, but not in the same way. All that is done is to tie their legs together a little above the instep, and in this manner they must also hobble off inland, often falling, rolling about at the small declivities; the harder they find it to advance, and the more they roll about, the slower will be the progress of the whale dragging the boat out with it, and it will not move far from the spot where it was harpooned.

When it has been observed from on shore that a whale is harpooned, no one is allowed to fetch water.

When out whaling, a boat must never be baled out. No one on board is allowed to make water or spit over the side; if spitting is absolutely necessary, one must spit on one's own person. As soon as the whaleboat with the whale in tow is about to land, all young mothers must try to be first down to it, running right out into the water, sometimes up to the waist, and then leap on board with water for their husbands; this will make their sons good hunters.

Women with infants, or women who have had a miscarriage, may not boil walrus meat until the backbone of the whale has been broken.

When the boat is within a stone's throw of the shore, maktak is cut up into strips, and the boys and girls divide into separate groups, and the maktak is thrown to them to scramble for. Older persons may also take part. The pieces obtained by women with infants or women who have their menses, or women who have had a miscarriage, are given to old women. The pieces thrown to the boys must be cut with a dice pattern along the strips, those thrown to the girls are marked crosswise.

In the olden days, when whales were hunted in kayaks, the boys had to do as the young mothers do nowadays, come down and pour water over the fore end of the kayaks as soon as they came towing in to shore. This would make them good whalers. The more one could smear oneself over with blood and blubber when a whale was being cut up, the better, for this would please the Mother of the Sea Beasts.

A big circle of stones was built up with a whole shelter wall behind and a flat stone in the middle, set up on another stone. On the flat stone were placed meat and maktak for the first common meal. The men sat here in a circle and feasted with the older women. Women with children were not allowed to take part in this meal. This maktak and all the meat were boiled in one large cooking pot which served for all, and drum dances were held after the feast.

For three days after the capture of a whale, no work was allowed to be done by men or women. In a village where a whale had been captured, no cooking was allowed to be done with fuel obtained from the ground, but only over fires made of bones and blubber, or over the lamp.

Clothing which had been worn at a whale hunt must never be taken inland in the spring for the caribou hunting.

During a whale hunt, the women were obliged to wear a head ornament consisting of a white quartzstone, fastened to a strap round the forehead. This was done to show a light for the soul of the whale.

Bear.

When a bear has been captured, its bladder, penis, ma^{v}sAq (spleen) and part of the tongue are hung up inside the house together with men's implements. This arrangement is to hang for three days.

At the end of that time, the man who got the bear must take it out into the passage and throw it down on the floor; the children in the house must then try which can be first to get hold of the implements and give them back to the owners.

When a she-bear is captured, sewing thread, needle and a woman's knife are hung up together with the bear's nakasuk, or bladder, its suŋᴀq, or gall, and ma^{v}sᴀq, spleen; this ceremony is called näciblugo, and means: "in order to wait for the time to pass". The soul only remains there on the spot for three days.

When a man has killed a bear and returns to his house he must take off all his outer clothing, including outer mittens and kamiks, before entering the house, and for a whole month he must not eat of the meat or blubber of the bear.

In a house where oil made from bear's fat is used for the lamps, it is forbidden to eat marrowbones. The souls of bears are very dangerous, and will not allow marrowbones to be eaten while bear's fat is burned.

People who have eaten human flesh never eat bear's meat; this because it is said that bear's meat is like human flesh.

Salmon or trout.

Persons on a journey and far from their relatives must, if they catch salmon, never eat the head. (Salmon nearly always means trout).

In winter, no one is allowed to eat salmon out of doors.

Water must not be spilled on the floor when salmon are sought for; if anyone does so, all the salmon will disappear.

Salmon must never be eaten at the spot where they are captured, whether raw or boiled, but only some distance away (especially on Back River).

The dorsal fin of the salmon and a narrow strip just below the fins must never be eaten (Back River).

If anyone out after salmon on a river during the ascent of the fish from the sea to a lake should chance to spill soup on the floor, the delinquent must utter a sound as if vomiting, and say "mᴇriʃ·ᴀq, mᴇriʃ·ᴀq" which means the vomit, that which is vomited. Unless this is done, the salmon will be afraid, and will not venture up the river. So also, children may not make water on the floor in tents pitched by these salmon rivers during the time when the salmon are moving up to spawn; altogether, special care has to be taken at this season, and anything spilt from a cooking pot is counted as an "insult to the spirits".

If a salmon is to be brought into a house where there is blubber, it must not come in the same way as the blubber, but a special hole must be cut in the wall (Back River).

When salmon is being cooked in a house where there is blubber, care must be taken that nothing falls on the floor, and that the soup does not drip on the floor. If salmon is to be passed from one side of the house to the other, it must be handed across the sleeping place, not over the floor (Back River).

If salmon is to be boiled in the same pot with meat (siŋmiuʃune: people who will live all the year round on the coast without going up country for the caribou hunting) then the pot must be washed very carefully, and some of its soot smeared on the inside; the salmon must not, however, be boiled over the same lamp as meat; a lamp has to be set up on the right of the ordinary one, and the salmon cooked there.

It is forbidden to eat walrus or bearded seal meat on the same day as salmon, but this does not apply to ordinary seal or caribou meat.

Salmon must never be eaten on the same day as flesh of seal or other marine animals.

It is very strictly forbidden to go walrus hunting with kamiks which have been used while after salmon. If there is absolutely nothing available with which to make new ones, then the upper laces — uŋɛrutit — are taken out of tuktɔqutit — shoes of caribou skin — and the kamik itself can be used with a new sole of bearded seal under.

Caribou.

The caribou is reckoned the most important of all the animals hunted; its taboo therefore, and all the special hunting rules associated with this animal are extremely complicated. The caribou is not only of enormous importance as food, but also as the animal which almost exclusively furnishes material for clothing and the sinew thread used in making the garments; it must therefore be treated with the greatest caution. Especially in the days when the natives had no firearms, and all the hunting took place at the swimming places, in kayaks and with spears or with bow and arrows from special hiding places called talut, it was so great an art to bring down the caribou required for food and clothing that all possible consideration was observed in order to propitiate the souls of the animals. The actual caribou hunting did not begin until summer, when it was no longer possible to go out on the sea ice after seal; as a rule at the beginning of July, the party would leave the coast and set out for a summer camp in one of those tracts where the great herds of caribou were known to pass. The main season for this hunting is as a rule in August, but the hunting parties would remain inland until the ice was firm enough to commence hunting seal. If the caribou hunting had been particularly good, the stay up country might be prolonged until about the New Year; if it had been bad, and there was need of meat and blubber, then as a rule the move down to the coast and out on to the sea ice would be made in November or December.

In all the rules and taboo regulations concerned with caribou and caribou hunting, a very marked and decisive line is drawn between these animals and those of the sea. As usual, it is the unclean women who have here to be most careful. From the moment the party leaves the coast and moves off up country, the women are not allowed to do any needlework, except small repairs, and even these must not be done in the tents, but always out in the hills, far away from the camp. This prohibition of needlework holds good throughout the whole of the autumn, and is not removed until the hunting is over and the party have again moved into snow huts. Women are not allowed to sew during that time, it is said, because amuklaiʃiʃuʷaŋmata tɔ·ʳŋʳʌ·r-mik: "they would draw an evil spirit to the place with their thread". This taboo against needlework is removed during the time when new clothes are being made in the first snow huts of autumn, and then all sewing is once more taboo as far as caribou skins are concerned, throughout the time when the party are living out on the sea ice, and when only sealskins may be used. This taboo lasts until the spring, when the sun is once more high in the heavens, and there is now a period of a couple of months where all the stricter rules of taboo are suspended. All the various rules associated with caribou and women's work are given in the following as formulated by Orulo:

No new garments may be made as long as the party are living in tents; not until they have moved into snow huts. If it should be absolutely necessary for a man to have a new garment before there is snow enough to make a proper snow hut, but some snow and ice have appeared on the lakes, then a little temporary snow hut is built, large enough for the woman who is to do the sewing, and in this she does the work. But the skin must not be softened in the usual way with a sak·ut, or scraper; it must be wetted on the inner side with water and softened with the feet, being stretched at the same time.

When the caribou have shed their old coats and the new ones have come, material of sealskin and used for footwear must no longer be used. If there are men who must absolutely have new soles to their boots, then the sole leather must be laid on the floor to be trodden on, so that it is no longer new, but soiled, and old kamiks may then be soled, but the work must be done out of doors, not in the tent.

No one is allowed to make new garments of caribou skin as long as the animals still have the "velvet" on their antlers.

It the snow is late in coming, i. e. before there is material available to build snow huts, and there is great need of new garments then instead of snow huts, ice huts may be built, and this is done in the form of qArmAq: i. e. with ice blocks for the walls and the tent placed over as a roof. The hairy side of the tent must be turned inward, in contrast to the usual custom when using skins for tents. Not until all items of caribou skin, clothing, outer furs, sleeping places, inner garments, footwear, sleeping rugs etc. are finished may the party move down to the coast and out on the sea ice to commence hunting the creatures of the sea.

At Iglulik, the walrus hunting might begin even though the women were still making clothes for the winter, as long as the snow huts were built on land; seal hunting, however, was absolutely forbidden. Three men were then chosen from the village; only one of them was allowed to use harpoon and lance; the others might go with him, but only to help in cutting up the catch. These three men were not allowed to eat caribou head or marrow, but only caribou meat, frozen, not boiled, and then only while wearing mittens. And the women who were doing needlework were not allowed to eat walrus meat, but only caribou meat from the summer stores; never meat of freshly killed beasts.

Usuarssuk was an exception; here, sealing and walrus hunting could be carried on at the same time. Heads and foreflippers of walrus however, were not allowed to be brought on land, but had to be cached out on the ice off the headland of Usuarssuk, where they were left until all needlework on the new caribou skin clothing was finished.

As long as caribou skin garments were being made, no walrus meat was allowed to be brought indoors. The observance of all taboo at Iglulik was especially necessary, as it is supposed to be from here that the sea spirit Takánâluk set out before going down to the bottom of the sea.

As soon as the needlework and all the new clothes were finished, and no one else required new garments of caribou skin, walrus meat could be brought into the house and be cooked and eaten by all. But caribou meat from the depots was now not allowed to be brought into the house, but had to be kept out in the sErluAq, and must not be eaten until the seals had their young (April). It was better to go hungry than offend against this rule.

Top left: The goblin woman Manîlaq, pack-ice. He met her last summer while wandering in the mountains; she looked so frightful that he fell and lost consciousness and only came to himself through his dog licking his navel. She became his helping spirit. Her speciality is to get quarry for the hunter from the mother of the sea animals. — Top right: Self portrait of Anarqâq, drawn as an expression of his thoughts; he is dragging a fat animal behind him, because he always has an appetite for dainties, and he has drawn his nose as a pipe-bowl, because tobacco is his dearest enjoyment. — Below: A vision while wandering in the mountains. The spirit had such a violent effect on him in its silent horribleness that he fled without first securing it as a helping spirit. Drawings by Anarqâq.

The gloomy helping spirit Issitôq, or giant eye. Soon after he had lost his parents this melancholy spirit came to him and said: "You must not be afraid of me, for I, too, struggle with sad thoughts; therefore will I go with you and be your helping spirit." It has short, bristly hair standing straight up; each eye is in two sections, and its mouth is vertical with a long tooth at the top and two shorter ones at the side. Its speciality is to find people who have broken taboo.

The spirit Nujaliaq, the hair woman. Nose at the side of the head, broad fold of skin on the neck, only one arm; long, unruly hair, sticking out to all sides; no body, only a behind; face white, otherwise covered with black, bare skin; carries a seal-skin line with which she catches caribou. Speciality: good for procuring land animals. Drawings by Anarqâq.

All this, however, did not apply to freshly caught caribou meat, which might freely be brought into the house together with walrus. These customs were observed more especially in the days when the natives had no guns, but hunted the caribou with bow and arrow only. It was then often necessary to pursue the animals for three or four days, a party of "beaters" shouting and screaming behind, until the animals grew so tired and hungry that they no longer heeded the hunter, who could then come up to quite close range and shoot them down.

At Iglulik it was forbidden to eat the flesh of walrus, whale or seal on the same day as caribou meat, nor was this allowed to be in the house at the same time. This taboo did not apply to Usuarssuk.

When walrus hunting gives place to caribou hunting or vice versa, taboo only applies to footwear, not to other articles of clothing.

Walrus hide, or things made from it, must not be taken inland when hunting caribou, but harpoon lines of bearded seal may be used, if they have not previously been used for walrus hunting.

When the women have finished making the new fur garments, and then proceed to eat sea meat and sew sealskins, they must first wash their hands.

Autumn skins of caribou, but only of animals killed while up inland, and meat of the same, must not be brought into a snow hut on sea ice through the passage entrance, but through a hole at the back of the house above the sleeping place. The same hole is used for bringing in bedding when seal are to be hunted. In the case of skins of animals killed in winter however, there is no particular taboo. All taboo comes to an end when the seals have their young, i. e. in April.

On first setting out for walrus or seal hunting after having hunted summer or autumn caribou up inland, a fire must be lighted in the snow hut, with fuel of dried seaweed, and over this are held clothing, mittens of caribou skin, harpoon with line and head, and the words "namᴀrmik-mamᴀrmik", meaning "give us something that tastes nice" are uttered. Then, in leaving the hut to set out on the hunt, one must step across the fire.

As soon as sealing begins after the close of the caribou season, a small narrow strip of pukᴇq (white skin from the belly of a caribou) is set out, and a piece of sinew thread from the short end (sinew thread is made from the back sinews of the caribou, and that part lying nearest the spine gives the longest threads, the outermost being quite short). This is a sacrifice to Takânâluk, and is called kivᴇrsautit: "that wherewith something is lowered down" meaning presumably that offences are thus lowered down into the deep.

If women have to sew caribou skins during the sealing season, they must go up inland, if they are living in snow huts built on the ice.

In spring, when old clothes have to be repaired with autumn skins while in snow huts, the skins must first be cut up as ilErnikut, i. e. that which is left over after cutting out a garment; these fragments are fastened on to the garments to be repaired, and not until they have been worn thus long enough to make the pieces old and dirty may they be used for needlework. Such patchwork, however, must not under any circumstances be done in winter during the dark season, but only when the sun has begun to give out warmth.

A woman must never sew while her husband is out at the ice-edge after seal.

When a caribou is cut up, a small piece of skin must always be left on round the eyes and genitals, for the caribou souls do not like women to touch those parts of their bodies.

When a caribou killed with an arrow is cut up, care must be taken not to break any of the bones, and when the animal has been cut up, a small piece of meat or suet is placed under a stone — qiŋaluklune — as a sacrifice to the dead — nErErquvlugit — piʃäkʃalik — manisinialuŋmat — it is desired that the dead shall eat, in the hope that they will procure game.

During the time when caribou are hunted with bow and arrows, the dogs are not allowed to gnaw the bones of the legs or any other bones. This would hurt the souls of the caribou, and the caribou themselves would disappear.

During the same period, men are not allowed to work on iron; if arrow heads have to be sharpened, the women must do it for them.

If a white caribou is brought down — a so called pukEq — then the hunter is subject to the same taboo as a man who has lost his sister. The meat must not be eaten, and the skin must be dried and then placed unused in the sErluAq. At Taserssuaq, a lake near Tununeq, no women are allowed; caribou killed here require the same taboo as is imposed upon a man who has lost his sister. Women must not look about in this neighbourhood, for if they should look out over the lake they would soon have bad eyes, a sort of snow-blindness; the eyes water continually and they cannot see anything. The reason of this is that two brothers were once attacked here; only the younger escaped, and he lived here afterwards in the neighbourhood, hunting, procuring fur clothing and in many ways obliged to do women's work because he was alone; this is said to be the reason why the taboo here is so strict in regard to women. Here also lived the Tunaluit, a man and woman of the Tunit tribe. It is said that when Tuneq, the husband, saw the solitary hunter, he was afraid and ran down with such violence to his kayak, leaping so high in the air, that deep tracks showed in the ground behind him; these tracks are still visible, and when they are particularly conspicuous it means that many caribou may be looked for that year. This Tûnâluk's "spy-glass" is still to be found here, a large piece of mica with specks of ɔqʃu[w]iʌq, or quartzite, which can shine in the dark; by looking through this stone, caribou may be seen far far away.

Caribou tongue must never be eaten while any one of the family is out on a journey.

Human beings must never eat of a caribou if any part of it has been eaten by fox or wolf. But it may be given to the dogs. A human being eating such meat will never again be able to satisfy his hunger.

Caribou skulls must never be cracked with hammer or stone. If this were done, the people of the village would have pains in the head.

If a visitor who has eaten caribou meat in the morning comes to a house where meat of sea animals is being eaten, and is to eat caribou meat in that house (for he must not eat sea meat), then the caribou meat he brings into the house must, when placed on the sleeping bench (it must never be placed on the side bench) be wrapped up, and while eating, he must take care that no pieces of meat fall on the floor.

During the time men are hunting caribou at Piling, the women are not allowed to sew in their absence; all needlework, even repairs, must be stopped, before a caribou hunt begins; for the land here is regarded as very "sensitive" and requires strict taboo.

At Tununeriseq: Admiralty Inlet, no work must be done for three days after caribou or bearded seal, narwhal, walrus or bear have been caught. During the same three days it is forbidden to break the soil, or to break fuel.

natlɔrsiɔrtut: i. e. people hunting caribou in kayaks on a river or lake, must, while hunting, lay out a piece of sealskin under a stone as a sacrifice to Tugtut Igfianut, the Mother of the Caribou.

If two caribou are seen fighting with their antlers locked, then bootlaces — siŋɛq — must be unfastened, as also the waistbelt: tɛqiʃ'ɛq̄, i. e. everything tight in one's clothing; one can then go straight up to them and they will not run away.

Marrowbones must never be thawed over a woman's drying frame.

Various rules and customs.

Women are not allowed to eat bear's meat or walrus meat during the time when the sun is low in the heavens. If they eat walrus meat, then the walrus will disappear; if they eat bear's meat, all the bears will become very shy.

Young women must never eat tongue, head or marrow of caribou, and little girls must not eat those of seals. Women who have ceased to bear children are exempt.

Widows are never allowed to pluck birds.

A widower during his first year must — like a widow — never mention any animal hunted by name. Nor may he strike his dogs, or even drive them himself, but must have a boy to act as driver.

If an animal with young is struck in the foetus, no woman is allowed to eat of the meat; otherwise, the meat of unborn tu·ga[d]lit "those with tusks" i. e. narwhal, may also be eaten by women, with exception, however, of mothers who have given birth to children during the current year.

Persons who have eaten human flesh are not allowed to eat at the spot where walrus meat is being cut up. It they wish to eat frozen walrus meat, this must only be eaten on land, and then not until after they have placed the pieces of meat on one foot, pretending to "boil" the meat with the foot as a cooking pot. A man who has eaten human flesh is likewise forbidden to crack the bones of animals other than those from old carcases stored in the depots; nor may he eat raw seal meat of newly captured seal, and only bearded seal of his own catch.

The first time a man rows out in a newly covered kayak, his wife places a cup full of water on the place where he sets out. This is done in order to give him good hunting; for the creatures of the sea are always thirsty.

If a SA·RVAQ, a small snipe, be placed in the bow of a kayak, the rower will not upset in a heavy sea.

Sickness and death.

If anyone lies ill in the house, drippings from the roof must not be wiped off, nor must the rime be cleared from the window, or the house itself cleaned out, as one might otherwise easily happen to throw out the soul of the sick person together with the dirt.

As long as anyone is ill in the house, no cracked marrowbones may be thrown outside; they must be collected in the passage, and only thrown out after the patient has recovered.

If dogs are to be fed from a house where anyone is ill, and the meat to be given them is inside the house where the patient is, then it must first be shifted out into the passage, and left there overnight, and only given to the dogs the day after.

A man who often has pains in any part of his body must never eat in company with a stranger; to do so would make the pain worse.

A man who has pains anywhere must, if the trouble occurs during the time when the sun is low in the heavens, never cut mud for shoeing sledge runners; should he do so, he will die before the winter is out.

If a man has a pain in the upper arm, he must not eat the upper foreleg of a caribou.

A man whose child is ill must not do any kind of work. Should he do so, it is believed that the child will never recover.

If a man loses his wits, it is because unclean women have secretly eaten of his catch or prepared skins from the legs of caribou which he has killed; the insane person is called pulamit'ɔq: i. e. one who falls-down flat on his face.

If a woman becomes insane, it is either because she has commited some serious breach of taboo, or because she has once seen i^{j}Erqät and thereafter visited a woman in childbirth. The i^{j}Erqät will not endure this; they feel such dread of women in childbirth that they deprive any woman who has done this of her wits.

If a man has lost one of his souls, he must not go out hunting for a whole month, but must remain quietly at home in hut or tent. This is in order that all his souls can get back properly into place.

When a spirit seance is held on behalf of a man to aid him in any way, he must, on first going out, set aside part of his catch as a sacrifice to the spirits.

A man who has regained his soul after illness and has recovered, must not do any work for five days.

A shaman is not allowed to hunt any kind of game during the time he is occupied in endeavouring to cure a sick person. Should he kill any animal in this way, he might easily happen to kill the soul of the persons for whom he is working at the same time.

If a patient on the point of death can manage to sneeze, he will get well.

As soon as it is evident that a person is mortally ill, the rugs and skins and all that he lies on, with the clothes he keeps in the house, not in use at the moment, are taken out and placed in the passage. Only the rugs belonging to the dying person may remain in the house. As soon as the dying person is about to expire, those present exclaim: "piujuŋ'nailErpɔq", i. e. "there is not much left of him", and as these words are uttered, loud weeping and lamentation are set up. The dead person is wrapped in graveclothes, only the inner jacket, inner breeches and stockings, and tied up in the sleeping rug. Anyone dressing a corpse for burial must stop up his or her nostrils with caribou hair. The manner in which the corpse is removed from the dwelling depends on whether it is in a snow hut or in a tent, and whether the deceased is a man or a woman. As a general rule, the body is not taken out through the usual exit, but through an opening in the side wall; among the Iglulingmiut however, the body of a man, but not of a woman, is taken out of a snow hut through the passage. From the snow hut, the corpse is hauled by a line fastened round the instep, to its resting place; from a tent, it is carried on the back.

In the case of a little child, the mother may take the body out of the house just before the child expires; in that case, no death taboo is imposed upon those in the house or the skins and clothing in the house, and the taboo affects only the mother of the dead child.

A woman who has lost an infant is called A·Rujɔq; whenever she goes out, she must have her hood pulled over her head, always have her head covered. The period depends on the age of the child. In the case of a newborn child, it is only a day, if the child is a couple of years old, then a couple of days. She must then make a small bonnet of skin without hair, and this she must have on her head whenever she goes out for a month or two according to the age of the child.

For a year, she must not eat raw meat caught by any other than her husband; she may eat of his catch if the child died in winter, but even then not until the spring, when the sun begins to melt the roof of the snow hut (i. e. in May). Apart from these special rules, she has to observe the ordinary mother taboo, i. e. not to eat entrails, heart etc. of any animal, or eggs; in a word, all that which applies to women who have to be particularly careful.

For instance, she must never drink water from melted ice, but only water from melted snow.

When parents have lost a child, the child's clothing is kept until they have to leave their place of residence. The clothing is then placed near the grave.

No visitors are allowed to be in a house when anyone is dying; they must go out into the passage and not come in again until the dying person has expired.

The face of a corpse is always covered when it is being taken to the grave. Here the face covering is removed, and carried round in the direction of the sun, to the cry of "ilɔrfak·ut", in order that the dead person may bring good weather. At the same time, the lashings with which the outer wrapping of the body is tied, are cut.

When the lashings of the skin in which the corpse is tied up are cut at the graveside, this must always be done with a knife that has belonged to the deceased; and the knife must never after be used for anything else, but is deposited by the grave.

When the men who have brought the corpse to the grave return to the house, they must all drink water from the dead person's cup, in order that the deceased may get something to drink, and not be thirsty.

The corpse is not placed in a cairn of stones, as was customary in Greenland, only a single circle of stones is placed round the body. At times a stone may also be laid under the head as a pillow.

If it is winter, a small snow hut is built over the body.

The dead are buried with their belongings, which are laid beside the grave. This applies both to men and women.

A dying person may, however, give away his or her possessions to any favoured friend, but all that is not so given away must be laid by the grave.

Apart from the implements proper, various articles in miniature are made for men, such as kayak, sledge, harpoon, bow and arrows, cup, these miniature objects being placed at the feet of the corpse. For women, a small lamp, meat fork, pot, cup and real needles and thimble are made; these are likewise laid at the feet. These things are made on the day before the na˙ce˙vik, or the stricter death taboo, comes to an end, and are placed in position on the day it ends. This is said to be done in order that the deceased may possess something. With these miniature objects the soul passes to Takánâluk as soon as the death taboo ceases. Until then, for 3 or 4 days, they remain with the body. The period of ṅa˙ce˙vɔq, i. e. maintaining the strict death taboo for men is three days, for women four days; during these days the persons concerned must do no work, must not wash, comb their hair or cut their nails; the lamp must not be cleaned, the dogs must not be fed, and the persons are not allowed to cut up their own meat for cooking. Sexual intercourse is forbidden, as also dancing or song festivals. The brother or sister of the deceased must during these days leave his or her own house and stay in that of the deceased, so that they may be together until the soul of the deceased passes away.

Sledges must not be driven during the days of strict death taboo. Should it be absolutely necessary to go out hunting, it must be done on foot. The noise of the sledge is offensive to the dead.

When the people of a village do not observe taboo after a death, the soul returns in the form of a tupiläk, an evil spirit, and strikes the disobedient with sickness; it is then necessary for a shaman to sakavɔq, i. e. to call up his helping spirits, and he can then stab the evil spirit to death with his sealing harpoon.

As soon as these three or four days have passed, one of those who have assisted in disposing of the body takes a piece of dog's excrement and carries it round the snow hut in all directions, saying "tu-tu-tu"; this done, all must wash, comb their hair and cut their nails, and then, rubbing their nails together, say in a kind of growling tone: "u·mh-u·mh-u·mh". Only when this has been done may all work be resumed.

When people are living in tents, and not in snow huts, the ceremony with the dog's excrement is not used after a death; instead, a fire stone or the toggle of the traces of an old dog is taken; sparks are struck with the stone, to cleanse the air in the tent. The reason for using a dog's excrement or toggle of an old dog is that it is desired to propitiate the dog which keeps watch in the passage of the house where the Mother of the Sea Beasts lives.

When the na·ce·nEq is over, all who have taken part in the setting of the stones round the grave, or have been in the house visited by death, must throw away their clothing and leave their snow huts with all inside, including the ilupErɔq, or skin hangings used to line the walls of the snow hut.

Those who have had anything to do with death are subject to various forms of taboo extending beyond the first few days; thus no one else is allowed to eat anything boiled in their pots, nor they to eat anything boiled in others' pots, for a whole year. Similarly, they may not eat raw meat of seals newly caught by others, only frozen meat caught some time beforehand; and neighbours, when making a catch, must speedily bring them meat for cooking; tɔquʃɔrɔ·q alianaŋusuniArmat, i. e. in order that the deceased may rejoice.

At a village where a man has died, no knife may be used for work on any implement for a whole year.

Women whose relatives or nearest neighbours have died within the year must not prepare raw skins, but only work on dried ones. Nor may they mention the animals by name, but only refer to them in the shaman language.

A·R·ujune, i. e. among people whose brother or sister has died, no animal may be cut up in a tent without placing a skin on the floor beneath the head. This custom is not observed in a snow hut.

If a brother has lost his sister, or *vice versa,* the bereaved is not allowed to pluck the feathers of the kaŋɔq (Canadian snow goose).

If there is seal meat in a house of death, the meat may be eaten, but the skins of these seals must not be used, dried, or in any way made into clothing.

When a man dies, no one is allowed to wear clothing made from animals he has caught. All such garments must be thrown away.

On the day when the news of a death is made known, no needlework is to be done in the evening.

When learning of a death in another village, one must sleep one night with all one's amulets under one's head.

When there are any dead in a village, one must get up very early in the morning.

A year after the death, the relatives visit the grave and walk round it three times in the direction of the sun, while when swinging his "face cloth" they only walked round once.

Persons wishing to put an end to their lives by hanging must do so in a house while they are alone, and must hang themselves from the bearing post of the drying frame, i. e. the piece of wood which is thrust unto the wall of the snow hut and frozen fast there, to support the drying frame. They must leave the lamp burning, not put it out, lest any should be frightened by coming upon them in the dark. After death, they do not pass to Ṭakánâluk or to the Narrow Land, nor to the Land of Day, but to qimiktun nunä·n the Land of the Hanged, where souls go about with their tongues hanging out. This country is nearer to the land of human beings generally than is any other region in the Land of the Dead.

The first time a man who has lost his wife goes out hunting and gets a seal, he must na·ce·vɔq it for three days, that is to say, he must observe a kind of taboo, as he is considered unclean in relation to game; in cutting up the carcase, he takes the meat, but leaves the bones whole without cutting them out (tanᴇʀ^{d}lugo); entrails, skin and blubber are likewise left untouched. It is this to which he must pay sacred attention for three days, wrapping the skin and blubber round the skeleton, after which it is placed out on the ice, as a sacrifice to the soul of his dead wife. In the case of the two next seals he catches, he is not required to na·ce·vɔq, but they must be cut up in the same fashion, skin, blubber and bones being laid out on the ice, care being taken also to see that the backbone is not broken. No stranger may eat of the meat of these three seals, only the man himeslf. Not until the fourth capture is normal procedure resumed, and only then is the death taboo removed from the seals he gets.

The first bearded seal he catches must be dealt with in a similar manner. In cutting it up, care must be taken not to break the spine; the meat is cut away from the bones, and skin and blubber flayed off, only the skeleton is sunk. Here also the catch is subject to some taboo; the meat may be eaten by others, but only by men, and in their own house, and no portion of blubber or skin may be given away; the hair must not be removed from the skin, but if the hide is required for thongs or sole leather, it must be left until the hair rots off (uti^{v}q). This applies only to his first bearded seal.

The first three caribou he kills must also be specially treated: he may only take the skin and lean meat, the skeleton must be covered up with stones. In the case of walrus there is no special taboo.

At Sentry Island (Arviaq), the death taboo lasts for three days; the following special customs are there observed:

If a person dies just after sunrise, burial must take place at once, and no special taboo is required of the immediate relatives, save that for five days they must not sleep out in the open. If on the other hand, a person dies after sunset, the body must remain in the tent or snow hut for five days, and during these five days none of the relatives may leave the hut.

A dead body must always be removed through a hole at the back of the house, never through the same hole that is used by living persons; otherwise, they would follow the deceased to death.

For the first five days after death, all in the village must lie down to sleep, the men with their knives, the women with their ulos, under their heads. And no one is allowed to go outside without carrying some weapon in the hand. This is done in order to guard against the dangerous spirits of the dead person.

After a death, a sledge must be at once raised on end in front of the house where anyone has died. This serves as a warning to strangers, so that they can take their knives in their hands at once before going up to the village.

A dead body must be handled by an old woman or a young woman who has only just reached marriageable age.

Views of life.

When it is winter in the land of human beings, it is summer among the aklivut, in the Land of Day; there are, however, the same seasons, and they follow one another in the same succession as on earth.

There are in the earth large white eggs, siläʃ·ät, as big as the bladder of a walrus. They turn to silät or silᴀ·ra·luit: these silᴀ·ra·luit are, when fully developed, shaped almost like caribou, but with large snouts, hair like that of a lemming, and legs as tall as tent poles. They look as if they were as big as an umiᴀq, but they are not dangerous, they have the nature of the caribou. Their footmarks are so large that two hands with outstretched fingers will not cover one. If it is killed, and one wishes to cut it up, it will take several days, so great are these animals, and that even if one only tries to deal with one side of the carcase. When one of these giant beasts is seen among caribou, it appears like a white mountain of snow; when it takes to flight and treads the ground, rain falls, pouring, drenching rain, and a thick mist covers the earth. The shaman Aua, who gave me this description, has seen such an animal at close quarters, and seen it take to flight in company with terrified caribou. To speak of them or describe them is like lying, no one believes it, but it is nevertheless true. They are called silAq, plural silät, and this means something of sila, of the earth, of the universe, of the air, of the weather. It is said that they are the children of the earth. Anyone killing such a silAq must observe the same taboo as a man who has lost his brother.

Round about the different villages are a few sacred stones. These stones are said to personify the Sea Spirit Takânâluk. Sacrifice is therefore made to them by those passing by. In case of sickness or dearth, a shaman may consult such a stone, sakablune, i. e. by consulting his helping spirits. If the shaman's wish be fulfilled, the stone will emit a grumbling sound, and the earth will tremble. Some declare that specially skilful shamans can consult any stone whatever, and get the "Mother of the Sea Beasts" to answer through it.

The souls can speak, but human beings cannot hear them, only shamans when invoking the spirits.

IX.

Mountain Spirits, Earth Spirits and other Spirits.

The Eskimos believe that they are surrounded on all sides by spirits, the same spirits which the angákut enlist in their service as helping spirits, and answering spirits. Distinction may be made between two different kinds of spirits, the more tangible, earth-bound spirits which in many ways correspond to those appearing in the folk-lore of other peoples as trolls and gnomes; and on the other hand, the personifications of such dissimilar things as fire, stone, a precipice, a feasting house or such like; these spirits are then referred to as the inua, the owner or lord, of the stone or house.

iʲErqät or Mountain spirits.

iʲEraq, plural iʲErqät, corresponds to the isErAq of Greenland. The word means literally: "those who have something about the eyes", and the name refers to the fact that the eyes of these mountain trolls are set lengthwise in the face, not transversely as ours are; they "blink sideways" with their eyes. The mouth is placed in a similar way to the eyes. They live up in the hills, or rather, inside the hills, which they have fitted up like great stone houses, much resembling those inhabited by white men. The shamans often see them disappearing into the cracks and fissures of rock that form their dwellings. They are not visible to human beings having no special relations with the supernatural, but only to shamans. Ordinary people are very much afraid of them, and hear only their whistling in the air; one must never show fright in any way, for they only attack the timid and cowardly.

The iʲErqät are famous especially for their running powers, and there is no animal which they cannot outrun. Caribou in full flight, for instance, they can overtake with ease. When, now and again, they capture a human being, the first thing they do is to make the captive a swift runner also. It is said that they have a method of cleansing the feet and shins of human beings through the action of worms in the earth or tiny creatures in the lakes. When these have eaten away the flesh from shinbones or toes, human beings become as lightfooted as the i^jErqät. They are of the same shape as human beings, and live in the same way. The men are dressed in human fashion, only the women's garments are otherwise, their breeches consisting of the white skin from the belly of the caribou; white belly skins all cut up into strips. They are as strong as wolves; when they have killed a caribou, they run home with it, slinging it over their shoulders just as a wolf does with its prey. They have always a great store of all manner of delicacies in the way of food, especially fat and suet from the caribou, which they boil down and leave to set in great skin bags made from the hides of bull caribou. When they capture human beings, they keep them, and do not allow them to go away again. Shamans have found among them strange implements very much like the mirrors used by white men. This implement is at once a mirror and a spyglass. It glitters like mica, and when one looks down into it, all that is passing far away among the dwellings of men is reflected in this mirror; therefore the i^jEqät know all about mankind.

Aua's father, Qingailisaq, called Oqâmineq: "the man with the sharp tọngue", gave the following account of his encounter with the i^jErqät: it is here reproduced according to Aua's version:

"My father was out once hunting caribou, and had killed four. He was just cutting them up when he saw four men coming towards him. They came over the crest of a hill, and he thought at first it was caribou. But they came closer, and he saw that they were i^jErqät, two men with their grown-up sons. One of the sons was quite a young man. All were big men, and they looked just like ordinary human beings, save that they had nostrils like those of the caribou. The oldest of the men seemed very excited, he at once grasped hold of Oqâmineq, pressed his hands against his chest to throw him down, but Oqâmineq remained calmly standing, and the angry i^jErAq could not do anything with him.

Then said the i^jErAq: "Will you do any harm?"

"I will do no harm; you need not be afraid of me" answered Oqâmineq.

Then the i^jErAq at once loosed hold of him, and proposed that they should sit down on a stone and talk. And he told his son to cut up the caribou my father had been cutting up himself. The work was speedily done, though he had no knife; he flayed them in the same way as one does a lemming, simply tearing open the skin, but it was done more rapidly than by a man working with a knife.

The i^{j}ErAq sat down on a stone and talked with my father. He said they lived in the country inland from Piling, near Nuvuk; they lived by hunting caribou. They had a small pocket in their tunics, in which they kept two small stones. They were mighty runners, and could outrun the caribou; when they came up quite close, they killed them with the stones in their pockets.

The old i^{j}ErAq was out looking for a son that was lost — a son who had not come home from his hunting, and he now thought he must have been killed by human beings, and had at first believed that it was Oqâmineq who had killed him. But Oqâmineq said he had never seen an i^{j}ErAq before, and the other then grew calm, and they parted in friendship and mutual understanding.

My father, who was a great shaman, went home and had a dress made like that of the i^{j}ErAq, but with a picture of the hands in front, on the chest, to show how the i^{j}ErAq had attacked him. It took several women to make that garment, and many caribou skins were used. There were a number of white patterns in the dress, and it became a famous dress, which was bought by him who was called: aŋak'ɔq (the well known whaler and collector for the American Museum of Natural History, Capt. George Comer), and my father was paid a high price for the garment, which is the only i^{j}ErAq tunic ever made by human hands.

A few of the best known stories of i^{j}Frqät are here given.

The two women who were stolen away by the i^{j}Erqät.

Two women who were out gathering fuel (Cassiope), were stolen away by the i^{j}Erqät. They stayed among them, and one of the girls had a child. It was feared that they might run away, and they were therefore always guarded. One day they were taken to a warm lake where it was the custom to remove the hair from caribou skins. They were made to stand with their feet in the warm water, and the big toe was then opened and some of the flesh cut away. Part of the skin and flesh of the big toe were cut away, and it was said that it was this which prevented human beings from running swiftly.

The two girls at last grew weary of living among the i^{j}Erqät, and went away, pretending they were going out to gather fuel, but as usual, there was one to keep watch over them. They managed nevertheless to hide in a fissure of rock near a river. One of the women had her child on her back. The other woman had no children.

It was at once discovered that they had run away, and a search was made at once, and dogs taken out.

When the i^{j}ᴇrqät came to the river and had to cross it, they leapt across, and that with such speed that one only heard the wind of their flight.

A dog found the women, but they said to it:

"We will kill you if you say anything".

The dog promised not to say anything, and simply went off after the others who were searching. It was afraid of being killed. The child on the woman's back tried to call to its father, but one of the women then took it by the throat and strangled it. The i^{j}ᴇrqät searched until evening then they went home.

The girls continued their flight and came to some human beings who were very fond of athletic sports. They took part in the sports, but without letting the others notice how swift they were; only when playing ball did they take rather more trouble. One day someone said to them:

"We have heard that people who have been stolen away by the i^{j}ᴇrqät become good runners".

The two girls would never show how good they were at running. They always said they could only run quite slowly, but once, when they were out playing ball, one of the girls threw the ball to her companion, and they began running.

One of the girls said:

"Run like a young caribou."

The other girl said:

"Try to run like a young cow with calf."

And then they ran. And the dust rose up behind them at every stride. They ran a long way, but came back again, and all the lookers-on stood staring.

"That is the way you should run when playing ball" said the two girls, and gave the ball to the others, but no one wanted to play ball any more, and all went home.

The two girls stayed on afterwards at that village and were married, and they were never again invited to take part in any kind of sport or ball game; they were left to themselves. But when they went out to gather fuel, they often came home with caribou. And their husbands loved them, because, though they were women, they brought meat to the house.

Told by

Inugpasugjuk.

The two old men who sought refuge among the iʲErqät.

There were once two old men who had nothing to live on. Not knowing what to do, they decided to seek refuge among the iʲErqät, for they had heard that one had only to cross a great river and follow it up, and would then come to the land of the iʲErqät.

So they left their own place, and walked and walked, and kept on walking until they came to a stream, and this they followed up inland. They passed a caribou lying dead on the ground, but they simply passed it by, and walked and walked and kept on walking.

On the way they saw more slain caribou, floating down the stream. Once, when there was a big fat bull among them, they hauled it ashore, cut it up and ate of it. After that they made up great loads of meat and carried these with them farther up inland.

Suddenly they were surrounded by iʲErqät, who called out to them that they were not to drag any more of the caribou carcases ashore. They looked round, and perceived many tents, and they were invited to come in as visitors; they went in, and were given sleeping rugs and shown their places. A tent was also given them, and they now lived here. They were given the most delicious rich tongues, and tender steaks, and every day fresh skins were given them for sleeping rugs and coverings. The iʲErqät were skilful hunters, and withal good and kindly folk, and the two old men stayed with them and lived in abundance to the end of their days.

Told by
Inugpasugjuk.

The iꞑnEriugjät, who are spirits both of sea and land.

iꞑnEriugjAq, plural iꞑnEriugjät, corresponds to the Greenland form iꞑnErʃuAq, plural iꞑnErʃuit, and means literally: "the great fire". The name refers to the fact that the windows of the sea spirits, or perhaps more correctly the shore spirits, are sometimes seen lighted up. The spirits of earth, on the other hand, have luminous lard bladders in their huts and take their name from this.

The iꞑnEriugjät, the sea or shore spirits, always have their houses on small reefs or rocky islets; they are exactly like human beings to look at, and not here, as in the Greenland stories, without noses. Some indeed say that they have very handsome noses; others again that their nostrils are like those of the caribou. All their clothes are made of sealskin. They never wear clothes of caribou skin, as the Eskimos

1) Nimeriarjuaq, or the hairy worm; moves by writhing its body sinuously; lives both on land and sea; smaller and narrower than the bearded seal, is very fast and only has hair on back and belly; acts as helping spirit, heals the sick; can also be used as defender. 2) Siggulik, or snout animal; big, melancholy eye, ears on its nose; very keen sense of hearing; short tusks in the mouth; heals the sick. 3) Nuatqeq, the water-man, is now a human being, now a dog, but always without a belly and with three tusks in the mouth; it has an excitable mind and split open his forehead at their first meeting; otherwise it is a very effective soul-seeker, can easily find stolen souls and is therefore good at healing the sick. 4) Umingmánguaq, the spirit of the musk-ox. No eyes, senses everything through its ears which are on stems and resemble horns. He met it first while hunting caribou; it spoke like a human being and said it was simply looking for a shaman whom it might serve. It would always follow him, he did not need to turn round to look for it; for then it would disappear. Good for healing all ailments. 5) Qarajaitjoq, the hole animal; the head merely consists of jaws, the opening runs backwards; has only one arm in prolongation of the lower jaw. The hand is formed as a loop; the eyes look like loose rings, one being on the back, the other below the lower jaw. He met it while out wandering and it became his helping spirit; its speciality is helping women who have difficulty in bearing children. Drawn by Anarqâq.

Harpooning a walrus from the ice. Below are a caribou and a polar bear. Drawn by Padloq.

Caribou, drawn by Ujarak.

in the neighbourhood of Hudson Bay otherwise do; they live on, and utilise exclusively, the animals of the sea. They are visited only by shamans, who state that they have warm and comfortable houses. They are not hostile to man, but on the contrary, often endeavour to help those who cannot get along by themselves, as they are very skilful hunters. The shamans often employ them as helping spirits. When the supply of meat runs out, the shamans often visit them and bring home meat from there. When game becomes scarce, the shaman will often visit their dwellings, which are just below the surface of the sea under the rocks where they live. From here they often send newly killed seal up to the surface as gifts to mankind. The only instance, as far as Aua's knowledge went, of harm done to human beings by the sea spirits was the following:

There was once a man who was left alone on the hunting grounds out on the ice, after all his companions had gone home. A seal came up to breathe at the blowhole where he was waiting, but when he harpooned it, both seal and harpoon disappeared in some way he could not understand. He then went homewards, and on the way, came to a house he had not seen before. He went inside, and was kindly received, and boiled meat was set before him that he might eat. An old woman asked him: "Do you like meat soup with blood in?"

The man answered: "If it is meat soup, I should be the last to despise it."

He drank the meat soup, stayed a little longer with the strangers, and then went home. He went homewards, and arrived at the place. But he had not been home long before he began to feel violent pains in his stomach, and then a remarkable thing happened, in that a harpoon suddenly appeared in his body, having passed through it from one side to the other. And the moment this took place, the man fell down dead. A shaman then explained that it was the iŋnᴇriugjät who had stolen his harpoon when he harpooned the seal, in order to kill him afterwards with his own weapon. The sea spirit had uttered a spell over the harpoon, changed it into seal meat, and this led him to swallow it, in order that it might bore its way out through his body after he got home, and kill him.

The iŋnᴇriugjät of earth lived far up inland, and hunted only caribou. They were mighty hunters, and had always abundance of meat and fine caribou skins. People who have visited them say that along the walls inside the houses were small shining things; they could not understand what they were, but they looked like intestines filled with suet and entrails, and resembled both intestines of caribou calves and of fully grown beasts. If only one could get hold of one of these mysterious luminous things, which they had no name for, one would become a very great shaman, provided one carried the light on one's person for the rest of one's life. This then became the shaman's aŋak'ua or qaumanᴇq. These luminous, transparent and oblong bags that shone out from the side walls of the house, have given those spirits the name of iŋnᴇriugjät. They too resembled human beings, but at the same time, their eyes and mouth were like those of the iʲerqät. They had very narrow faces and long noses.

A young man who was out hunting caribou once came to the land of the iŋnᴇriugjät. He entered a large and comfortable house, but hardly had he got inside before he was forbidden to go out again. These fire spirits never slept, they were always awake, they did not understand how to sleep. The young hunter, who had walked far and was now tired, soon began to feel sleepy, and as he had been awake for a long time, he made ready to sleep on the spirits' bench, but every time he lay down and closed his eyes, the iŋnᴇriugjät cried: "he is dying, he is dying!" and raised him up and woke him.

At last the man was tired and sleepy beyond endurance, and said: "You must not raise me up because I lie down and close my eyes. I am not dying, I am only going to sleep."

But the spirits, who did not know what sleep was, raised him up every time he tried to sleep, and the man, who was never allowed to sleep, at last grew ill with exhaustion and died.

Since then, only very great shamans have dared to visit the iŋnᴇr-iugjät, for though they are not otherwise hostile to men, there is this dangerous thing about them, that they cannot endure to see a human being sleep.

The tᴀrqajägʒuit or shadow folk.

tᴀrqajägʒuᴀq, plural tᴀrqajägʒuit, the Shadow Folk, are quite like ordinary human beings, but there is this peculiar thing about them: that one never sees the beings themselves, only their shadows; they are not dangerous, but always good to human beings, and the shamans are very glad to make use of them as helping spirits. They hunt by running, and can only bring down an animal if they are able to overtake it on foot. These Shadow Folk correspond to the tᴀʀajaⁱt of the Greenlanders, and Ivaluardjuk related of them as follows:

"It is said that there is this remarkable thing about the Shadow Folk, that one can never catch sight of them, by looking straight at them. The Shadow Folk once had land near Tununeq (Ponds Inlet). One day, an elderly man appeared among them and stayed with them. And the Shadow Folk came and brought food both for him and his dogs. The Shadow Folk themselves had also dogs; one of them was named Sorpâq.

"One day, the Shadow Folk spoke to the old man who was visiting them as follows: 'If you should ever be in fear of Indians, just call Sorpâq. There is nothing on earth it is afraid of.'

"The man remained for some time among the Shadow Folk, and then went home again. He came home, and some time after he had come home, his village was attacked by Indians, and the old man then fell to calling Sorpâq. Sorpâq at once appeared, and began to pursue the Indians. Every time Sorpâq overtook an Indian, it bit him and threw him to the ground, killing him on the spot. Thus Sorpâq saved all the people of the village, who would otherwise have been exterminated by the Indians.

"It is said that these Shadow Folk are just like ordinary human beings, save that one cannot see them; otherwise, they have the same kind of houses and the same kind of weapons, harpoons and bladder harpoons, just like everyone else."

Told by
Ivaluardjuk.

The kukiliga·ciait or claw-trolls.

kukiliga·ciait is the plural form of kukiliga·ciᴀq and means: "those with the great claws", corresponding to the Greenlanders' kukiʃ·a·jɔ·q, plural kukiʃ·a·jo·t.

The Claw-Trolls live far up inland, where in winter they dwell in snow huts, just in the same way as human beings do. They are very dangerous on account of their long claws. If they come upon human beings, or human beings come to them, they will attack with their long claws, and keep on scratching and tearing at them all over the body as long as there is any flesh left. Only the greatest of shamans ever escape alive from such an encounter.

These Claw-Trolls are best known in the stories from their encounter with the Moon and his sister the Sun, when the pair were wandering out into the world after having killed their wicked grandmother. The story is given elsewhere. Only very bold and skilful shamans dare to have a kukiliga·ciᴀq for a helping spirit; but the shaman who does so venture is held in high esteem and feared by all.

The amajɔr uk or amaut-witch.

The amajɔrʒuk is an ogress, hated and feared beyond all the other earth spirits. The naughtiest children can be made to stop crying at the mere mention of her name. She is said to be great ogress, with a big amaut on her back; it is made of untanned hide of great male walrus; it is filled with old rotten seawed, and the human beings whom she captures smell of seaweed long after, even when they escape without delay.

The amarjɔrʒuk attacks both adults and children, and as soon as she has overtaken her victim, she puts it down into her amaut, from which none can escape without aid. She is the most feared of all soul-stealers, and only the greatest shamans dare to set out against her.

amajɔrʒuk was one of Aua's helping spirits.

amajɔrʒuk corresponds to the Greenland amᴀrsiniɔ·q.

The inɔrᴀrutligᴀ·rʒuit or mountain dwarfs.

inɔrᴀrutligᴀ·rʒuk, plural inɔrᴀrutligᴀ·rʒuit, answer to the Greenlanders' inuᴀruL·igᴀq, plural inuᴀruL·ik·at, meaning literally: "the Little People, the Dwarfs".

It is said that the inɔrᴀrutligᴀ·rʒuit live in the mountains just in the same way as human beings, and are just like them to look at, but quite small. They are no bigger than the lumbar vertebra of a walrus set on end. Their clothes are made of caribou skin, often cut to the same pattern as those of human beings. They are as a rule mischievous and hostile. When they meet a human being, they suddenly grow, and as soon as they have grown as tall as their opponent, they fall upon him and throw him down, if they are strong enough; then they remain lying on the victim until the latter is starved to death. Should they on the other hand be overthrown themselves, they pretend to die, and the human being leaves them, believing them killed; but if one turns round a moment after leaving them, they have always disappeared without a trace. The inɔrᴀrutligᴀ·rʒuit kill their game by following up an animal's track and keeping on until they overtake the beast. If a human being has killed it meanwhile, they nevertheless consider it their own catch, and grow angry if the hunter refuses to give it up. They are very swift-footed, and can outrun every animal there is.

They are good and effective helping spirits, and much sought after as such.

Many different stories are told about them. Here is one of the best-known:

The old woman and her granddaughter, who were visited by mountain dwarfs and shadow folk.

inɔrʌrugligʌ·rʒuk, a little Mountain Dwarf, once came with his wife on a visit to a village where there lived none but an old woman and her granddaughter. They built their house close to that of the old woman, as a double house with a single entrance, and the old woman entertained her guests as well as she could, but the guests returned to their part of the house without having eaten their fill, and being hungry after their journey, they took the after-part of a caribou and the tail fin of a whale in to thaw, and began eating of these.

inɔrʌrugligʌ·rʒuit made a long stay, and when the day came for them to leave, the old woman invited them to stay on, but in vain; they wished to go, and they went. The old woman wished to keep the hindquarters of the caribou bull and the tail fin of the whale, of which they had eaten, and so she spat on them, to make them freeze fast to the bench. The dwarf and his wife came in to fetch them, but as they could not get the meat loose from where it lay, they left it behind in the snow hut.

"It is impossible to get it loose, it is frozen fast" said the dwarf's wife.

"When a thing is impossible, one must leave it" answered her husband, and so they left the meat where it was. But after they were gone, the old woman and her granddaughter went in to fetch it, and lo! the hindquarters af the caribou bull had changed into that of a gull, and what had been the tail fin of a whale was now no more than the stump of a bird's tail.

The possessions of a dwarf, and his game, are always directly proportional to the size of the dwarf himself, but as long as they are being dealt with by one of the dwarf race, they appear to human beings as if they were real large animals, of the type they represent.

Some time after, other visitors came to the village. They heard the noise of dogs and the talking of human beings, but could see nothing but some shadows moving over the snow. They had received a visit from the tʌrqajʌ·qjuit.

Then they heard a voice, which came from the wife of the visiting tʌrqajʌ·qjuʌq:

"We have come to the house of poor folk who appear to have nothing to eat. We will give them some meat".

And then the shadow folk built them a new house, and the old woman and her granddaughter moved in, and they brought meat into the new house, and said:

"Take this, though it is not very much. All the meat on our sledge is frozen".

The Shadow Folk were clever hunters, and the man caught seal, caribou and salmon, and the old woman and her grandchild lived in abundance.

One day there came other visitors again. This time it was a party of real human beings, and the Shadow Man wanted them to go out hunting with him. They went out together, and it often happened that the Shadow Man vanished from the sight of his companion, and they had to search for him. The man was ill at ease about having such a comrade while out hunting, and when he saw a shadow close beside him, he stabbed that shadow with a knife. He killed him, and the moment he was dead he became visible. He was a young and handsome man.

The Shadow Folk mourned deeply at his death, and went away, though the old woman and her granddaughter did all they could to make them stay, for they had grown very fond of them.

Told by
Inugpasugjuk.

inukpait or the Giants.

Inukpäk, plural inukpait, means a giant, and answers to the Greenland term, which is the same.

It is said that the inukpait are fashioned just like ordinary human beings, save that they are mighty and huge, but otherwise harmless, and indeed well disposed towards mankind. So large are their bodies, that when a man of the human race marries an inukpäk woman and goes to lie with her, he is altogether lost in her genitals and dies. But if an inukpäk man lies with a human woman, it has happened that he has thrust his penis right through her and killed her. The following story is told wherever Eskimos are to be found, but in different versions. Right over in East Greenland men know this story of the giant who was treated with scorn because he had only two teeth.

The giant and the mountain dwarf and the human beings from the umiᴀq.

There was once a giant who stood astride of a fjord, catching sea-scorpions. He was so big himself that he called the whales sea-seorpions.

A little mountain dwarf stood on the shore watching him. He cried:

"You giant, you great giant, your catch is a morsel for two teeth."

The giant did not answer. But the dwarf kept on calling out, and so at last the giant went up after him.

The dwarfs, inɔrᴀrugligᴀ·rʒuit, who are mountain spirits, have the faculty of growing to suit the size of the things they meet, and so it happened now; the little dwarf suddenly became big, when the giant fell upon him to thrash him. But the giant threw him down all the same, with such force that he lost one leg, and the giant left him lying there, and went back to the fjord where he was catching sea-scorpions.

One day when the giant was out, he swept up a whole umiᴀq with its crew in the hollow of his hand, and took them home. He lived on a shelf, a rocky shelf on a steep cliff. Thither he carried the umiᴀq and its crew, and whenever he wanted to sleep, he laid them on his cheek.

The people of the umiᴀq were soon weary of dwelling on the rocky shelf, and one day when the giant lay down to sleep, they bored a hole in his nose and lowered themselves down to the ground.

There were still two remaining when the giant woke, but those who had fled hid among the rocks.

"Where are my children?" asked the giant, when he awoke. Then one of those who had been left behind sang:

"Through a hole in your nose
Your children let themselves down,
It is true, it is true.
Through a hole in your nose,
They let themselves down,
Ijaja, ijaja."

Then the giant began digging in the ground to make a new channel for a river, and the river then burst through the country and flooded it, carrying with it all those who had hidden among the rocks, so that they perished.

But the giant remained up on his rocky shelf with his human children, and whenever he lay down to sleep, he set them on his cheek so that they should not run away.

One evening when the giant lay dozing, the two men caught sight of a bear, a great he-bear. At first they did not know how to wake the giant, but then one of the men picked up a piece of rock and began hammering at the giant's head. It was no use, the giant would not wake up. So they took a bigger piece of rock and began hammering at his head with that. Then at last the giant woke, and they cried to him:

'There is a bear down there".

The giant got up and went to meet the bear, sticking one of the men in under his belt and the other in the lace of his kamik. On the way, the man under the belt was crushed and killed, and only the one in the lace was left alive.

The giant went up to the bear, took it in his fingers and killed it.

Whenever the giant ate, the man who was with him used to gather up great stores of meat from the crumbs that fell from his food. And now I know no more of that story.

Told by
Naukatjik.

nᴀra˙je˙ or the great glutton spirit.

Nᴀra˙je˙ answers to the Greenland form nᴀʀaje˙, and means properly: the one with the big belly. They are excellent helping spirits, as their enormous voracity renders them very swift. When a nᴀra˙je˙ girds up his stomach, there is not a living creature that he cannot outrun. All else that is known of them is told in the following story:

The great glutton spirit nᴀra˙je˙.

A nᴀra˙je˙ spirit once took a human being to live with it. One day they sighted some caribou. They went into hiding, so that the caribou could not see them, and here the nᴀra˙je˙ spirit began girding up his belly with a long strip of hide. He had so huge a belly that it almost hung down to the ground. His adopted son was afraid he might burst if he tied himself up like that, and suggested that he himself should run after the caribou. But the nᴀra˙je˙ spirit went in chase of them all the same, and though they had a long start, he ran so swiftly once he had fastened up his belly, that he overtook them all. Then he struck them one by one over the legs so that they could not walk, and then he killed them. He was a glutton, who could eat a whole caribou at once, and it was his custom, when about to feed, to make a hollow in the ground for his belly, and there he would lie down and begin to eat.

The nᴀra˙je˙ spirit ate a whole caribou, and when the adopted son came near, he was frightened, and cried:

"When I have eaten sō much you must go a long way round and keep well away from me": "avu'nakan'ᴇq" (A long way round; keeping some distance off).

Here ends this story.

Told by
Inugpasugjuk.

There are spirits which take care that human beings shall not become too devoted to songs and festivals; they--also dislike to hear children making too much noise out in the open or in the houses when alone without adults.

tc·ʳɳʳa·luk ugjuɳmik unatautilik: The thrashing spirit that used a live bearded seal for a whip.

There was once a great village where the people were very fond of assembling for festivals in the dancing house. When the huts were deserted, the children were gathered together in a big house. In this house there was a very large drying frame, made of sealskin thongs tied together, and it was the children's custom to do gymnastic exercises in these, and not infrequently, one or another of them would get hurt; for they were only children, and had no one to look after them. When the children were not playing inside the house, they would run outside and scream and shout, or they would play at being shamans, and pretend to be calling up spirits.

Once when the grown ups were at a singing festival, the children played as usual, shouting and making a noise, and when the lamps, with no one to tend them, began to smoke, they ran outside. But here they suddenly discovered that the great Thrashing Spirit was coming towards them. Ahead of it ran its whip, which was a live bearded seal. The children, terrified, ran back to the house to hide. In the confusion, while all were trying to conceal themselves, there was a little boy who asked the others to lift him up on to the great drying frame of sealskin thongs, and the others lifted him up, and he hid away there. Some hid in the space under the bench, others crept into the side cupboards of the house where skins and furs were kept. The children had just hidden themselves when the Thrashing Spirit came in through the passage. In front of it crawled its whip, which was a live bearded seal. Once inside the house, the Thrashing Spirit picked up the bearded seal by its hind flippers, swung it like a whip and thrashed all the children to death. Only the little boy who had clambered up on to the drying frame remained undiscovered. Then the Thrashing Spirit went out of the house and disappeared.

All the grown ups had been in the dancing house, and stayed a long while at their singing. When at last they came home, they found all their children had been killed. The boy up on the drying frame climbed down and told who it was that had killed all the others. All the men at once set about preparations for vengeance, and made ready their weapons. Next day they again held a song festival in the house they used for dancing, just as if nothing had happened, but some of the men hid in the house where the children had been murdered. Now and again the men went out of the house to see if anyone was coming, and at last they saw the Thrashing Spirit approaching. One of the men then clambered up on to the great drying frame, taking with him a lamp and some oil which had been heated over the lamp. The oil was just thoroughly scalding hot when the Thrashing Spirit at last came into the house. In front of it crawled its whip, the live bearded seal. Hardly had the bearded seal entered the house, when the man up on the drying frame poured the boiling oil down over it. There was a fizzling sound, and at the same time, the other men, who had hidden themselves about the house, sprang out and stabbed it. The bearded seal died almost at once. But the Thrashing Spirit itself escaped out of the house, and though the men ran after it, none of them could overtake it.

But it is said that after that, the Thrashing Spirit never visited people who were singing in their feasting house, now that it had lost its whip.

Told by
Ivaluardjuk.

— — —

Some stories concerning various spirits are given in the following pages. They are set down without comment, as all that is known about the spirits in question is given in the stories themselves.

The spirit of the stone (inua) that married a woman.

There was once a woman who saw two Indians come rowing across a lake, and she sat down to wait for them. When they reached her, they proposed that she should sit down in the back of their kayak, as one of the men had no wife, and would like to marry her; but the woman did not want to get married, she rejected the men and let the kayak row on. But as she turned her back upon them, she laid her hands on a big stone, and suddenly it was as if the stone began dragging her towards it. It was the Stone Spirit that took her, because she had rejected her fellow human beings, and when the stone drew her to it, she began to grow stiff, and as soon as she felt this, she cried out to the men in the kayak, at the top of her voice:

"Dear kayak men, come back, you may have me for your wife if you like."

But the men in the kayak rowed on, and again the woman cried out:

"Dear kayak men, come back, you may have me for your wife if you like. Now my feet are turning to stone, now my legs are turning to stone, now my body is turning to stone."

But the men in the kayak paid no heed to her cries, and so the Stone Spirit took the woman to itself, and she was turned into a pillar of stone.

Told by
Inugpasugjuk.

Ipiup inua or the spirit of the precipice.

It happened that people disappeared, and no one knew how. It happened that children running about outside at their play were suddenly lost, or that caribou hunters up inland did not return. And then it is said that three children of the same parents were out one day playing together. The oldest carried the youngest in an amaut. One of them found a little bird carved out of walrus tusk, and at that they all fell to searching eagerly about in the hope of finding more, and so intent were they on their search, that suddenly, without knowing how, they found themselves in a house. The moment they got in, a woman came and placed herself in their way, so that they could not get out again.

The oldest girl understood that they had come to the house of a spirit which ate human beings, and so she said:

"Before we begin eating this tender calf I am carrying, just turn round and eat a little of the earth by the door opening; and close your eyes, and cover them with your hands, and howl at the top of your voice."

The girl had the jaw of a seal in her hand, and as the Spirit of the Precipice began eating away at the passage, she herself fell to digging in the ground with the jawbone. The girl had just managed to dig a hole through the ground when the Spirit of the Precipice was about to open her eyes, so she said:

"Do not open your eyes, eat a little more of the earth by the doorway; then you shall soon have the tender little calf to eat."

The Spirit of the Precipice closed her eyes again and fell to howling with all her might, and at the same moment the girl sent out her two little sisters, making them go first through the hole she had dug; then as she herself was about to follow them, the Spirit tried to grasp her, but only managed to get hold of a piece of her clothing, which she tore off and kept in her hand. Thus the girl got away. The Spirit of the Precipice called after her:

"Did you see all the heads lying about in here, all the human heads? When I have nothing to eat, I suck the snot from their noses."

The girl took her little sisters by the hand and they fled homewards as hard as they could. They had got a good way when the Spirit came out of her house and cried after them:

"I had not thought you could be so artful!"

When they got home, the children told what had happened, and thus it became known what had happened to all the children and all the caribou hunters that had disappeared. It was the Spirit of the Precipice that had taken them. None of the men were at home, so the women of the village all set about to take vengeance on the Spirit of the Precipice. One of the women took down a new sealskin thong, one that had never been used, and then they tried to do exactly as the children had done. They began looking about on the ground for small figures of birds carved out of walrus tusk. One of the women found such a figure, and before she knew where she was, she had been drawn into the house, and at once she spoke to the Spirit, and said:

"The whalers cannot kill the whales they catch, and therefore I have come to cut your claws."

At these words, the Spirit stretched out her hands, and said:

"You are right. My nails have got so long."

"Let me see your feet as well," said the woman. But as soon as the Spirit had stretched out hands and feet, she bound them with the sealskin thong and cried out to the others outside the house to pull. The Spirit tried to resist with her feet, but the women outside pulled so violently that one of the Spirit's hips was broken, and at last they pulled her out of the house. Then they dragged her away, hauling her along over the ground. They tried to pick out the most uneven parts, so it was no wonder the Spirit was soon on the point of death. Then suddenly it said:

"Wait a little before you kill me, wait a little. Let me tell you a little story first. My entrails are made of beads, wait a little, wait a little before you kill me. My liver is made of copper, wait a little, wait a little before you kill me. My lungs are made of a hard white stone, but I do not know what my heart is made of."

Hardly had the Spirit spoken of her heart when she breathed her last and died.

Then they cut up the dead body to see if what she had said was true, and sure enough: hardly had they slit up the belly when they saw that it was full of beads, and they took out the beads and made bracelets and necklaces of them, but there were many more than they could use, and they took the rest home.

They lay down to sleep, decked out in all their fine beads, but when they awoke next morning, all the beads had turned into ordinary human entrails.

Told by
Inugpasugjuk.

The spirit that could not catch seals.

There was once a woman who could not get married, and so she married a spirit. The spirit could not eat the same food as the woman, and though she always invited him to partake of every meal, he wasted away and was at last nothing but skin and bone. One day he left the house and went out on to a great plain. He cut a hole in the ground in the same way as one cuts a hole in the ice of a lake, and began fishing. It was not long before he brought up a whole caribou, a fine big beast with plenty of suet. He took the caribou home with him, and they lived on that. He himself was able to eat of it. But when the caribou was all gone, the spirit went down to the sea and set about hunting seal. Here, however, he never caught anything, and again he wasted away; for he could not eat meat that others had caught. Once, when the hunters had been out, and the spirit as usual came home without having caught anything, he pulled out a piece of his own intestine and came home with it in his hand. His wife's parents, who thought he had made a catch, received him with pleasure, and made preparations to cook the piece of intestine, which they supposed was from a seal. They put it into the pot and began to boil it, but before long a horrible smell spread through the house. Then said the spirit:

"I think it must be cooked now." And he got up and took a step across the floor, but at the same moment he fell down dead.

Told by
Inugpasugjuk.

täcip inua (The spirit of the lake) that loved a woman.

The story begins with a man who lived somewhere or other and had a real woman for a wife. The man was a great caribou hunter, who went out on long, long hunting expeditions, often remaining away for many days. One day he came home from his hunting, and as he approached his dwelling, he saw his wife wading out in a lake. He hid himself in order to see what she was about; and then he heard her say:

"Oh penis of the Lake Spirit, come up to the surface and show yourself."

At these words a great penis appeared in the middle of the lake and the woman went out to it and let it go up into her genitals. The man stood watching, then went home, but said nothing to his wife of what he had seen. On the next day he did not go out hunting, but went up to the lake. He placed himself by the edge of the water, and imitating his wife's voice, uttered the same words he had heard her say the day before; and sure enough, a penis at once rose up to the surface of the water, and the man waded out, cut it off and carried it home to his house. He then set to work to boil it. When it was done, he said to his wife:

"Here you are, eat."

The woman took the food her husband gave her and began to eat.

Then said her husband:

"What is that you are eating?"

"I do not know," answered his wife.

But then he said:

"It is your lover's penis."

"Then no wonder it tastes so nice," said the woman.

Then said her husband again:

"Which are you more afraid of: a knife, or maggots?"

"Maggots one can crush, but I am afraid of a knife," answered the woman.

After that the husband said nothing, but went out hunting as usual, only now he nearly always came home with one mitten. The other one he had lost, so he said. It was because he was collecting maggots in his mittens. When he had got together a great number of maggots, he brought them home, spread a skin on the floor and told his wife to undress and sit down on it.

The woman tried to keep her tunic on by clutching the tails between her thighs, but her husband cut away the ends of the stuff and pulled off the tunic, and then he poured all the maggots out over her. And the maggots crawled into the woman, in through her mouth, her nostrils and every opening of the body. Thus they came into her body and killed her.

This the husband did because his wife had the Spirit of the Lake for a lover.

Told by
Ivaluardjuk.

After that the man set out on a journey, and when he had come far from his own place, he put up a tent and settled down there and began hunting in those parts. He went out hunting caribou as usual, but now it happened that sometimes, on returning home to his tent, he would find cooked meat in the pot. When this happened several times, and he had found a meal ready waiting for him on his return, he determined to try to find out who it was that cooked his food for him. He pretended to go out hunting, but hid himself near the tent and kept watch.

He had not been waiting long when a little fox appeared and stole into the tent. Before going in, it took off its skin and laid it out to dry on the stones; and thus it turned into a young woman, and went into the tent. She only stayed in the tent a little while at a time, and kept coming out and looking round, in fear of being taken by surprise; but whenever the woman went into the tent, the man ran towards it as hard as he could; then as soon as she came out he hid again; when she went in, he ran a little way again, and in this manner he approached the tent. At last he was near enough to run up and snatch the fox skin just as she was coming out of the tent. The woman at once came up to him and begged and prayed him to give her back the skin, and when he would not, she burst into tears..

"I will marry you" said the man.

"No, I will not" answered the woman.

„You shall not have the skin unless promise to marry me".

"Well then you may have me for your wife, but now give me the skin".

Thus the man obtained a wife, and they lived together in his dwelling.

The summer passed, and the winter set in, and there came a raven in human form to visit them.

One day the raven said suddenly that he noticed a strange smell of urine in the house.

At these words the husband said:

"My wife feels uncomfortable when you say such things. Please never speak of it when she is within hearing".

This warning had no effect. The raven said again:

"How can it be there is such a strange smell of fox in here."

At these words the young wife burst into tears, drew forth her bag, and took out a fox skin and began chewing it to make it soft. As soon as the skin was soft enough, she put it on, and ran out into the passage and disappeared.

"Oh, oh, now I have made my dear host a widower" said the raven.

At these words the man said:

"Ugh, what is that horrible stink I can smell? It is like dog's dirt."

He said that because the raven's wife was a piece of dog's dirt in human form.

After that the man went outside to try to follow up his wife's tracks. He followed the tracks in the snow, there was one of a fox and one of a human being. Thus he came to a village. He went straight into the house and found his wife, who was in there. But every time he sat down beside his wife, she slipped away from him; so he spat on his first finger and touched her with that, and then she did not try to escape from him any more. And in that way he got back his wife again.

Told by
Ivaluardjuk.

The spirit of the feasting house.

There was once a family who had put their drying frame away in a feasting house, and so they sent a young girl in to fetch it. It was a dark evening, and when the girl came into the dark house, she said:

"Where is the spirit of the feasting house?"

"Here he is" answered the spirit, He was quite naked, and had no hair.

"Where are your eyes?" asked the woman.

"They are here," answered the spirit in a very deep voice and he spoke in a deep voice because he was not a human being, but a spirit.

"And where is your nose?"

"It is here!"

"And your ears?"

"They are here!"

"And your mouth?"

"It is here!"

„And your hands?"

"They are here!"

"And your feet?"

"They are here!"

"And your penis?"

"It is here?"

"And your testicles?"

"They are here!"

But at these words the spirit leaped forth from the bench and grasped hold of the girl, and she cried:

"Oh, do let me take my drying frame down first!"

At these words the spirit let the girl go, and she managed to slip out of the feasting house and run off home.

Hunting scenes, drawn by Ujarak.

Musk-ox hunt.

A bear breaking into a tent and attacking a child.

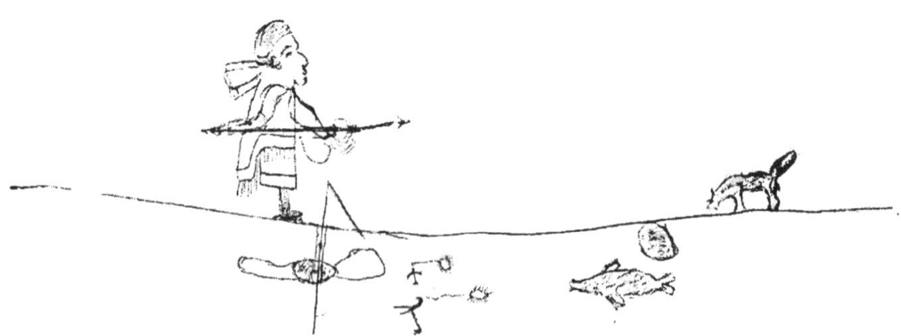

Breathing-hole hunting. Drawn by Taparte.

Old people say that the spirit would never have appeared to the girl if she had not asked after it herself. One should never ask after spirits, or attempt to speak to them, for if so, they will appear.

Told by
Unaleq.
(immigrant Netsilingmio).

ikuma·lu·p inua, or the spirit of the flame.

There was once an old woman, who went out to look to the traps she had set, and took her dog with her. She was anxious to get back to her snow hut the same day, but when darkness fell, she stopped to wait for the moon to come up. She had come to some snow huts, which were deserted, and here she sought out the narrowest, and here she went in to rest. Having climbed up on to the sleeping place, she crept right inside her breeches, closed them at the top, laid her dog down beside her and tried to sleep. (Women's breeches reach almost to the armpits at the top, and when women have to sleep without coverings, they can pull their breeches right over their shoulders and curl up in them as in a sleeping bag).

While she lay there, she heard a voice say:

"Whose a·papa· are you?"

The dog answered of its own accord:

"It is my a·papa·" (an untranslatable word, that was used to frighten people).

But every time the voice asked, the dog answered:

"It is my a·papa·."

At last the dog was silent, but the voice kept on asking. Then the old woman made ready to slip out of the snow hut, taking the little dog in her amaut. The moon was now in the sky, and it had grown light; and now, following her tracks, she hurried homewards as fast as she could. She had already gone a good distance away from the snow hut, when suddenly a crackling flame darted out from the window opening of the snow hut, and the flame rushed along the road after the old woman. The old woman threw herself down beside the tracks, out in the clean snow, where there were no footmarks, hiding her head in the snow; she had turned round, and pulled up the tail of her tunic. The Spirit of the Flame (ikuma·lu·p inua), came rushing forward, but did not notice the old woman, as she lay outside the line of tracks, while she herself distinctly saw the face of the Spirit through the flickering fire in the flame itself with hood pulled down, just like a human being in a hurry; but as the Spirit of the Flame passed by the old woman, it broke up, as it were, into a whole lot of little flames, that flickered for a moment and then went out. Now that the Spirit of the Flame was gone, the old woman tried to get her little dog to stand up, taking it out of the amaut; and the dog was now none the worse, and stood up as lively as could be, there in the snow; and the old woman hurried home with her dog, after having overcome the Spirit of the Flame by her cunning.

Told by
Inugpasugjuk.

X.

Songs and Dances, Games and Pastimes.

The Eskimo temperament finds a lively and characteristic expression in the mode of entertainment chosen as soon as but a few individuals are gathered together. The natural healthy joy of life must have an outlet, and this is found in boisterous games as well as in song and dance. Underlying all the games is the dominant passion of rivalry, always seeking to show who is best in various forms of activity: the swiftest, the strongest, the cleverest and most adroit. There are many different kinds of games, often in the form of gymnastic exercises, which are associated with the festivals invariably held when guests are to be entertained, and the party as a whole are otherwise fit and well, with meat enough for a banquet. There are ball games, races, trials of strength, boxing contests, archery etc.; but the same spirit of rivalry which makes all this kind of sport exciting, is also found in the song contests which are held in the feasting house as the culmination of all the merry items in the entertainment. And where there are several families living in one village, there is no need of visitors to provide the occasion, the party is then sufficient in itself. The autumn and the dark season naturally form the great time for song; as if it were desired to chase away the thoughts of the winter now inevitably approaching, in the course of which so much may happen in the way of unlooked-for, undesirable events, if Sila and the other guiding powers are not favourably disposed towards mankind.

The great song festivals at which I have been present during the dark season are the most original and the prettiest kind of pastime I have ever witnessed. Every man and every woman, sometimes also the children, will have his or her own songs, with appropriate melodies, which are sung in the qag̡·e, the great snow hut which is set up in every village where life and good spirits abound. Those taking part in a song festival are called qag̡·iʃut; the poem recited is called pisᴇq, the melody of a song i^{v}ŋᴇrut: and to sing is i^{v}ŋᴇrtᴀ·rnᴇq; the combination of song, words and dance is expressed by the word mumErnEq: "changing about"; having reference to the fact that as soon as the leading singer has finished, another comes forward; he sings: mumErpɔq, plural mumErtut. The chorus, which must always accompany the leading singer, who beats time with his drum while dancing, is called iŋiɔrtut: those who accompany in song.

A qaɢ·e is heated and lighted by one or more lamps; to make it thoroughly festive, there must be no lack of blubber, and that is one reason why it is difficult to celebrate these festivals unless there is abundance of everything. If the hunting has been such as to require economy, no special feasting house is built, but the whole community assemble in the largest house in the place. An essential preliminary to the success of the general entertainment is the careful practising of the songs by each family at home in their own huts. These people have no written characters, and no means of breaking the monotony of indoor life but what they can make for themselves, so that the songs are apt to be their chief method of entertainment. Where all are well, and have meat enough, everyone is cheerful and always ready to sing, consequently there is nearly always singing in every hut of an evening, before the family retire to rest. Each sits in his or her own usual place, the housewife with her needlework, the husband with his hunting implements, while one of the younger members takes the drum and beats time; all the rest then hum the melodies and try to fix the words in their minds.

When the song festivals are held in the qaɢ·e, the party assemble there every evening. Among villagers still living inland, because their womenfolk have not yet finished their needlework, the gathering begins early in the afternoon, and lasts until late in the evening, song and dance continuing uninterruptedly all the time. Should there happen to be visitors, the entertainment may last all night. The men who have most meat contribute the most delicious kinds of food, and the festival opens with a great banquet, at which everyone may eat as much as he can stuff.

Then, when the singing is to begin, the performers are drawn up in a circle, the men inside, the women outside. The one who is to lead off with an original composition now steps forward, holding the large drum or tambourine, called qilaut, a term possibly related to the qilavɔq previously mentioned: the art of getting into touch with spirits apart from the ordinary invocation. For qilaut means literally: "that by means of which the spirits are called up". This term for the drum, which with its mysterious rumbling dominates the general tone of the songs, is doubtless a reminiscence of the time when all song was sacred. For the old ones believe that song came to man from the souls in the Land of the Dead, brought thence by a shaman; spirit songs are therefore the beginning of all song. And the direct relation of the songs to the spirits is also explained by the fact that every Eskimo who under the influence of powerful emotion loses control of himself, often breaks into song, whether the occasion be pleasurable or the reverse.

Compare here, the manner in which Aua the shaman could suddenly fall a prey to an inexplicable dread, burst into tears and sing the song of joy. Or the case of Uvavnuk, when struck by the meteor suddenly bursting into song over the theme of all that moved her and made her a shaman (p. 123).

As a rule, each leading singer has to sing a certain number of songs, but not too many; three, for instance, and often it is so arranged that the one who comes after him must sing at least as many as the first. Should he fail to equal the number of his predecessor, he is accounted a poor singer, a man without experience or imagination. Before the song festival begins, the drum has to be carefully tuned up. The skin, which is stretched on a wooden frame, sometimes quite round, sometimes oval in shape, is made from the hide of a caribou cow or calf with the hair removed. This is called ija', the "eye" of the drum, and must be moistened with water and well stretched before use. Only thus will it give the true, mysterious rumbling and thundering sound.

The singer generally opens with a modest declaration to the effect that he cannot remember his insignificant songs. This is intended to suggest that he considers himself but a poor singer; the idea being, that the less one leads the audience to expect, the humbler one's estimation of one's own performance, the more likelihood there will be of producing a good effect. A conceited singer, who thinks himself a master of his art, has little power over his audience.

The singer stands in the middle of the floor, with knees slightly bent, the upper part of the body bowed slightly forward, swaying from the hips, and rising and sinking from the knees with a rhythmic movement, keeping time throughout with his own beating of the drum. Then he begins to sing, keeping his eyes shut all the time; for a singer and a poet must always look inward in thought, concentrating on his own emotion.

There are very precise rules for the use of the qilaut. The skin of the drum itself is never struck, the edge of the wooden frame being beaten instead, with a short and rather thick stick. The drum is held in the left hand, by a short handle attached to the frame, and as it is fairly heavy, and has to be constantly moved to and fro, it requires not only skill, but also considerable muscular power, to keep this going sometimes for hours on end. The singer's own movements, the beating of the drum, and the words of the song must fit in one with another according to certain definite rules, which appear easy and obvious to an onlooker, but anyone trying to imitate the performance will inevitably get out of time. It is a great art to keep one's attention fixed on the rhythmic movements of the body, the beats of the drum, which must accompany, yet not coincide with, the bending of the knees; then there is also the time of the melody itself, which must likewise follow the movements, and finally the words, which have to be remembered very accurately, with the inconceivably numerous repetitions recurring at certain particular parts of the song. And the singer, while keeping all this in mind, must at the came time inspire his chorus so that it is led up to that ecstasy which can at times carry a simple melody for hours, supported only by a refrain consisting of ajaja, ajaja. I have been present at song festivals lasting for 14—16 hours, which shows what song means to these people. Imagine a concert in any civilised community lasting for that length of time! But the secret of the Eskimos' endurance lies of course in the fact that they are simple and primitive natures, working themselves up collectively into an ecstasy which makes them forget all else.

I have many a time endeavoured to learn their songs so as to be able myself to take part in a performance at the qaġ'e, but with no great success. I never found any difficulty in making up a song that should fulfil the ordinary requirements, though it was not easy to equal the natural primitive temperament in its power of finding simple and yet poetic forms of expression; but as soon as I tried to accompany myself on the drum, with the very precise movements of the body that go with it, I invariably got out of time, and thus lost my grip of those whom it was my business to inspire as my chorus. These attempts of my own to take part gave me an increased respect for this particular form of the art of singing, and now that I have to describe, as far as I can, the performance as a whole, I can only say that the general feeling, the emotional atmosphere in a qaġ'e among men and women enlivened by song is something that cannot be conveyed save by actual experience. Some slight idea of it may perhaps be given some day, when the "talking film" has attained a higher degree of technical perfection — if it gets there in time; it would then have to be by a combination of the songs in the Eskimo tongue and the dancing in living pictures. Unfortunately, I was unable to record their melodies on the phonograph, as our instrument was out of order. I hope then at some future date to be able to revert to this complicated but humanly speaking highly interesting subject; for the present, I must confine myself to the Eskimos' own view.

There are various kinds of songs. Firstly those inspired originally by some great joy or sorrow, in a word, an emotion so powerful that it cannot find vent in ordinary everyday language. Then there are songs merely intended to give the joy of life, of hunting, rejoicing in the beasts of the chase, and all the good and ill that man can experience when among his fellow men. Then again, every man who aspires to be considered one with any power of gathering his neighbours together must also have challenged some one else to a song contest; and in this he must have his own particular rival, one whom he delights to compete with, either in the beauty of his songs as such. or in the skilful composition and delivery of metrical abuse. He describes the experiences which he considers most out of the ordinary, and best calculated to impress others with the idea of his own prowess as a hunter and courage as a man. Two such opponents in song contests must be the very best of friends; they call themselves, indeed, iglɔre˙k, which means "song cousins", and must endeavour, not only in their verses but also in all manner of sport, each to outdo the other; when they meet, they must exchange costly gifts, here also endeavouring each to surpass the other in extravagant generosity. Song cousins regard themselves as so intimately associated that whenever they meet, they change wives for the duration of their stay. On first meeting after a prolonged absence, they must embrace and kiss each other by rubbing noses.

Song cousins may very well expose each other in their respective songs, and thus deliver home truths, but it must always be done in a humorous form, and in words so chosen as to excite no feeling among the audience but that of merriment.

These cheerful duels of song must not be confused with those songs of abuse which, albeit cast in humorous form for greater effect, have nevertheless an entirely different background in the insolence with which the singer here endeavours to present his opponent in a ludicrous light and hold him up to derision. Such songs always originate in some old grudge or unsettled dispute, some incautious criticism, some words or action felt as an insult, and perhaps breaking up an old friendship. The only means then of restoring amicable relations is by vilifying each other in song before the whole community assembled in the qaɢ˙e. Here, no mercy must be shown; it is indeed considered manly to expose another's weakness with the utmost sharpness and severity; but behind all such castigation there must be a touch of humour, for mere abuse in itself is barren, and cannot bring about any reconciliation. It is legitimate to "be nasty", but one must be amusing at the same time, so as to make the audience laugh; and the one who can thus silence his opponent amid the laughter of the whole assembly, is the victor, and has put an end to the unfriendly feeling. Manly rivals must, as soon as they have given vent to their feelings, whether they lose or win, regard their quarrel as a thing of the past, and once more become good friends, exchanging valuable presents to celebrate the reconciliation. Sometimes the songs are accompanied by a kind of boxing, the parties striking each other with their fists, first on the shoulders, then in the face, not as a fight, but only to test each other's endurance and power of controlling emotion despite the pain. This form of boxing, which is called tiklu't'ut, is well known among the Aivilingmiut and Iglúlingmiut, but is especially prevalent among the Netsilingmiut.

I shall frequently have occasion to revert to the Eskimo songs when dealing with the various tribes encountered on my last journeys. The best singers I met during our winters at Hudson's Bay were Aua and his brother Ivaluardjuk, whose most characteristic song I have already given in the introductory section. When sung, it produced an altogether extraordinary effect on those present. And anyone who understands the Eskimo tongue will be able to appreciate the great power of expression and the elegance of form in the original text. For my own part, what impressed me most was the individuality of conception in the poet's endeavouring to further the expression of his inspiration, or of his hunting experience, by lying down on the ice on a winter's day and in a vision recalling the contrast to the harshness of the moment in his fight with the gnats, which are the pests that accompany the delightful warmth of summer. The Eskimo poet does not mind if here and there some item be omitted in the chain of his associations; as long as he is sure of being understood, he is careful to avoid all weakening explanations. Here is the old man, his limbs awry with the gout, shivering with cold one bitter winter's day, and, in order to give warmth to his description of a distant memory of the chase, he cries out into the driving snow:

Cold and mosquitoes
These two pests
Come never together.
I lay me down on the ice,
Lay me down on the snow and ice,
Till my teeth fall chattering.
It is I,
Aja — aja — ja.

This reference to the mosquitoes at once calls up recollections of summer in the minds of his hearers, and he drives them away again at once to bring forward the situation he has in view. The same poetic adroitness is also apparent in Tûglik's play song, which is given in the description of the shaman Unaleq. This also must be heard to produce the full effect; it needs the clear-children's voices to give it at its best. The description of the evil days of dearth could not be more intensely given than in the second and sixth verses, where the subject is introduced as follows:

Hard times, dearth times
Plague us every one,
Stomachs are shrunken,
Dishes are empty.

The hallucinations which almost invariably accompany actual starvation are then given in the following lines, where things of solid earth become but as a floating mirage to those whose entrails are racked with emptiness:

Joy bewitches
All about us,
Skin boats rise up.
Out of their moorings,
The fastenings go with them,
Earth itself hovers
Loose in the air.
aja· — ja· — japape.
aja· — ja· — japape,

And then comes finally the joyous vision of food:

Know you the smell
Of pots on the boil?
And lumps of blubber
Slapped down by the side bench?
aja· — ja· — japape
Hu — hue! Joyfully
greet we those,
who brought us plenty!

This little song, which is given on p. 41, is nothing but a scrap of nursery rhyme, known to all children at play, yet it shows to the full the high level of Eskimo poetry.

But when one tries to talk to one of these poets on the subject of poetry as an art, he will of course not understand in the least what we civilised people mean by the term. He will not admit that there is any special art associated with such productions, but at the most may grant it is a gift, and even then a gift which everyone should possess in some degree. I shall never forget Ivaluardjuk's astonishment and confusion when I tried to explain to him that in our country, there were people who devoted themselves exclusively to the production of poems and melodies. His first attempt at an explanation of this inconceivable suggestion was that such persons must be great shamans who had perhaps attained to some intimate relationship with the spirits, these then inspiring them continually with utterances of spiritual force. But as soon as he was informed that our poets were not shamans, merely people who handled words, thoughts and feelings according to the technique of a particular art, the problem appeared altogether beyond him. And it is precisely in this that we find the difference between the natural temperament of the uncultured native and the mind of more advanced humanity; between the Eskimo singer and the poet of any civilised race; the work of the latter being more a conscious attempt to create beauty and power in rhythm and rhyme. The word "inspiration", as we understand it, does not, of course, exist for the Eskimo; when he wishes to express anything corresponding to our conception of the term, he uses the simple phrase: "to feel emotion". But every normal human being must feel emotion at some time or other in the course of a lifetime, and thus all human beings are poets in the Eskimo sense of the word.

In order further to make clear Ivaluardjuk's ideas, I would once more refer to the woman Uvavnuk, who one dark night experienced her great emotion, the decisive inspiration of her life, through the medium of a meteor which came rushing down out of space and took up its abode in her, so that she, who had until then been quite an ordinary person, became clairvoyant, became a shaman, and could sing songs that had in themselves the warmth of the glowing meteor.

Finally, the Eskimo poet must — as far as I have been able to understand — in his spells of emotion, draw inspiration from the old spirit songs, which were the first songs mankind ever had; he must cry aloud to the empty air, shout incomprehensible, often meaningless words at the governing powers, yet withal words which are an attempt at a form of expression unlike that of everyday speech. Consequently, no one can become a poet who has not complete faith in the power of words. When I asked Ivaluardjuk about the power of words, he would smile shyly and answer that it was something no one could explain; for the rest, he would refer me to the old magic song I had already learned, and which made all difficult things easy. Or to the magic words which had power to stop the bleeding from a wound: "This is blood, that flowed from a piece of wood".

His idea in citing this example was to show that the singer's faith in the power of words should be so enormous that he should be capable of *believing* that a piece of dry wood could bleed, could shed warm, red blood — wood, the driest thing there is.

— — —

Some poems are so fashioned that they can be reproduced without difficulty, almost word for word, as they are recited and sung. Such are the songs I have quoted here and there in the foregoing. But there are others which presuppose a thorough acquaintance with the events described or referred to, and would thus be untranslatable without commentaries that would altogether spoil the effect. This applies more especially to hunting songs, where the animals are not mentioned by name, but indicated by some descriptive phrase, and where various details are explained beforehand, apart from the text proper, the latter being then often rather a kind of encouraging refrain, an incitement to the chorus, who, once in the grip of the tune, simply shout out the words among the other singers, and thus make the singing more pleasing and effective. In such cases, I have been obliged to seek explanatory information from the composers, who then interpreted the text for me into ordinary language, so that it was possible to translate it. I give here some examples of such songs, which would have been the merest guesswork in translation, if the poet himself had not furnished the needful commentary. All these songs are by Aua.

Walrus hunting.

ajaja^{i}ja aja aja^{i}ja
ajaja^{i}ja aja aja^{i}ja
ajaja^{i}ja aja aja^{i}ja
tupaguatᴀrivuŋa
imᴀq man·a
sailᴇrata·talᴇrmät

ajaja^{i}ja aja aja^{i}ja
ajaja^{i}ja aja aja^{i}ja
ajaja^{i}ja aja aja^{i}ja
tautuŋ·uᴀrpäk·iga
nap·ᴀriᴀratatlᴀrmät
(aiwᴇq una)
kauligjuᴀq una

ajaja^{i}ja aja aja^{i}ja
ajaja^{i}ja aja aja^{i}ja
ajaja^{i}ja aja aja^{i}ja
tuŋnᴇriʃuŋᴀrivᴀra
tu·^{v}ka^{v}nik

ajaja^{i}ja aja aja^{i}ja
ajaja^{i}ja aja aja^{i}ja
tautuŋ·uᴀrpäk·iga
avatᴀra ꜱᴇrqisᴀ·ratätlarmät
tautuŋ·uᴀrpäk·iga
ajäp·ᴇriᴀriätlarmät

ajaja^{i}ja aja aja^{i}ja
ajaja^{i}ja aja aja^{i}ja
ajaja^{i}ja aja aja^{i}ja
tulɔrsa·talᴇrmago
aksɔruku·lᴀ·rpᴀra

(awiŋakuluŋmik
pit·ɔrqutᴇqalʌ·rmän)
ajaja^{i}ja aja aja^{i}ja
ajaja^{i}ja aja ája^{i}ja
tʌrqatigigamiuk ima
tuŋnᴇriʃuŋʌrivʌra
aŋu^{w}ik·a^{v}nikle·
ajaja^{i}ja aja aja^{i}ja
ajaja^{i}ja aja aja^{i}ja
anᴇrsʌ·qʌrpām·ata
avaklivun piʒamiŋnik
ajaja^{i}ja aja aja^{i}ja
ajaja^{i}ja aja aja^{i}ja
ajaja^{i}ja aja aja^{i}ja

This hunting song can however, be directly translated without comment beyond the two parenthetical passages inserted by Aua out of consideration for "the white men". The first of these passages merely indicates that the object of the chase was a walrus, which, he states, need not have been explained to his fellow-countrymen, as it would be apparent from the song itself. The second interpolation tells us that the amulet belonging to the hunting float was a lemming; this explanation likewise would be superfluous to an Eskimo audience, as a lemming is the regular amulet for hunting floats. The translation then runs as follows, save that the refrain ajaja^{i}ja aja aja^{i}ja, incessantly repeated for the sake of the melody, and otherwise only chosen as easily vocalised words, is here omitted. These words alone however, can work up the chorus to full pitch when constantly repeated, and all can join in. And thus general participation, where everyone present can feel, as it were, a part of the song itself, is perhaps what makes it possible for a song festival to go on for many hours without anyone growing tired.

I could not sleep,
For the sea lay so smooth
near at hand.
So I rowed out,
and a walrus came up
close beside my kayak.
It was too near to throw,
And I thrust the harpoon into its side,
and the hunting float bounded over the water.
But it kept coming up again
And set its flippers angrily
like elbows on the surface of the water,
trying to tear the hunting float to pieces.
In vain it spent its utmost strength,
for the skin of an unborn lemming

was sewn inside as a guardian amulet,
and when it drew back, blowing viciously,
to gather strength again,
I rowed up and stabbed it
With my lance.
And this I sing
because the men who dwell
south and north of us here
fill their breathing with self-praise.

Bear song.

The following song is typical of the indirect method, where the poet takes it for granted that the situation referred to is known in all its details, and therefore contents himself with throwing out a few words to the chorus, who then, steadily repeating a refrain, allow their own imagination to work on the theme. Anyone not familiar with the underlying idea of this poetic brevity would be quite unable to understand the meaning, and may then, like a wellknown whaling captain, otherwise fully acquainted with the language and customs of these people, form the impression that the text is a kind of poetic riddle-me-re.

tautuŋuᴀrpăk·ivᴀra
nanɔralik
kiglimile·
ajaja^{i}ja aja aja^{i}ja
ajaja^{i}ja aja aja^{i}ja
ᴇrsisạ·ŋ·uăŋ·iŋmăt
saŋuniᴀrniniuna
akuŋniŋin·ᴀriƀlugo
ajaja^{i}ja aja aja^{i}ja
ajaja^{i}ja aja aja^{i}ja
tᴀrqatigigamiŋa
tuŋnᴇrʃuŋᴀrivᴀra
aŋu^{w}ik·a^{v}nikle·
ajaja^{i}ja aja aja^{i}ja
ajaja^{i}ja aja aja^{i}ja
ᴇrqasuŋᴀrsin·ᴀrpᴀra
anᴇrsᴀ·qᴀrpäm·ata
avaklivun.

Literally translated, the meaning is as follows:

It chanced that I caught sight of
one wearing the skin of a bear
out in the drifting pack ice.
ajaja^{i}ja aja aja^{i}ja.
It came not threateningly.
Turning about
was the only thing that seemed to hamper it.
ajaja^{i}ja aja aja^{i}ja.

It wore out its strength against me,
And I thrust my lance
into its body.
ajaja^{i}ja aja aja^{i}ja.
ajaja^{i}ja aja aja^{i}ja.
I call this to mind
Merely because they are ever breathing self-praise,
Those neighbours of ours to the south and to the north.

I asked Aua to give me an explanation of the actual event which forms the theme of this song, and he told the story as follows:

He was out one day hunting walrus with his brother Ivaluardjuk, when they caught sight of a huge bear, a male. It came forward at once to attack them, running at full speed, looking delighted at the prospect of fresh meat, almost like a cheerful dog that comes running up at a gallop, wagging its tail. And so assured did it seem of the inferiority of its prey that it appeared quite annoyed at having to take the trouble of turning when Aua sprang aside. And now commenced a hunt that lasted the whole day. Ivaluardjuk·had clambered up to a ridge of ice and was shouting at the top of his voice to frighten the bear away. So swift and fierce was the bear in its movements that Aua was unable to harpoon it, while Aua himself was so agile that the bear could not get at him. At last the great fat bear became so exhausted that it sat down in the snow, growling like a little puppy in a nasty temper. Then Aua ran up and thrust his lance into its heart. Ivaluardjuk stood up on his ridge of ice a little distance from the scene of the combat and waved his arms delightedly. He was so hoarse with shouting that he could no longer speak.

This is the hunting episode of which the song treats. It has been related so often that Aua can make do with but the briefest reference in his text to the course of events. At my request, he filled in the gaps so as to give the action in full, the result being as follows:

tautuŋuᴀrpäkˑivᴀra
nanɔralik
kiglimileˑ
ᴇrsisaˑŋˑuàŋˑiŋmät
qiŋmizut
unazutut paŋaliŋmaŋa
qilamik ᴀqajäktuˑtigiumaƀluŋa
saŋuniᴀrniniuna
akuŋniŋinˑᴀriƀluƀlugo
pikʃilᴀˑrama
aˑmakitaujualᴀrpuguk
uvlaˑmin u^{w}alimun
tᴀrquatigigamiŋa
uŋnᴇrisuŋᴀrivᴀra
aŋu^{w}ikˑamikleˑ

I sighted a bear
On the drifting ice,
It seemed like a harmless dog
That came running towards me gladly,
So eager was it to eat me up on the spot,
That it swung round angrily
when I swiftly sprang aside out of its way.
And now we played catch-as-catch can
From morning to late in the day.
But by then it was so wearied
It could do no more,
And I thrust my lance into its side.

Another song was even more fragmentary, the text being spun out into incessant repetitions, with the customary refrain of aja^{i}ja; in its original form, as Aua sang it for me the first time, it ran as follows:

Caribou Hunting.

aja^{i}ja^{i}ja aja aja^{i}ja^{i}ja aja
misikʃa^{i}giga
ajaja^{i}ja aja
ajaja^{i}ja aja
natᴇʀɴᴀʀmiutᴀq
ajaja^{i}ja ajã
misikʃa^{i}gigale
ajaja^{i}ja aja
pᴇʀaläktik·ig̣a·
ajaja^{i}ja.

All unexpected I came and took by surprise
The heedless dweller of the plains,
All unexpected I came and took by surprise
The heedless dweller of the plains,
And I scattered the herd
In headlong flight.

— — —

I now begged Aua to give me the song in detail, and it then ran as follows:

I came creeping along over the marsh
With bow and arrows in my mouth.
The marsh was broad and the water icy cold,
And there was no cover to be seen.
Slowly I wriggled along,
Soaking wet, but crawling unseen
Up within range.
The caribou were feeding, carelessly nibbling the
juicy moss,

Until my arrow stood quivering, deep
In the chest of the bull.
Then terror seized the heedless dwellers of the
plain.
The herd scattered apace,
And trotting their fastest, were lost to sight
Behind sheltering hills.

— — —

Of course it is by no means all songs that are abbreviated in the text. It is done occasionally, because this also is reckoned something of a gift, to be able to convey the essence of a great event by the slightest indication. Finally, there is also the self-consciousness of the great hunter, underlying the view that one's adventures are so generally known that there is no need to describe them in detail. Accompanied by the weird rumble of the drum, one then flings out now and again, between repetitions of the stirring aja[i]ja, such simple words as:

"All unexpected I came and took by surprise the heedless!"

The voice is raised and lowered in accord with the melody:

"All unexpected I came and took by surprise the heedless!"

The dancer and singer suits the movements of his body to the steadily increasing force of the chorus:

"All unexpected I came and took by surprise the heedless!"

And at last all believe they are themselves taking part in the happenings described.

— — —

I have already mentioned that the qaɢ·iʃut as a rule celebrated their festivals standing in a circle, with the men inside and the women outside, and in the middle the leading singer, called qila·uʃᴀrtɔq: "the one that beats the drum". Sometimes, when the qaɢ·e is big enough, the participants will, especially among the Iglulingmiut, arrange themselves in such a fashion that the women kneel in a circle on the large raised platform of snow, while the men stand up out on the floor. The men awaiting their turn for dance and song stand innermost in the circle, nearest the one performing, who is called mumᴇrtɔq. Every wife must know her husband's songs, for the woman is supposed to be the man's memory. The mumᴇrtɔq will therefore often content himself with flinging out a few lines of the text, while his wife leads the chorus. A woman thus conducting the performance of her husband's productions is called iᵥᵥɳᴇrtɔq: the chorus being termed iɳiɔrtut. A man without a wife, in other words, a singer with no one to take this important part, simply stands erect and sings his words.

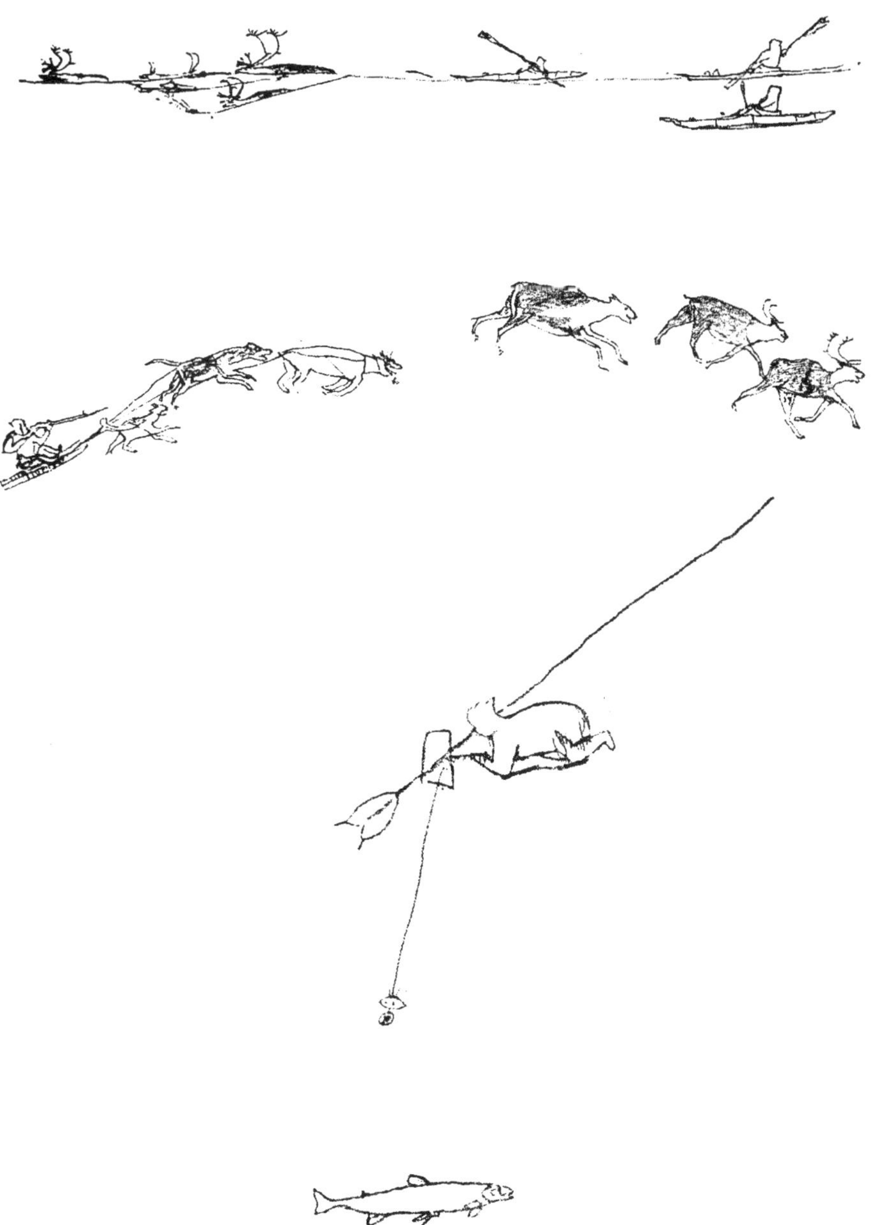

Above: Caribou, swimming over a river, hunted from the kayak. — Middle: Caribou-hunting from dog sledge. — Below: Trout-fishing with the leister through a hole in the ice.

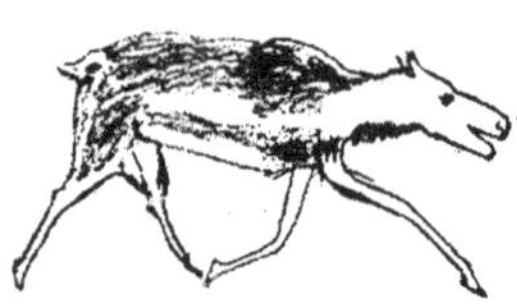

Caribou hunt. Drawn by Usuglâq.

He is called iʷŋe·nᴀrtɔq: one who only sings. The nearest rendering of iʷŋᴇrpɔq is: utters his thoughts in song.

On the evening when any man of the village gives a banquet and festival in the qaɡ·e, the following cry is used to call the people together: "qaɡ·iava·, qaɡ·iava·", this is shouted about the place until all have heard.

Many remarkable customs are associated with song festivals in the qaɡ·e. I will give some further particulars of a few of the most characteristic, which, though known among the Aivilingmiut, belong more especially to the Iglulingmiut, where there are always many people together and an abundance of walrus meat.

There was the tivaju·t. When an ordinary qaɡ·e festival had taken place, and all those who so desired had sung their songs, the snow platform was pulled down and thrown out. Two men would then dress up, hidden from the inquisitive in one of the houses near by, one as a man, the other as a woman, and both wearing masks of skin. The idea was to make the masked figures appear as comical as possible. The woman's dress would be drawn in tight wherever it should ordinarily be loose and full, as for instance the large baggy kamiks, the big hood and the broad shoulder pieces; the dress in itself should also be too small. The same principle was observed in the case of the man's costume, which was barely large enough for him to get it on at all. The man dressed as a woman should have an anautᴀq, or snowbeating stick, in his hand, that is, a stick used for beating or brushing snow from one's garments; the male figure should carry a te·ᵍᴀrut, or short dog whip. Finally, the "man" should have fastened in the crutch a huge penis, grotesque in its effect, fashioned either of wood or of stuffed intestines.

In the middle of the qaɡ·e, from which the platform has now been removed, two blocks of snow are set out, one about the height of a man, the other half as high. These blocks should be roughly squared. The lower of the two snow pillars is called atᴇrᴀrtᴀrwik: the jumping block, the higher is called quᵈlᴇqᴀrwik: the lamp block.

As soon as the necessary preparations have been made, all the men and women assemble in the qaɡ·e, and now the two masked dancers, who are called tivaju·t, come bounding in. They are dumb performers, and may only endeavour to make themselves understood by signs, and only puff out breath between the lips and ejaculate "pust, pust" exactly as if they were trying to blow something out. They come bounding in, taking great leaps through the entrance hole, and must jump over the atᴇrᴀrtᴀrwik, this also to be done whenever they re-enter after an exit. The first thing the tivaju·t now do is to chase out all the men with blows, the woman striking with her anautᴀq, the man with his te·ɡᴀrut, the women of the audience being suffered to remain behind. They then caper about, with light, adroit movements, among the women, peering everywhere to see if any man has concealed himself in their ranks. Should a man be so discovered, he is recklessly and mercilessly thrashed out of the house. As soon as the tivaju·t are sure all the men have gone, they themselves must dash out of the qaɡ‘e, to where the men are assembled in a group outside. One of these men then steps up to the tivaju·t, and with his face close to the mask, whispers with a smile the name of the woman inside the qaɡ·e, with whom he wishes to lie the coming night. The two tivaju·t then at once rush back, gaily into the qaɡ·e, go up to the woman whose name has been whispered to them outside, and touch the soles of her feet with anautᴀq and te·ɡᴀrut respectively. This is called ikuʃ·iʃut: the ones who hack out something for themselves with an axe or a big, sharp knife. Great rejoicing is now apparent among all the women, and the one woman chosen: ikut·aujɔq, goes out and comes in again with the man who has asked for her. Both are expected to look very serious; all the women in the qaɡ·e however, must be quite the reverse, laughing and joking and making fun, and trying all they can to make the couple laugh; should they succeed, however, it means a short life for the pair. The women in the qaɡ·e make faces, and murmur, in alle kinds of surprising tones: unununununun, unununun, unununun! The two who are to lie together must then solemnly and slowly and without moving a muscle of their faces, walk round the lamp block twice, while the following song is sung:

tivajo· katuma·
ata·lune
kunige·cialaɳmᴀriga·
mamᴀri·̣cialaɳmᴀriga·
kisume·tɔq kan·a
a·t·ɔrtaile manᴇrmit·ɔq
kan·a a·t·ɔrtaile
tivajo· tivajo·, tivajo· tivajo·.

The words of this song are difficult to translate literally, but the following rather free rendering comes nearest to the sense as given by Orulo:

Masquerader,
teasing, capering Dancer-in-a-mask,
Twist yourself round and kiss yourself behind,
you will find it very sweet.
Give him gifts,
dried moss for lamp wicks,
masquerader, masquerader,
teasing, capering Dancer-in-a-mask!

While this song is being sung, the two maskers stand facing each other and making all manner of lascivious and grotesque gestures; now and again the man strikes his great penis with his te'gArut, and the woman strikes it with her anautAq, and then they pretend to effect a coition standing up. This is intended partly to demonstrate the joys of sexual intercourse, and partly also to elicit a laugh from the couple walking round the lamp block. The game is carried on throughout the evening, until all the men and woman have been paired off, the party then dispersing, each man leading home to his own house the woman he has chosen.

Another favourite game was tɔrlɔrtut. When two song cousins met at a village, and one of them wished to challenge his iglɔq to a song contest, he would very secretly approach all the other men in the place, so that his iglɔq should have no idea of what was going on. Then in the evening, all would pretend to retire to rest as usual, but a watch would be kept over the house of the man to be challenged. As soon as it was known for certain that he was asleep, all the rest would get up, and, armed with their dog whips and snow beaters, steal up to his house and suddenly, with wild howlings and a terrible commotion, wake the sleeper by beating on the roof. This meant that there was to be a contest on the following evening in the qaɢ'e.

Another festival, only celebrated when there are many people, is called qulungErtut. It opens with a challenge between two iglɔre'k, first to all manner of contests out in the open, and ending with a song contest in the qaɢ'e. The two rivals, each with a knife, embrace and kiss each other as they meet. The women are then divided into two parties. One party has to sing a song, a long, long song which they keep on repeating; meantime, the other group stand with uplifted arms waving gulls' wings, the object being to see which side can hold out the longer. Here is a fragment of the song that is sung on this occasion:

See, they come,
gaily dressed in new fur garments,
women, women, youthful women.
See, with mittens on their hands,
gulls' wings they are holding high,
and the long, loose-flapping coat tails
wave with every swaying motion.
Here are women, youthful women,
No mistaking when they stride
forth to meet the men awaiting
prize of victory in the contest.

The women of the losing party then had to "stride" over to the others, who surrounded them in a circle, when the men had to try to kiss them.

After this game an archery contest was held. A target was set up on a long pole, and the one who first made ten hits was counted the winner. Then came ball games and fierce boxing bouts. In these, it was permissible to soften the effect of the blows by wearing a fur mitten with the fur inside. The combatants had to strike each other first on the shoulders, then in the eyes or on the temples, and in spite of the glove, it was not unusual for a collarbone to be broken, or for a blow in the face to do serious damage. I have at any rate seen a man who had had one eye knocked out in the course of one of these tests of strength and manliness. After all these sporting events, which in the respective games required the two iglɔre·k to be unceasingly up to the mark and to show themselves at their very best, the conelusion took place in the qaɡ·e, where the two rivals had again to finish off their duel by a song contest lasting as a rule the whole night.

Apart from these festive customs more or less associated with the qaɡ·e, there were also the numerous kinds of games which, at any rate in the more cheerful villages, were practised not only by children but also by adults of all ages. Persons playing a game are called qitiktut.

Greatly in favour were the gymnastic exercises with sealskin thongs stretched across the room, either in the qaɡ·e or in an ordinary dwelling. This was called akluŋᴇrtᴀrtut: those who played with thongs. The thongs were made fast by cutting holes through the wall of the snow hut and attaching the ends of the hide to sticks placed across outside. With these strips of hide, which were not very thick, and therefore cut into arms and legs with painful effect, exercises in strength and agility were performed, resembling in many ways our Reck exercises. I would here refer to Pakak's illustrations, which are an attempt at showing how these were carried out.

But then, besides all this, there were the real games. When the day's work was done, and the young hunters came home from their various expeditions, all those who were of a lively temperament would assemble out on the ice or on a piece of smooth ground behind the houses, if on land, and here the games would be played, preferably in the twilight or in the evening by moonlight. The following are some of the most common:

amᴀru ʝᴀ rtut: the wolf game.

First, all form up in a long line and at a given signal run each to the place where he wishes to stand. The object is to pass a certain goal, a hole in the snow or a pole set up, or something of the sort;

the one who is last to pass the spot has to be the wolf. The wolf has now to run after all the others, and every time he catches any one must touch him either on the neck or at the waist up under the tunic, but always on the bare skin; to touch the dress does not count. The moment the wolf touches one of the others he must say: u^{w}iniɡɔrᴀra: "I have touched his skin" and the one so touched is then wolf in his turn. And so the game goes on until all have been wolf.

a·mákitaujuᴀrnᴇq: "Touch".

This is often played by children. It is precisely the ordinary game as we know it, the object being merely for one to run after and touch another. In doing so, he cries "a·mak", and hence the name a·makitaujuᴀrnᴇq, which means "to say a·mak to one another".

anauliɡᴀ·rnᴇq: Rounders.

There is also a ball game in which the players endeavour to run certain marked distances set out in a square, with stops only allowed at the corners, a kind of rounders. There are two sides, one first throwing the ball to one of the other side, who strikes at it with a kind of bat. Having struck the ball, the striker has to run from one place of safety to another without being hit; thus one player after another runs in turn. As soon as one of a side is hit by one of the other, they change over, the batting side handing the bat to the others.

at·aujᴀ·rnᴇq.

The players divide into two sides, which, however, do not form up in separate groups, but mingle together. One side has the ball, and throws to those of the same side, the other players trying to take the ball from them. At every throw, there is a wild scrimmage, the object all through being for one side to get the ball from the other.

ijᴇrᴀ·rnᴇq: Hide-and-seek.

One of the players hides, and the others look for him. As soon as the one in hiding is found, all must run after him, and the first to touch him is the next to hide. When one has gone into hiding, the rest cry: "ilak kuk·umiᴀrit": "comrade, utter a sound". The one in hiding must then whistle, and should as often as possible change his hiding place and whistle again, so as to deceive the others as to his position.

qimuksiŋ·uArnEq.

Children find a small piece of wood and make of it a little sledge; then all their companions come and are harnessed to it, or more correctly, pretend to be harnessed. The boy on the sledge then pretends to whip his dogs. This is called: Driving the sledge.

am·iArmE·rtArnEq.

Children select a small hill and slide down it on a skin, a piece of sealskin or caribou skin. If the hill is steep enough, they simply lie flat face downwards, and slide down in the furs they are wearing.

pat·A·rtut.

This game is played with a ball, the player striking it up in the air again and again with one hand. The player who can keep this up for the greatest number of times without letting the ball fall to the ground is the winner, and receives a prize from the rest.

uŋa·jA·rnEq.

A child runs in to the passage way of a house, and while there, is beaten about the body by one of the others with clenched fist. The one thus beaten must then begin to run after the others. Some run into the house to escape, others run out, and the object now is to catch them in the same way as in the wolf game, by touching them on the bare body. Every time the pursuer touches one of the others, he must say "uŋa·", and at last, when he has touched every one, another takes his place and the game begins anew.

tArquᵗᴶA·rnEq: The moon game.

Children form up in a long line. The one who is to be moon takes another player, and the pair place themselves a little distance from the rest. Some of those in the line now move off, pretending to search for fuel. As they pass by the one playing moon, they must pretend not to see him, and try to carry off the child. When the latter resists, they must cry out: "ana·luk, ana·luk" (an excrement). When they then add: "A piece of caribou suet, a piece of caribou suet" the child consents, and goes off with them. Thus they take the child with them, and hide it behind those in the line. The moon now suddenly discovers that its child is gone, and must then say: "But where is my child gone?"

He goes off in search of the child, and must pick up all the pieces of dogs' dirt he sees on the ground and rub them over his belly and hindquarters, then smell them and throw them away, and leaping high in the air, exclaim once more: "But where is my child gone?"

Then he comes up to those in the line, and sniffing at them, says: "Of course he has been enticed away with caribou suet and dainty eyes and tongue. What did you have it in?"

"A piece of a mitten."

"What did he use for a knife?"

"A piece of flint."

The one playing moon must now strike those in the line, tread on their feet and kick at them, saying:

"What is it making all that noise over there?"

Then those in the line answer: "Dogs."

And then they all begin saying "miam, miam, miam" and pretending to eat the child. The one playing moon now asks the child: "Who was the first one that took you?" And the child answers: "That one there". And now the moon begins to go for the others in earnest, trying to frighten them, and every time he gets hold of one, tickles him and ill-treats him as hard as he can. The game ends when he has gone the whole way round.

A·RA·rneq.

A party of children join hands and form up in a circle, crying: "A·Ra·," repeating it again and again. When they have stood thus for a time, one of the players attempts to break out of the circle, the rest doing all they can to prevent it. If one succeeds in breaking away, he must run over to two other children, standing some distance from the group, hand in hand, and try to force himself in between these two; should he succeed, one of the pair thus divided must strike him, saying: "umiAq" a skin boat, and after a pause, adding: "May you have the strength of a wolverine!"

The next time one comes up to the pair standing hand in hand a little way from the group, the same process is repeated. They must say "umiAq" to the one who joins their group, but this time, after striking him, they must add: "May you have the strength of a wolf." And so the game goes on, with wolf and wolverine alternately. When this has gone all round, wolves and wolverines fight, two and two but the pair that stood holding hands, and named the others wolf and wolverine respectively, are now themselves called grandmothers, and must cry out: "Wolverines, use your strength, wolves, use your strength." They now fight and keep on until one side wins.

ArʃArnEq.

A piece of caribou skin is filled with all manner of articles, giving it the shape of a big ball, and sewn up; it is then played with as follows:

The players take sides, with the passage way of a house for goal on either side. The side that kicks the ball into the other's goal wins. Next day the game is resumed, the losers of the day before endeavouring to make matters even.

täta·ujA·rnEq: Blind man's buff.

The players are assembled in the qaɡ·e, and the one to be blindfolded is given a blow to start off with. He must then at once close his eyes so that he can see nothing, and then endeavour to touch the others; on touching anyone, he strikes him in the same way as he himself was struck at first and may then open his eyes. The player caught must then be blind man, and so the game goes on.

kaluErtArtut: Skipping rope.

Two players take a sealhide thong, one holding each end, and swing it, a third trying to jump over and under.

avatAq.

An inflated sealing float is used for this, with a line attached at either end, and swung round in the same way as the skipping rope, the players trying to jump over and under.

inuɡArnEq.

The player collects the knuckle bones from the flippers of a seal, shakes them in one hand and drops them. Each bone is named after a man, and the man whose name-bones stand on end when thrown will be lucky in hunting.

sa·qat·Aq.

A mug or dipper with a handle, such as is used for water, is taken and twirled round, the players sitting about in a circle. The one to whom the handle points when it stops must hand out some article belonging to him. Next time the handle points, the player indicated picks up the article deposited by the first, forfeiting something of his own instead. And so the game goes on.

*nuglukt*ᴀ*q.*

A piece of bone with a small hole in it is hung from the roof and swung backwards and forwards. Each player has a thin stick and tries to thrust it into the hole as the bone passes before him. The first to do so must pay a forfeit, which is claimed by the next to succeed, and so on as in the previous game.

*iglukit*ᴀ*·rut.*

The player takes two, three or four pebbles, and juggles with them, singing the following song:

qulukpa· qulukpai
tun·it tun·it tun·e·t
aja[i]jᴀrujuɳ·ne· aja[i]jᴀrujuɳ·ne·
kam·aɳ-ukua put·atlᴀrtᴇrute·ɳ
auɳmiɳ tᴀrtautiⱼuɳ, tᴀrtalat·iuɳ
alᴇqāmauna siu[w]aliut,
anᴀrnicualukʒuaq
u[w]a·tale u[w]a·tale u[w]a·tale;
alᴇqāciᴀra piɳasuniɳ
u[w]aɳale ataucimiɳ
kak·e·k·ak najɔrtuᴀri[w]ak·ak
imᴇrpak·a, imᴇrpak·a ajai ajai
kitutle aɳagigaluᴀrpagit?
a·ija[i]lu·t·ik·ut qatlᴀrialinik·ut
nigāƀjulik·ut te·[ɢ]ᴀrutik·ut
sun·iala·k·ut nu[w]uk·ut
ajija· aja·ja· ajija aja!

The text is incoherent and almost untranslatable. It is recited or sung very rapidly, to make the juggling more difficult; I give here the untranslatable portions in the original, and a literal rendering of the remainder:

"Qulukpa· qulukpai
Tattoo marks, tattoo marks, tattoo marks
— Little children, little children —
They make one's anger overflow,
They make the blood swell in the veins,
My elder sister was the first,
A big one that smelt of dirt,
u[w]a·tale u[w]a·tale u[w]a·tale
My little elder sister had three
I had one,
my elder sister two
I one,
I sniffed up the dirt from my nose and swallowed it,
I drank it, I drank it, ajai, ajai.

Whore are your mother's brothers?
Are they a·ijalu·te or qatlʌrianilik?
Are they nigäbjulik or te·gʌrut?
Are they sun·ialʌ·q or nuʷuk?
ajija· aja·ja· ajija aja!

qäcipʌ·q.

Two little girls jump up and down keeping time together, and sing:

a·jäŋaja·-a a·jäŋaja·-a
a·jäŋaja·jäŋaja·jäŋaja·
tukliliutik·ik qailak·it
ʌrnʌqatiʃautiginiʌrapkit
a·jäŋaja·-a a·jäŋaja·-a
a·jäŋaja·jäŋaja·jäŋaja·

Bring hither your wooden hair ornament,
I will deck myself with it,
To make me look like a real woman,
a·jäŋaja·-a
etc.

This song also is sung very rapidly, the singers jumping up and down and bending the knees to the full each time.

These are briefly the games specially played by children and women. In good seasons, when game is plentiful and parties remain for a long time at one place, the women will, unlike the men, have very little exercise, and it is therefore not a mere coincidence that nearly all the games include some form of gymnastic activity. Thus nature regulates itself at all times, and the people keep themselves in health and good spirits by means of pastimes which in a pleasant and festive manner fill the space about the houses with merry cries and laughter.

There is also an Eskimo proverb which says that those who know how to play can easily leap over the adversities of life. And one who can sing and laugh never brews mischief.

XI.

Folk Tales and Myths.

Old men and women among the Iglulingmiut and Aivilingmiut, remember but few of the common Eskimo folk tales as compared with many other tribes; this is due to the fact that their interest in the stories is not particularly great, thanks to certain "modern" views which they have acquired through intercourse with white men. There were at any rate no professional story-tellers among them, such as we find in Greenland, where there are still persons who live during winter by telling stories to shorten the long nights for their fellows. The stories were narrated in a naive and incoherent fashion, so that it was often difficult to follow the plot. Often they could not understand that anyone should not have heard all their stories before, and would therefore have no hesitation about starting off in the middle of a tale, or leaving out whole episodes which they themselves considered uninteresting.

In writing down these folk tales, I received very valuable assistance from Jacob Olsen, and as a rule, none was written down until we both knew it and had heard it several times, preferably from different sources. But once we had got hold of the action and details of the story, we could check the version given by any particular story-teller, and the Eskimo text was then written down from his own dictation. The translations follow as closely as possible the original text.

Through the medium of these folk tales, children and adults learn of the events concerning which any tradition has been preserved, and which have become myths forming part of the life of the tribe. They are always regarded as history, and as referring to actual happenings which once took place. Little will be needed in the way of commentary to these tales, and only in the case of those which the Eskimos themselves regard as belonging to the very earliest chapters of their history. Otherwise, a brief introduction will suffice, similar to that given in my previous collections of folk tales and myths from Greenland. Stories known in Greenland are marked with a (G) in brackets. As soon as the collections from all the different tribes have been published, a general survey will be given, in the last volume, showing how the same story is repeated in the different districts.

Earliest history of earth and mankind.

With regard to the creation, there is not, as for instance among the Polar Eskimos of North Greenland or the Eskimos of Alaska, any detailed tradition preserved. When questioned on the subject, the natives will generally answer that they know nothing about the creation of the earth; they know it simply at it is and as they have seen it for themselves. One old shaman, however, Unaleq, was able to give the following account, which was subsequently found to be generally known also among the Iglulingmiut:

"It is said that once upon a time the world fell to pieces, and every living thing was destroyed. There came mighty downpours of rain from the heavens, and the earth itself was destroyed. Afterwards, two men appeared on earth. They came from hummocks of earth; they were born so. They were already fully grown when they emerged from the ground. They lived together as man and wife, and soon one of them was with child. Then the one who had been husband sang a magic song:

Inuk una,
usuk una
pa·tulune
nᴇrutulune
pa· pa· pa·!

A human being here
A penis here.
May its opening be wide
And roomy.
Opening, opening, opening!.

When these words were sung, the man's penis split with a loud noise and he became a woman, and gave birth to a child. From these three mankind grew to be many".

Unaleq's wife, Tûglik, gave us the following version, which she had from her great-grandmother. I include it here, although it is very much like Unaleq's, because it mentions that the earth "stands on pillars", which is in accordance with ancient Greenland traditions.

"There was once a world before this, and in it lived people who were not of our tribe. But the pillars of the earth collapsed, and all was destroyed. And the world was emptiness. Then two men grew up from a hummock of earth. They were born and fully grown all at once. And they wished to have children. A magic song changed one of them into a woman, and they had children. These were our earliest forefathers, and from them all the lands were peopled."

Light comes to mankind.

During the first period after the creation of the earth, all was darkness. Among the earliest living beings were the raven and the fox. One day they met, and fell into talk, as follows:

"Let us keep the dark and be without daylight," said the fox.

But the raven answered: „May the light come and daylight alternate with the dark of night."

The raven kept on shrieking: "qa·ᵓrɳ, qa·ᵓrɳ!" (Thus the Eskimos interpret the cry of the raven, qa·ᵓrɳ, roughly as qa·ᵓq, which means dawn and light. The raven is thus born calling for light). And at the raven's cry, light came, and day began to alternate with night.

It is said that in the days when the earth was dark, the only creatures men had to hunt were ptarmigan and hare, and these were hunted by wetting the forefinger and holding it out in the air; the finger then became luminous and it was possible to see the animal hunted.

To this account, given by Ivaluardjuk, the following was added by Inugpasugjuk, who however, was a Netsilingmio:

When men had only earth for food.

"In the very earliest times, it was very difficult for men to hunt. They were not such skilful hunters as those who live now. They had not so many hunting implements, and had not the pleasure of abundant and varied food that we now have. When I was a child, I heard old people say that once, long long ago, men ate of the earth. Our forefathers ate of the earth; when they halted on a journey and camped, they worked at the soil with picks made of caribou horn, breaking up the earth and searching for food. That was in the days when it was a very difficult matter to kill a caribou, and it is said they had to make a single animal last all summer and autumn. Therefore they were obliged to seek other food.

"In those days, men were not clad as now, in warm caribou skins, but had to use skins of birds and foxes. So men lived in those days. In summer, when they were starting up country, they had to be content with a little unborn seal, a tiny thing too small even to be frightened away down through the mother's blow hole when people came up to it on the ice to kill it.

"In those days, earth was the principal food of man."

Where the first human beings came from cannot be stated with certainty, but the Aivilingmiut have an old tradition referring to a story current among the Qaernermiut near Baker Lake, and heard down at Aksarneq, Chesterfield Inlet:

"The first human beings came from among the Pâdlermiut (the natives living on the shores of Hikuligjuaq, or Lake Yathkyed). It was from here, up inland, that the first human beings began to come, but where they came from before they reached those parts, or how they came to be many, no one can say. All that we know is that in the olden days, mankind did not multiply so rapidly as now, it was a very long time before there were many, and therefore the earth itself had to help:

Earth gives the first men their children.

It is said that in very ancient times, in the earliest ages, women were often unable to have children. And when people were out on a journey and settled at a place, one might see them going round about the camping ground, bending down and searching about in the earth. It is said that in that way they sought for children from the earth, the children of earth. And with the children they found on the ground it was in this wise: a long search was needed to find boys, but one had not to go far to find girls. Not all however, were equally lucky. Some found only girls, perhaps because they would not take the trouble to go far, being lazy, but those who were not afraid of walking, those who were not lazy, they had sons. As soon as a child was found on the ground, it was picked up at once and put in the amaut, and carried off home. The women who came home with children they had found, observed precisely the same taboo and the same rules as those who had themselves given birth to a child, and were similarly regarded as unclean. They were given a birth hut of snow, or if it happened in summer, a small tent, and there they stayed for the time prescribed after childbirth, during which the woman must live apart from her husband, and they were treated exactly as if they had borne children of their own flesh and blood. Some found children very easily, others found none, however much they sought about.

Thus the earth gave the first people their children, and in that way they grew to be many.

Told by
Ivaluardjuk.

When it had grown light on earth, human beings lived in the same way as they do now. They lived by pursuing game, and chose for preference places where there was abundance of game. It was far easier then to move from one place to another than it is now, for every house had its own particular inua, its own spirit, which, when the household wished to move to another place, shifted the whole house with all the people in it and all their household goods, away to the spot where they wished to be. And in regard to this is the following story:

When houses were alive.

One night a house suddenly rose up from the ground and went floating through the air. It was dark, and it is said that a swishing, rushing noise was heard as it flew through the air. The house had not yet reached the end of its road when the people inside begged it to stop. So the house stopped.

They had no blubber when they stopped. So they took soft, freshly drifted snow and put in their lamps, and it burned.

They had come down at a village. A man came in to their house and said:

"Look, they are burning snow in their lamps. Snow can burn."

But the moment these words were uttered, the lamp went out.

This happened in the days when the houses had spirits and were alive, and would move with all the people in them from one hunting ground to another. In those days, people out on hunting expeditions could also burn soft, freshly drifted snow.

Told by
Inugpasugjuk.

The first human beings had no kayaks for hunting caribou on the lakes, nor had they umiᴀqs as up at Tununeq, for voyaging on the sea and hunting off the coast. All they could do then was to sit on an inflated skin, when they wanted to cross a piece of water. We have knowledge of this from an old story, which runs as follows:

When inflated sealskins served as boats.

Eqivdlertuarjuk and Qungasinaitjoq were two old men, and they were friends. One day they sat together telling each other stories, and the talk turned on those old times when men were wont to make boats of inflated skins. The two old men grew more and more excited as they talked, and then they began to compete with each other as to which of them could make the better boat out of an inflated skin. They took a sealskin tent, sewed it up and blew it full of air, and when that was done, they set it out into the water. They now wished to have their wives with them, and took them on board the inflated sealskin and sailed away. They paddled round the island of Iglorjuartalik, south of Tajarneq (Beach Point). When they had rounded the point, they rowed on further southward to another point of land called Suloraq. Here they set their wives on shore, and the women walked on along the beach, while the men paddled ahead to Petigtorjik. They were not far from land when suddenly their boat sprang a leak, and they came near to sinking. The waves closed over Eqivdlertuarjuk's white beard, and he sank. But Qungasinaitjoq caught hold of the tail of a dog they had with them, and it swam with him in to shore, and so he was saved.

Inflated skins were good boats in those days when no other craft were known.

Told by

Inugpasugjuk.

It is believed that the different kinds of people are descended from the woman who was married to a dog. From her come the Indians in the woods, and the white men who come in the great ships. There are also some who believe that the iJErqät, the mountain spirits, which occupy all countries, are descended from the dog-children of that girl. No one can say anything with certainty; it is simply said that mankind did not grow to be many until after a girl had married a dog and later went down to the bottom of the sea and procured game for men. (This story is told under the heading of Takánakapsâluk).

Before the present Iglulingmiut and Aivilingmiut came to the land where they now live, it was inhabited by a great and strong people called Tunit. They lived in stone houses in winter, and were mighty men in all manner of hunting by sea. But they were very quarrelsome, and easily angered. At first the tribes lived peaceably together down by the coast, but the Tunit were too easily angered, and were at last driven out of the country.

Tunit, the strong folk and lovers of women.

It is said that the Tunit had many villages at Uglit near Iglulik. They lived in houses built of stone and the bones of whales. They were strong folk, skilful in hunting by sea. They hunted the walrus with a long harpoon line and a short one. When they had harpooned a walrus with the short line, they gave it a jerk, and so strong were they, that this broke the creature's neck.

A walrus hauled up on the ice was dragged home just like an

Musk-ox hunt. Drawn by Usugtâq.

ordinary fjord seal, by thongs fastened to its body; so strong were those men. Their hunting grounds were far away from their houses, and it might therefore happen that they felt tired when at last they approached their houses with one of these walrus in tow. When they were at the extremity of weariness, the women would come out of the houses, and these Tunit, who loved their womenfolk, were so rejoiced at seeing them outside the houses, that they forgot their weariness in a moment, and with renewed strength dragged the walrus up to the houses.

The Tunit were a strong people, and yet they were driven from their villages by others who were more numerous, by many people of great ancestors; but so greatly did they love their country, that when they were leaving Uglit, there was a man who, out of desperate love for his village, harpooned the rocks with his harpoon and made the stones fly about like bits of ice.

Told by
Ivaluardjuk.

Life and events in the days when all sorts of unbelievable things might happen.

Whenever I talked with Ivaluardjuk or his brother Aua about their views of life and human beings, they were very fond of referring to the folk tales when there was anything they could not explain, for "Those stories were made when all unbelievable things could happen". They would also take the events of the stories as examples showing how everything recoils on oneself if one does not try to be good to one's fellow. The folk-tales therefore not only give an idea of the Eskimo moral code, but, viewed in the same light as themselves afford likewise a reflection of their feelings, of what they admire and what they despise or condemn. They love strength and fearlessness, helpfulness and kindliness. We should be kind one to another; cruelty not only hurts the person ill-treated, but recoils upon the doer. Nothing is more certain than Nemesis. This is illustrated in the three following stories:

The girl who became a land bear.

There were once a man and his wife who had three daughters, two grown-up daughters and a little tiny girl. They lived happily together until it happened that the father, for no reason, began to starve his eldest daughter, who was now of an age to be married. This took place after all the other people of the village had gone off on a hunting expedition, and the father with his wife and children were left alone in the village. The neighbours on setting out had left their snow huts empty, and the father shut up his grown-up daughter in one of these, and kept her there without food.

Her mother and the two younger sisters wished to help her, but could find no way to do it. Whenever the imprisoned daughter slipped out and tried to get in to the others, her father drove her out into the empty, cold and deserted snow hut, without giving her sleeping rugs to lie on, for he wanted her to freeze to death, so that he should not have the trouble of keeping her. He closed up the entrance so that she could not get out; and to make it thoroughly cold inside, the father made an opening up in the roof, through which the cold came in, so that the hut could not even be warmed the least little bit by the heat of her body. But as it happened, the girl lived all the same. She suffered from cold, suffered so that she was near to perishing, and that was not surprising since there was no lamp in the snow hut; but all the same she did not die. One day her younger sisters came over to the hut and stood outside to hear how she was, and the girl inside spoke to them as follows:

"Say I will not die, I cannot freeze to death; ask then if I might not as well be allowed to come home to you. Hair is growing on my calves and hands, hair like that of an animal."

The two sisters went home and told their father and mother, but the father nevertheless would not give her leave to come home. So the two sisters went back to the snow hut, and once more the girl inside said to them:

"I am turning into a land bear, therefore I cannot die. The hair is growing on my body. Do let me come home and be with you. I feel ashamed at the thought of becoming a land bear. In order that I should not die of cold, hair has now grown all over my body."

But the father was implacable. At last hair began to grow on her face as well, and then she called her mother over to the snow hut, and the mother and the two sisters went over to the snow hut and stood close to the hole in the roof, and the girl inside talked to them, till the mother wept and the two little sisters wept.

The elder of the two little sisters, who used to come over to the snow hut to hear how it fared with their sister who was shut up inside, had some skin stretchers (small wooden sticks used for stretching out skins) and these she kept in a small skin bag. Now the imprisoned girl talked to this sister and said:

„Soon I shall run away up into the hills, because I have turned into a land bear, and should I now come after you, all you have to do is to thrust these sticks into the ground so as to form a ring. Once inside that ring you will be safe, and I shall not be able to hurt you."

Night came, and all slept. Next morning, when it was light, a deep growling was heard outside, and one could hear an animal gnawing with great teeth at something hard. It was the imprisoned girl, who had turned into a land bear, and was now burrowing a way out of the hut. Then the others hurriedly set to work, the wicked father and the mother and the two sisters. They loaded up their sledges, harnessed their dogs, and as soon as they were ready, they drove off. The land bear was then so far out through the wall of the hut that one could see its chest. The father bade his wife run in front of the dogs, and the wife ran in front of the dogs; they followed the sledge tracks. The father had stayed behind to fetch something, and before he had time to get away, the land bear flung itself upon him and bit him to death. The land bear then at once looked round after more prey, sniffed at the tracks and set off in pursuit of the fugitives. The mother and the two sisters, who saw it coming, now stuck the skin-stretchers down into the snow in a circle and placed themselves inside the circle. They wept with fright when they saw the wild beast come running up; it reached the skin-stretchers, sniffed at them, but kept on running round them in a ring without going inside, and when it had done this a few times, it turned its back on them and trotted off up country as a real land bear.

Told by
Ivaluardjuk.

Be helpful to one another in time of need.

There was once a village of two houses, and in both houses there was dearth of food. When the trouble was at its worst, those in the one house caught a seal. It was the custom always to give one another gifts of meat when a catch was made, but this time, the people in the house where they had meat wished to keep the whole seal for themselves, and said therefore to their neighbours:

"We know it is not the right thing to do, but this time we are going to keep the whole seal for ourselves."

In the house where they had no meat there was an old man who was so exhausted that he could no longer rise from where he lay. He had a son, who went out every day trying to find game, but was never lucky enough to come upon any living thing. He redoubled his efforts now that they could no longer look for help from their neighbours in the other house, and he went out early in the morning and did not return until the evening. One day while he was out he espied a giant bear that had made a shelter for itself among some pressure ridges in the ice, and lay there with its cubs. He went off home at once to fetch heavier weapons than those he had with him, and made himself a huge harpoon out of a tent pole. As soon as the big harpoon was finished, he set out to try to kill the giant bear, and his father rose up from where he lay and went with him. They came to the lair, and the son at once set about making an opening in the ice from above, while his old father stood there on the ice looking on. As soon as he had made an opening, the young man thrust his harpoon down into the body of the giant bear and stabbed it again and again. The bear crawled out from its lair growling. The old man saw the bear coming at him with jaws agape, and ran straight towards it. At the same moment the bear drew in its breath, and the old man flew right down its throat. The man went right down into the belly of the bear, but slit it open as rapidly as he could with his knife; his clothes were almost boiled when he came out, and the skin was scalded off his face. He was half suffocated. Meantime the yound man stabbed the giant bear with his harpoon as often as he could get at it, and dodged in between its feet every time. Thus the giant bear was killed. This time they contented themselves with cutting off a small piece of meat, and then went to their village, and as they passed by their neighbours' house, the old man called in to them:

"Neighbours! My son has got a bear, but we will not give you any gift of meat, not even a scrap of blubber for the children!"

The old man and his son ate up the piece of meat they had brought home with them, and then they moved away from that house over to the spot where they had killed the giant bear, and built a snow hut there. They had now meat enough for the whole winter.

But their neighbours, who had not helped them with gifts of meat when they themselves had caught a seal, all starved to death.

Cruelty to animals punished in the end.

In the olden days it often happened that people gathered together to play and engage in various kinds of sport. Once the people of the village were playing ataujᴀq, a game played with a ball, in which the players must take care to keep the ball up in the air all the time and not let it fall to the ground. While they were playing, a loon came flying low close over their heads.

When the players caught sight of the loon, they shouted out loudly to frighten it. The bird was so terrified that it fell to the ground, and then one ran and picked it up before it could recover strength enough to rise, and plucked off all its feathers, leaving it bare all except the wings; then they set it free to fly away.

But the loon, having lost all its feathers, sickened and grew thin, and felt a great anger within itself.

And the winter came, and much soft snow fell, and people starved to death.

That was the loon's revenge upon those who had tormented it.

Told by
Ivaluardjuk.

Views of nature.

The splendour of the heavens.

Two men came to a hole in the sky. One asked the other to lift him up. If only he would do so, then he in turn would lend him a hand.

His comrade lifted him up, but hardly was he up when he shouted aloud for joy, forgot his comrade and ran into heaven.

The other could just manage to peep in over the edge of the hole; it was full of feathers inside. But so beautiful was it in heaven that the man who looked in over the edge forgot everything, forgot his comrade whom he had promised to help up and simply ran off in to all the splendour of heaven.

Told by
Inugpasugjuk.

The thunder girls.

There were once two young girls, both unmarried, though they were old enough to have husbands. It was a habit of theirs to stay up at night. Their father did not approve of this, and when he had scolded them, the girls ran away from their village. They lived on ptarmigan, which the older sister caught on the way, but she always divided the meat with her sister in such a manner that she herself had the breast, while the younger one had to be content with the bony part.

The little sister, who was always cheated of her share, once began singing a song of questions to her sister:

"Elder sister, elder sister,
What shall we make of ourselves?
Elder sister, elder sister,
What shall we make of ourselves?
Shall we make ourselves bears?
If we turn into bears
We can bite with our teeth if need be.
Shall we not, shall we not?

"No," answered the elder sister, and the younger said:

"I cannot satisfy my hunger with bony scraps of bird,
Those bony scraps
Are not enough for me.
What shall we make of ourselves?
Shall we turn into wolves?
Our fangs would help us then."

"No," answered the elder sister, and the younger said again:

"What shall we make of ourselves?
What shall we make of ourselves?
Shall we turn into caribou, caribou?
If we turn into caribou, then we can strike
With our antlers.
Shall we not, shall we not?"

"No," said the elder sister; and the younger then named all the animals one after another.

"What shall we be, what shall we be?
Walrus, walrus?
As walrus we could strike
with our tusks.
Shall we not, shall we not?"

"No," answered the elder sister, and again the little one said:

"I cannot satisfy my hunger
with bony scraps of bird.
Sister, Sister,
What shall we be, what shall we be?
Thunder, thunder,
Shall we be thunder?
Then we can strike
with lightning, with lightning!

"Yes!" answered her sister.

And then one of them picked up a piece of dry skin and the other a small piece of firestone (iron pyrites), and when one crumpled the stiff hide with a rattling noise, and the other struck sparks from the stone and both made water at the same time, then came thunder and lightning and rain all together.

And that is how thunder and lightning first came. To begin with, the two girls kept to the neighbourhood of their own village, but people grew afraid of them, and the shamans drove them away, and after that the two girls fled to the white men's country, where they now live; only now and then in summer do they visit their own country. They are never in want of food now, for whenever they like they can kill a caribou with lightning and eat it, and it is said that they grew to be very old.

Told by
Ivaluardjuk.

The Pleiades (u^{v}dläktut).

One evening a bear suddenly appeared in a village and the people came out to hunt it. The men harnessed their teams to the sledges, and went off in chase. A boy who was with them said:

"I have dropped my mitten of caribou skin."

The man with whom he was driving said to him:

"Well you can go and look for it by yourself. There is nothing to be afraid of, it is bright moonlight."

The boy dropped from the sledge, but as he did so, the sledge suddenly began to rise up in the air, with dogs and those in it as well.

"Where are we driving to now?" asked the man in surprise.

"Where are we driving to?" asked the other.

"We are driving right up into heaven," said others again. And the sledge with the dogs kept on rising and rising; and at last it came up to heaven, and there it turned into the u^{v}dläktut (literally, those hunting a bear).

The land bear that turned into fog.

A land bear in human form often used to come to a village and steal meat from the stores. He did this at night, while people were asleep, and therefore no one could discover it. But it happened again and again, and at last an old man hid in one of the meat stores to find out who was the thief. In the night he heard a creaking in the snow, and a little after a bear in human form came up to the spot. The man in hiding kept quiet, and took care not to breathe. The bear listened for his breathing, but as it could not hear anything, it flung him over its shoulder and carried him off.

The bear went a long distance with its burden, then laid it down on the ground again and examined it, but still found no sign of life, and so hoisted it on its shoulder again and went on. When it had gone some little way, the man caught hold of a willow twig. He was being carried head downwards. It happened so suddenly that the bear nearly fell over backwards. Again he laid down his burden, listened for his breathing, but could hear none. Then it went on again, but once more the man caught hold of a willow twig, and once more the bear nearly fell backwards. Again it examined the body, but finding no sign of life, went on again, and at last, after a long time, came in sight of a house. The bear's children came out chattering gaily to meet them, and one said:

"I will eat the hands",

the other said:

"I will have the eyes".

The bear laid the man down beside its house, and its wife came. The wife also laid her ear to the man's mouth and listened for his breathing, but as there seemed to be none, she dragged the man into the house, laid him on the floor and threw an adze on top of him. The bear's wife waited a while, expecting him to thaw, but at last she grew impatient, and snatching up her knife, tried to slit him open. But the man set his muscles hard, and the knife slipped, and the bear's wife said:

"Oh, he is frozen hard. I had better wait until he has thawed a bit more."

The land bear lay down on the bench to rest, and presently fell asleep. His wife went outside. Just then the man opened his eyes and picked up the adze. The children saw it and cried out at once:

"Our dainty morsel has opened his eyes. Look, he has opened his eyes".

"No wonder, then" said the land bear, "that he was able to make himself such a weight today. If he is alive, I can better understand it".

But now the man jumped up, grasping the adze, and slew the land bear and fled out of the house. He ran off homewards at full speed, the bear's wife after him. She was just on the point of overtaking him when the man said:

"May a ridge of mountain rise up behind me!" And at once a ridge of mountain rose up behind him as he ran, and the bear's wife had first to get over that. But it soon got across, and was again on the point of overtaking him when he said:

"May a river spring out behind me." And at once a river sprang out behind him, and the bear's wife called out to him as he ran:

"How did you manage to get across that river?"

"I chewed at it and swallowed it down!"

The bear's wife began drinking from the river, but at last she could drink no more, and turned into a real land bear again and went swimming across the river. On reaching the other side, it shook the water from its coat, but it was full of water inside as well, and when it shook itself, it burst with a loud noise and a fog spread over the country.

It is from this land bear that the fog first came.

Told by
Ivaluardjuk.
(G.)

Beast fables.

The man who travelled to the land of birds.

There was once a man who had married a wild goose. It had flown away from him, and so he wandered off alone and came to a village where there lived gulls and ravens in a double house with one entrance to the two sides.

Before we go on with the story, I must tell you that the man in this story had once been out walking when he came upon a party of young women running about and playing on the open ground without any clothes on. He saw their clothes, and stole up to them, and just as he had reached the clothes, all the women came running towards him. Now he wanted a wife, a strong wife, so he showed them a bit of line made from the hide of a bearded seal and told them to pull. He wanted to try their strength, and choose the strongest for his wife. He chose the strongest, and she became his wife. After that they lived together and had children, but one day when the autumn had come, and the wild geese were flying away, the man was left alone. He tried to follow in the same direction as the wild geese had taken, and it was thus he came to the village of gulls and ravens.

He went in to the ravens first, and they received him hospitably, and were at once eager to find him something to eat. The host said to one of the others in the house:

"You, broad-chested one, go out and fetch the breast of a bird."

The broad-chested one went out and came in with a piece of frozen dog's dirt. When the man saw that he said:

"We human beings cannot eat such stuff as that."

The raven answered:

"Kra, kra, then I will eat it myself." And it ate it.

Then the man heard a whistling noise from the other side of the house:

"Kty, kty, come in here, come in here!"

The man went in, and the gull took out a dried fish from the space under the bench. The man thought this was nice, and ate it. He slept in the gull's house, and next day went on again to find the land of the wild geese. He walked on and on for many days, and when he felt lonely, he would sing and sing of all that had happened to him:

"Far, far will I go,
Ajajai, ajajai,
Far away beyond the high hills,
Ajajai, ajajai,
Where the birds live,
Far away over yonder, far away over yonder,
Ajajai, ajajai,

A stone pot barred the way,
barred the way,
bubbling and boiling,
Only by stepping
On pieces of meat in it
Could one pass by — — —
Ajajai, ajajai.

I jumped into the pot
Set my foot on pieces of meat,
And wandered on,
Wishing to reach the land over there, beyond,
Beyond the high hills,
To the birds' land
Over yonder away,
Ajai, ajaja.

A stone pot stood there,
Barring the way,
There was no room to pass
And he who would over it
Must put in his mouth
Bits of burnt out blubber.
Ajajai, ajajai.

I ate of them greedily,
Those bits of blubber,
And on I went
Wishing to reach
The land beyond and away,
Ajaja, ajaja,
Beyond the high hills,
The birds' land
Beyond and away.
Ajajai aja.

Two pieces of rock barred the way,
Two mighty rocks,
That opened and closed
Like a pair of jaws.
There was no way past,
One must go in between them
To reach the land beyond and away,
Ajajai aja,
Beyond the high hills,
The birds' land.

Two land bears barred the way,
Two land bears fighting
And barring the way,
There was no road,
And yet I would gladly
Ajajai aja,

Pass on and away
To the farther side of the high hills,
To the birds' land,
Ajajai aja.

Thus the man sang of all that happened to him, but he overcame all obstacles, and at last one day he reached the land of birds.

And there in the village was his youngest son playing outside the house, and when he saw his father, he called in to his mother:

"I have seen Father. Father has come, Father has come.

His mother answered:

„Do not speak of your father. We left him behind far far away in another country".

But the son answered:

"Father has come, Father has come."

"Well then, try to get him to come in" answered his mother.

Then the father went in, but when he tried to sit down beside his wife, she flew away from him, and settled in the other part of the house, for it was a double house. But the man went after her and sat down again beside his wife; but now she flew off again to the spot where she had been sitting at first. The man moved over to her again, but this time he wetted his first finger with spittle and touched her with it before sitting down. Then she stayed where she was and did not fly away from him again.

Thus this man found his way to his wife and lived ever after in the Land of Birds.

Told by
Ivaluardjuk.
(G.)

The old woman who adopted a bear.

There was once an old woman who took in a bear's cub to live with her. She brought it up and taught it, and soon it was big enough to go out and play with the children in the village, and the bear and the children fought and wrestled and played together.

The bear grew up and was soon so big that some of the people in the village wanted to kill and eat it. But the old woman wept, and prayed for her bear and did so wish that it might live. When at last she dared not keep it any longer, she urged it to run away. But before the bear left its foster-mother, it spoke to her thus:

"You shall never suffer want. If you should be in want, go down to the edge of the ice, and there you will see some bears. Call them, and they will come."

The old woman did as the bear had said. When she began to be in want, she went out on to the sea ice and began looking about for bears. She saw a bear on a drifting icefloe, and called to it, but when the bear saw and heard her it fled away.

The old woman went on until she saw another bear, and called to this one also. The bear heard her, and as soon as it had seen her, it ran over to the other bear, that was close by, and began fighting with it. It soon killed the bear it was fighting, and hauled it in to land, and left it there even before the foster-mother had reached the spot. After that the old woman lived in abundance on the meat of the bear that had been given her, and even gave her neighbours some for themselves. Thus it came about that greedy people in the village themselves caused a bear, that might have procured meat for them all, to go away and leave them.

Told by
Inugpasugjuk.
(G.)

The woman who took in a larva to nurse.

There was once a barren woman, who could never have any children; at last she took in a larva and nursed it in her armpits, and it was not long before the larva began to grow up. But the more it grew, the less blood the woman had for it to suck. Therefore she often went visiting the houses near by, to set the blood in motion, but she never stayed long away from home, for she was always thinking of her dear larva, and hurried back to it. So greatly did she long for it, so fond of it had she grown, that whenever she came to the entrance of her house, she would call out to it:

"Tit'it'ᴀ'q tᴇʀumiᴀrit!": "Oh, little one that can hiss, say 'te-e-e-ᴇ'r'.

And when she said that, the larva would say in answer:

"Te-e-e-e-ᴇ'r".

The woman then hurried into the house, took the larva on her lap and sang to it:

"Little one that will bring me snow
when you grow up,
Little one that will find meat for me
When you grow up!"

And then she would bite it out of pure love.

The larva grew up and became a big thing. At last it began to move about the village among the houses, and the people were afraid of it and wanted to kill it, partly because they were afraid and partly because they thought it was a pity to let the woman go on growing paler and paler from loss of blood.

So one day when the woman was out visiting, they went into her house and threw the larva out into the passage. Then the dogs flung themselves on it and bit it to death. It was completely filled with blood, and the blood poured out of it.

The woman who had been out visiting came home all unsuspecting, and when she got to the entrance of her house, called out to the larva as she was wont to do. But no one answered, and the woman exclaimed:

"Oh, they have thrown my dear child out of the house". And she burst into tears and went into the house weeping.

Told by
Ivaluardjuk.
(G.)

The owls that talked and lived like human beings.

There were once a father owl and a mother owl with their children, and the children were big enough to go out hunting already. Some of the bigger ones were out hunting marmot, while the younger ones remained at home. Then said the old father and mother owl:

"Children, look out and see if you cannot see your big brothers coming home with a marmot."

The children went out and looked about, and sure enough, they came in and said:

"Here come our brothers, each dragging a marmot".

Then said the old owl to his wife:

"Where is the dog's harness?"

"It is lying down there beside the passage" answered his wife. "But one of the breast straps is missing. I was going to mend it yesterday, but I forgot."

Then the old owl raised his voice and cried:

"What were you so busy with yesterday to make you so forgetful?"

And here ends this story, which shows that the owls talk, live and quarrel among themselves just like human beings.

Told by
Inugpasugjuk.

The shaman who visited the fox in human form.

Once in the winter a man was out walking. And he came to a village. He was a shaman, and therefore went in to the people there without fear. There was only one house, and when he entered it, there lay the old father very ill. In the course of the visit, the sick man's wife gave the shaman two caribou skins, and asked if he could not help her husband to get better. The shaman called up his helping spirits, and afterwards, the sick man said he felt better. In the evening, the shaman went back to his own village, and when he got home, he laid the skins that had been given him in payment on top of the passage way to the house. He went into the house and told what had happened, and asked his wife to fetch in the skins. The woman could not find them, and came in and asked her husband to help her to look for them, but all they found was two lemming skins. The man could not understand what had happened, and next day, he went off with his wife, following his tracks of the day before, to the village he had visited. They came to the spot where the village and the house had been, but all they found was a fox's earth; there was nothing else. The shaman had visited foxes in human form.

Told by
Inugpasugjuk.

The musk oxen that spoke in human speech.

Two musk oxen, both bulls, were discovered and pursued by human beings, and endeavoured to escape. The dogs were sent after them, and the musk oxen ran up to the top of a hill, and one of them then suddenly began talking like a human being:

"My dear little cousin, the dogs are after us. Let us try to get up to the top of a mountain".

The musk oxen took to flight once more and came to the top of a mountain and placed themselves back to back, ready to meet the dogs. At first the hunters were afraid, and dared not approach, but later they took courage and killed them.

This, it is said, was the first time musk oxen were ever killed by human beings, who were formerly afraid to hunt them.

Told by
Inugpasugjuk.

How the mosquitoes first came.

There was once a village where the people were dying of starvation. At last there were only two women left alive, and they managed to exist by eating each other's lice. When all the rest were dead, they left their village and tried to save their lives. They reached the dwellings of men, and told how they had kept themselves alive simply by eating lice. But no one in that village would believe what they said, thinking rather that they must have lived on the dead bodies of their neighbours. And thinking this to be the case, they killed the two women. They killed them and cut them open to see what was inside them; and lo, not a single scrap of human flesh was there in the stomachs; they were full of lice. But now all the lice suddenly came to life, and this time they had wings, and flew out of the bellies of the dead women and darkened the sky.

Thus mosquitoes first came.

Told by
Inugpasugjuk.

The bear and the owl that talked together.

A bear was out walking, and there sat an owl on its hill. The bear came up to the owl. Then the owl spoke up and said:

"Old wanderer, are you out walking as usual, out wandering again?"

The bear answered:

"You that always stand straight up like a pillar, are you standing there staring as usual?"

Again the owl said:

"Old wanderer, out walking again, walking, walking?"

The bear did not bother to say more, but started up suddenly to catch the owl. But the owl spread its wings and flew away.

Told by
Inugpasugjuk.

The woman who visited the bears and the wolves.

There was a woman who was often scolded by her husband. At last she grew tired of it, and went off with her little son in her amaut. She walked all day, and when evening came, she came to the dwelling of a pair of wolves in human form. She was well received, and entertained with suet and caribou steaks. After the meal, they lay down to rest. They were all lying down, when the woman heard the wolf say ot his wife:

"Where shall we put her? Shall we lay her up on top or underneath?"

At these words the woman struck her child, to make it cry. At first she tried to make it cry in the house, but as she did not succeed in this, she took the child out again to quiet it. She was outside for a little while, then she came in again, and so she kept on. Meantime, she was looking about to see which was the best way to escape. At last she fixed on the way to go, and set off. She walked all night, and next day came to a house where there lived bears in human form. She went into the house, which was empty, and got up on the bench and hid at the back behind the skin hangings. Here she remained, and towards evening the bears came home. They sat down to eat, and from her hiding place she noticed that one of them, an old bear, had had one of its back teeth knocked loose, so that it hung half out of its mouth. And the old bear now told his house-mates that he had that day tried to bite a bearded seal to death, but it had been so strong that it had pulled one of his teeth loose.

Suddenly the little child began calling out for its father, and the woman was so frightened that she strangled it at once. The bears listened a moment, thinking they had heard something, but soon went on again as if nothing had happened, and one of them began again:

"Today I stole up to one of the 'Stand-uprights'; one of those creatures that stand straight up like a tent pole, and killed him. It was great fun."

By 'stand upright' and 'tent pole' the bear meant a human being, because human beings walk upright.

At these words an old bear joined in and said:

"You should not speak so carelessly of those that walk upright. They are dangerous, when they throw their weapons at us. If they were to find this hut of ours, they would break in and kill us."

In the evening, when they had finished telling their hunting stories, they went to rest. The bears lay down on the bench, but there was one of them that could not quite find room, and that was the one lying where the woman had hidden. So it kicked out at the skins at the foot end to make more room, but though it hurt most dreadfully, the woman set her teeth and took care not to utter a sound.

The bears slept all through the night, and next morning, some of them went out hunting, while others remained at home to get their boots dried. But the bears who had stayed behind were restless, as if they were afraid of something, and at last they put on their boots and went off after the others.

As soon as the house was empty, the woman came out from her hiding place, laid the strangled child in among the bears' bedclothes, and ran off home. She came home and told what had happened, and the people at once made ready to attack the bears in their lair. The bears came home and found the dead child among their sleeping rugs, and were very much afraid. They knew now that there would be human beings coming to attack them, and therefore hurried away from their house.

And thus it came about that the men who went to seek out the bears in their lair found it empty.

Told by
Ivaluardjuk.
(G.)

The man who came to the house of the wolves.

There was once a man who had two wives. In summer he did not go out hunting caribou, but made do with walrus, bearded seal and fjord seal. One of his wives at last began to envy all the people who went hunting caribou in summer, and so one day she said:

"It is said that the people of Nerránâq have got a number of caribou. What sort of a husband is this of ours? Here are we simply getting our clothes in a mess with blubber and grease."

The winter was at an end, and spring had come, when the man asked his wives to make him some kamiks. So his wives made him some kamiks, and when the spring was fairly come, and the kamiks were finished, the man went off up inland. He stayed away all the summer.

It was nearing autumn when he came in sight of a great lake. There it lay, sometimes white, sometimes black and sometimes red. It was shadows cast by children at play. It was their clothes, reflected in the lake. He waited until evening, and then he went down. He stole up to the tent farthest out, and saw a married woman sitting inside. Her husband was not at home. So he went in, laid his knife in front of the woman and said:

"I will give this in payment if I may have something."

The woman took the knife, and then hid her guest at the back of the bench and hung up his kamiks to dry.

In the course of the evening, many people came to visit her, and always they said as they came in:

"There is a smell of human beings in Uviarasugiaq's house."

It was late in the evening when at last her husband came home. The first thing he said when he came in was:

"There is a smell of human beings in here."

At this the woman picked up the knife which the stranger had given her, and said:

"Hide it, hide it, hide it." And then she began howling like a wolf.

Later in the evening, when they were going to rest, they let their guest come out in order to give him something to eat. The master of the house now declared that there was no one in the village whom he feared; his guest might then be quite at ease.

After the meal, they took out some caribou skins, many beautiful skins, and arranged a dress which their guest could take with him when he left.

The guest stayed a whole day in that place. On the day after, when evening had fallen once more, and the people had gone to rest, he set off. The man accompanied his guest a good part of the way, and then turned back and went home; the other went on homewards, in like wise. So far had he to go that it was winter when at last he reached home. When he got home, he let his wives and several of the neighbours make new garments for themselves of the skins he had brought with him. But one of those in the village, who had not been given any caribou skin, was envious, and decided to go off himself and visit the wolf people. Others tried to dissuade him, but in vain.

He set out, and walked and walked and went on walking and came at last to the dwellings of the wolf people. He went into the first hut he saw, without troubling to look about him. Then he did the same as the first man had done. He took out his knife, laid it on the floor, and said:

"If anyone here will give me something, I have this to give in return."

But hardly had the man laid down his knife when the wolf people fell upon him and tore him to pieces. Thus it fared with the envious one, who insisted on going though others had sought to dissuade him. He was eaten up.

Told by
Ivaluardjuk.

Kâkuarshuk, who came to the bears in human form.

It is said that Kâkuarshuk only hunted at the blowholes by night. One day when he was out after seal, there came a bear, and stood by the shelter wall the man had built close to the blowhole, and said to him:

"Seat yourself on top of me."

Kâkuarshuk was so frightened that he at once seated himself on the bear, but the bear said quite calmly:

"Bring your hunting things with you."

Kâkuarshuk laid his hunting implements on top of the bear, and the bear trotted off with him. The bear went out towards the sea, in the direction of the ice edge. As soon as they came to open water, the bear told Kâkuarshuk to get down, and when he stood on the ice, the bear said to him:

"First you must make water."

Then the bear plunged into the water and told Kâkuarshuk to climb on its back again, and said also:

"Close your eyes, get a good grip of my fur, and lay your head against my shoulders."

Then the bear swam off. At first one could hear from the shoulder-blades how hard the bear was working, but after a little while there was no longer anything to be heard. The bear at first swam straight out to sea, but after a little while it changed its course and turned in towards land. Now Kâkuarshuk no longer heard the sound of the water, they were moving quietly forward. Again some time elapsed, and then Kâkuarshuk seemed to feel the bear clambering up on shore, and to hear its footsteps creaking in the snow.

"Now you may open your eyes," said the bear. Kâkuarshuk opened his eyes and discovered that it was now moonlight, and the moon shone on a great number of tracks. There were also sledge tracks to be seen. They followed the sledge tracks, and soon came in sight of people running about at play. They went towards the people, and as soon as the latter saw them coming, they came forward to meet them. The newcomers made straight for Kâkuarshuk and would have attacked him, but the bear who was with him struck them with a little stick and kept them off. When they came over by the house, the bear took off his bearskin coat and went in with his guest. Meantime, the man sat and waited for the bear. Then they came into a big, light house. Here Kâkuarshuk stayed as a guest. They went out hunting, going from the village to hunt at the blowholes, but at first Kâkuarshuk did not go with the others; not until he had grown accustomed to the bear folk and was no longer afraid of them did he go with the rest, and then he often got a seal. Whenever Kâkuarshuk got a seal, the others all came gallopping up to him and were given some of the meat. If he got a seal and the people were very hungry, they would run up to his catch with such a ravening speed that he only wanted to get away.

Kâkuarshuk had been there a long time before he grew so accustomed to them that he could begin to go visiting in their houses. When Kâkuarshuk began to go visiting, his foster-father said to him:

"You must keep away from that house there farthest off. The man who lives there is a dangerous man, who often kills people."

Afterwards it happened that the dangerous man always wanted to go out hunting when Kâkuarshuk was of the party, and therefore his foster-father forbade Kâkuarshuk to go to the blowholes; for he was afraid the Dangerous One was only waiting for a chance to kill him. But Kâkuarshuk kept on begging his foster-father to let him go with the rest, and plagued him so that at last he was allowed to go.

One day they were out hunting when the dangerous bear suddenly came running towards Kâkuarshuk with jaws agape. Kâkuarshuk snatched up his harpoon, and when the bear came up to him, he sprang aside and thrust the harpoon deep into its body. Then he ran off home at full speed. As soon as he came home, he told what had happened, and his foster-father said to him:

"Good, good; it was a good thing you struck down the Dangerous One first."

Evening came, and they went to rest. Next morning, before it was yet light, a voice called in through the window:

"Come outside a little, Kâkuarshuk!"

"Do not go out whatever you do," said his foster-father.

Then the voice from without cried again, but this time less loudly:

"Come outside a little, Kâkuarshuk!"

This time, the foster-father told Kâkuarshuk he had better go out a little, as he was afraid the bear might come in, and Kâkuarshuk went out believing he was now to be killed. But all that happened was, that when Kâkuarshuk came out, there stood the bear he had just wounded, and handed him back his harpoon, smiling all over its face. The dangerous bear afterwards became a good neighbour, and Kâkuarshuk resumed his old habits and went out hunting with the other men and visited them in their houses, without need to go in fear of anyone. And all the bears were fond of him, because he was an active and courageous man, as skilful at catching seal as any bear.

Told by
Ivaluardjuk.

The bear in human form, that visited a village.

There were once a bear and its wife and their two childen, that came in human form to visit a village. After they had got there, they set about building a snow hut. While their parents were building the house, the children, a brother and a sister, went visiting about the village. In the course of their visits there was a man who asked them:

"What is the name of your father?"

"Bear," answered the boy.

"And what is your mother's name?"

"Mouth."

"What then is your brother called?"

"Hide."

"And you yourself?"

"I am called Miserly."

During the night, the bears felt anxious lest the human beings should attack them, now they had learned who they were, and so they fled away before the people of the village were awake.

Told by
Ivaluardjuk.

The fox and the hare that married.

There was once a vixen that married a hare, and afterwards, when they were living together, it was always the wife who hunted game for her husband, he himself never cared to go out hunting. The hare, thinking it was too bad that his wife should always go hunting on his behalf, at last suggested that she should go away and leave him, for he feared lest his own wife should at last go hungry, and that through his own fault. But the vixen would not leave her husband. At last the hare himself decided to go away, and so he did, not caring to live merely as an eater up of food procured by another. But the little vixen, who was very fond of him, burst into tears, and sang a song:

"My husband, my dear little husband
Wished us to part,
And now I am alone.
He never went out hunting,
And now I am alone.
Aja — aja.

My husband, my dear little husband,
Wished us to part,
And now I am alone.
But I was really so fond of him,
Really so fond of him,
Aja — aja"

Told by
Ivaluardjuk.

The raven and the loon that tattooed each other.

Once a raven and a loon happened to meet, and they agreed to tattoo each other. First the raven tattooed the loon, and when it was done, the loon set about tattooing the raven. But the raven was very ill pleased with its tattooing, and would not keep still, and again and again the loon said:

"If you wont keep still, I will pour the soot I am using all over you."

At last the loon lost patience, and poured all the soot over the raven, and then ran out of the house. But just as the loon was on the point of disappearing, the raven picked up the fire stones that lay in the house and threw them at the loon. The fire stones struck the loon on the thighs, and it sank down and could hardly walk.

From that day all ravens are black, and all loons awkward on their feet.

Told by
Ivaluardjuk.
(G.)

The owl that tried to take two hares at once.

An owl was out hunting one day when it caught sight of two hares sitting close together. The owl came down on the hares from above, gliding down slowly and noiselessly on its wings, and when it was just over them, it grabbed at them both at once. The hares leapt up in a fright and ran opposite ways, but the owl had got its claws fixed in their flesh and could not get them out again. And such was the strength of the hares that they tore both thighs from the owl, as they ran their different ways, and the thighs went with them as they ran away.

So it came about that the owl caused its own death.

Told by
Ivaluardjuk.
(G.)

The owl and the marmot.

An owl once caught sight of a little marmot, that was out looking for food, and so it placed itself at the entrance to the marmot's lair and waited there.

The owl did not kill the marmot, but called out to his family:

"I have barred the entrance to a creature's lair; come and fetch it, with the best sledges and the best dogs."

When the owl had cried out thus, the marmot turned to it and said:

"Now that you are going to eat me up, going to eat my chops and smack your lips over my kidney suet, you might show your satisfaction by dancing for me a little. But you must look up to the highest part of the sky, spread your legs wide apart and bend down properly as for a real song and dance." The owl did so, and when it had begun dancing, the marmot sang:

"Look up at the dome of the sky overhead
As you do your song and dance,
Spread wide your legs
And bend your knees,
Swaying in time with the song!"

But the moment the owl spread its legs wide apart and began dancing, the marmot slipped in between its legs and disappeared down into its hole.

Then shrieked the owl:

"Alas, the beast I had caught escaped,
Alas, the beast I had caught escaped.
Take back the sledges
Turn back with the sledges!"

And then it called down to the marmot:

"Don't be afraid, you can come out again, I wont hurt you."

"What can he be thinking of, that fellow up there?" said the marmot to his wife. "He had better go away."

But his wife answered:

"I think I will go out to him. You heard what he said, that he would not hurt us."

"Well go out then if you like, and let him first kiss your genitals," said the husband marmot. And here ends this story.

Told by
Ivaluardjuk.

The bear that thought it was stronger than a caribou.

A caribou came slowly down wind, grazing as it went, when it met a bear, and when they met, they spoke to each other in this wise. The caribou was the first to speak, and it said: "Let us try pulling arms."

The bear looked at it a little, and then said:

"Oh, I am afraid I shall break your upper arm."

The caribou answered:

"I can use it without fear of breaking it. Let us try."

The bear looked once more at the other's forelegs, and then said:

"No, we have better not, I am afraid of breaking it."

The caribou answered:

"I often run at a gallop, and I am never afraid of breaking my forelegs."

So they set to and began pulling arms. At first they did as men do when pulling arms, to show their confidence and give their opponent a chance; they each stretched out an arm now and again towards the other. But at last the bear dared not do so any more, and kept his arm in the same position all the time. Then the caribou began to pull, and very slowly, straightened out the bear's foreleg with such force that it tore the skin and flesh from the whole of the upper arm and broke the bone.

Wild with pain and shame, the bear bit at its opponent, but the caribou had already made a great leap and was gone.

Told by
Ivaluardjuk.

The raven that married wild geese.

There was once a raven that married wild geese. It took two wild geese to wife.

When the time came for the wild geese to go off to their own country, where there is no winter, they begged the raven stay behind, fearing lest the way should be too long for him. They told him how they flew over lands far away and distant one from another, and they explained:

"The way we have to fly is so long that you will grow tired; you had better stay behind, and when we come back, we can meet again."

But the raven was so fond of its wives that it would not part from them, and when the day came for them to set out, it went with them. Off they flew towards the south. Soon the wild geese were so far ahead of the raven that it could not see them at all, then again it could just make out where they were. Sometimes they flew away from him, sometimes he would overtake them a little, and when at last the wild geese grew tired and sat down on the surface of the sea to rest, the raven managed to come up with them, but had to keep hovering in the air above them, and could not get any rest itself. As soon as the geese had rested, they went on again. The raven followed after. Then again the wild geese grew tired and sat down on the water to rest, and once more the raven hovered in the air above them. As soon as the wild geese had rested sufficiently, they flew on again. This happened four times; four times they sat down on the water to rest, and four times they flew on again when they had rested enough. Then, when they settled down on the water for the fifth time, the raven had grown so tired that it could do no more, and said to its wives:

"Wives, place yourselves close together."

And the wives placed themselves close together on the water, and the raven sat on top of them. But it was afraid of the water, and kept on saying:

"Dear wives, do keep close together."

After a short rest, they flew on again, and when the wild geese once more wanted to rest, they did as before; the raven's two wives placed themselves close together, and the raven sat down on top of them. But it clutched at their necks so hard that all the feathers were worn away. Their brothers noticed it, and were afraid their sisters might freeze to death if they lost their feathers, so they said to them later on, when the raven had dropped behind and was far away:

"Next time he comes and begs you to sit close together so that he can sit on top of you, wait till he has settled himself comfortably and then swim suddenly apart."

It was not long before the raven came, and cried pitifully to his wives:

"Place yourselves close together, wives, place yourselves close together." And the wild geese placed themselves close together, but the moment the raven sat down on them, they suddenly swam apart, and the raven fell into the sea. It called after the wild geese in despair:

"Oh, come and help me, come and hold my chest above water." But no one heeded the raven's words, and so it was left behind far out at sea.

Told by
Ivaluardjuk.
(G.)

The whale, the sea scorpion, the stone and the eagle, that married human wives.

There were once four young girls who had nearly reached an age to be married; they played together, pretending they had to choose a husband.

One of them saw a whale spouting out at sea, and said: "That shall be my husband." And so it came about. Another of the girls caught sight of a sea-scorpion lying in shallow water, and said: "That shall be my husband." And so it came about. A third found a stone, which she thought very handsome, and she said: "This shall be my husband." And so it came about. The fourth saw an eagle hovering high in the air, and said: "That eagle shall be my husband." And so it came about.

The girl who wanted to marry the whale was taken and carried off by a whale and brought to an island, and here on this island the whale made a house for the girl of its own bones, a house of whale's bones[1]) and gave her food of its own maktak and its own flesh.

The whale was so fond of its wife, and so afraid lest she should run away, that it would never let her go out, not even to make water. And he kissed her so often, and lay with her so often, that maktak skin began to form about her nose and genitals.

The girl's parents knew quite well that she was out on the island, and went out there themselves now and again, but as they could not get hold of her, they always had to go back home without having accomplished their errand.

The girl knew that her parents were in the habit of coming to the island to try to carry her off home with them, and one day when she was expecting them, she asked her husband to let her go outside and make water, and something more. When she said this, the whale answered: "You can make water in my mouth, and if there is anything more you can do it in my hand."

But at last one day it chanced that the whale gave his wife leave to go out on condition that she was tethered to a line. She tied the line to a bone, a whale's bone, that lay outside the house, and then said to the bone:

"When my husband inside there asks you if I have done making water, and the rest of it, all you have to do is to answer in my voice: 'No, I have not yet finished, I have not finished yet!'"

Then she ran as hard as she could down to her parents' umiAq, which lay close up to the beach waiting for her. The girl had not been gone long when the whale began tugging impatiently at the line, and called out:

"Have you not yet finished making water, and all the rest of it?"

And the bone to which the line was fastened answered:

"No, I have not finished yet."

A little while after the whale tugged at the line again, and only now did it discover that it was not the girl, but a bone, it was tugging at. Then it rushed but of the house, gathered up all its bones, so that it became a whale again, and set off in chase of the fugitives, who were already far away. But in its haste, it forgot its hip bones.

The whale rapidly overtook the umiAq, and those on board, in their fright, threw the wife's outer coat into the sea. The whale came up to the garment, and flung itself upon it, and the boat drew a little way ahead while it was busy with that. Then it took up the pursuit again, and now they threw out one of her boots. The kamik again

[1]) There are still to be found remains of the houses built by the Tunit out of whales' bones, and it is doubtless this which has given rise to the story of the whale building a house with its own bones. Moreover, this whale exists so exclusively as a soul that it is able to feed the girl on its own flesh.

delayed the whale for some little time, and then they threw out the other one, and then her breeches. The breeches, which smelt of her body, kept the whale back so long that the boat got far ahead, and reached the shore, running in with such force that it dashed up on land, over two high terraces on the beach. The whale, following close behind, made after it at such speed that it cleared one of the heights, but stopped a little way behind the boat, and the moment it got on shore, it died. So the whale lost, because it had forgotten its hip bones.

But the girl who married a sea scorpion was carried off and stowed away under a stone, and there she stayed and was never found again.

The little girl who married a stone was herself turned into a stone. and as she was turning into a stone, she sang this song:

"Men in kayaks,
come hither to me
and be my husbands:
this stone here
has clung fast to me,
and lo, my feet
are now turning to stone.

Men in kayaks,
come hither to me
and be my husbands;
this stone here
has clung fast to me
and lo, my legs
are now turning to stone.

Men in kayaks,
come hither to me,
and be my husbands:
this stone here
has clung fast to me,
and lo, now my thighs
are turning to stone

Men in kayaks,
come hither to me
and be my husbands;
this stone here
has clung fast to me,
and lo, from the waist down,
I am turning to stone.

Men in kayaks,
come hither to me
and be my husbands;

this stone here
has clung fast to me,
and lo, my entrails
are turning to stone.

Men in kayaks,
come hither to me,
and be my husbands;
this stone here
has clung fast to me,
and lo, my lungs
are now turning to stone.",

She sang one more verse, but the moment she mentioned her heart, which had now also turned into stone, she died.

The little girl that married an eagle was also carried off, and placed on the top of a high mountain. The eagle was a skilful hunter, and often caught small caribou calves, and his wife had plenty of food and plenty of warm skins. The girl found out that her kinsfolk were coming in an umiᴀq to see her, and now she began plaiting a long line of caribou sinews. She lived on a high cliff falling sheer away down to the sea, and when the line she had plaited was so long that she thought it would reach right down, she made up her mind to try. One day when the eagle was out hunting, the umiᴀq came to the bird cliff, and she fastened the line of caribou sinews to the rock and lowered herself down. But the cliff was so high that in lowering herself down she scraped all the skin from the palms of her hands and the inner side of her thighs. But the umiᴀq sailed home with her to her own village.

It was not long before the eagle came flying along, and when it stood above the house, it raised a storm with its wings. It remained hovering above the village and the men called up to it:

"Eagle, let us see what a handsome fellow you are; spread your wings wide!"

The eagle did so, and the girl's kinsmen shot off their arrows; they struck it under the wings, and it fell down dead.

There lay the eagle and rotted away, and so big was it, that when its huge head had lost all the flesh and only the skull remained, dogs crept into it to litter, and brought forth their young inside the skull.

And here ends this story.

Told by
Ivaluardjuk.
(G.)

Epic tales.

Atungait, who set out to travel round the world.

It is said that Atungait determined to travel round the world, and therefore set about carefully breeding dogs. They would have to be strong and of great endurance. When he thought the dogs were as they should be, he decided to go up a steep mountain, that was close by their village, and he said:

"If I can manage to climb this steep cliff face near our village, I will set out. If not, I will stay at home."

He set off on his way, and climbed the cliff without the slightest difficulty. Then he called from the top to his dogs which stood down below at the foot. The dogs came up at once, and with those which had been chosen for the journey there came also one that had received no special training. This dog, which was not specially hardened to strength and endurance, came halfway up the cliff, but then it slipped, and fell down and was killed. Atungait assembled his team on top of the cliff and drove off. He travelled night and day at one spell without resting, and when many days and many nights had passed, he came to a people that were lame from the hips, and they had a curious throwing game, a red and a white ajagʌq. These lame folk all had sledges. Atungait soon grew tired of staying with them, and wishing to possess this curious throwing game, he cut through the lashings of the cross bars on all the sledges, and then going into the house, took the red game and drove away. The lame folk tried to set out in pursuit, but all their sledges fell to pieces, all save one that Atungait har forgotten when cutting the lashings of the rest, and this one drove after him. It was a long time before it overtook him, but at last it did, and Atungait then, turning round, shot the leader of the lame driver's team with his arrow. The dog with the arrow in its body then ran off away from the sledge tracks, and took the rest of the team with it, and the lame driver as well, for he could not get down from the sledge. It went on and on until it came right out to the edge of the ice; here it flung itself into the water with all the other dogs, and they were all drowned, the lame man and all his dogs.

Atungait then travelled on, night and day in one, until at last he came to a steep cliff, a precipice, where there was no way round. The ice had gathered round the steep rock, and it was impossible to go farther. Atungait then drove his team out into the open water, and they swam along with him and the sledge. Once or twice, when they came to places which he thought they would never manage to pass, he closed his eyes, but opened them again immediately. So Atungait drove round the steep cliff and continued his journey.

One day he came to a big village, but the people who lived there were dangerous. They wanted to kill him, and therefore Atungait travelled on again without stopping to sleep. He travelled on again, night and day in one, and came to a glacier. There was no other way to go, so he drove up into the ice. It was steep and smooth, and at all the places where there was a sheer descent, it was only his dogs that saved him from being dashed down, for they had long, sharp claws and did not slip on the smooth ice.

Thus Atungait managed to cross the ice and travelled on, night and day in one; and it is said that he travelled right round the world. But how he came home again to his own village nobody knows. And therefore I end the story here.

Told by
Ivaluardjuk.

Agdlumaloqâq, who hunted at the blowholes in a far, foreign land.

Agdlumaloqâq told his fellow-villagers that the places where he went hunting every day at the blowholes were so far far away from their customary hunting grounds that it was like hunting in a far, foreign land. But nobody believed him. And since nobody would believe him, he invited one of the neighbours to go with him to the place where he generally went. They set off very early in the morning, but it was dark before they got to the hunting ground. During the night they passed two small cracks in the ice. It was now well on in the night, and they still kept on. Then they came to a piece of land, crossed over that, and went on over the ice on the farther side. Here at last they came to a blowhole, and Agdlumaloqâq made ready his implements and prepared to wait until a seal should come up to breathe. Towards morning, Agdlumaloqâq got a seal, and they now prepared to set off home with it. Agdlumaloqâq proposed that they should go home together, without waiting for his companion to try his luck; for, he said, if the other once got a seal to drag behind him, he would be unable to keep up all the long way home. But his companion would not believe this, and said he would first try what he could get himself.

Agdlumaloqâq then hurried off home alone, and arrived on the same day he had caught the seal. Now that he was alone, he got along quickly. But the whole day passed, and his companion did not return. At last several days had passed, and still he had not returned.

It happened in this wise with his companion: he had got a seal, and had set off homewards with that seal, and had gone on day after day and at last he had eaten up the whole seal, and was now near dying of hunger. At last he came back to his village, half dead with hunger. And now at last the unbelieving neighbours understood that Agdlumaloqâq had been telling the thruth when he said he was wont to hunt in a far, foreign land.

Told by
Inugpasugjuk.

Kivioq.

In the spring, when the young seal were moving close in along the coast, the men of one large village used to go out hunting them in kayaks. There were many men, and when they came home from their hunting, it was their custom to play at·aujᴀ·q (a ball game, in which the players take sides, those of one side throwing to their fellows and trying to keep the ball from those of the other).

A little boy used to go over to where they were playing, but whenever he came up to them, they cut the tails off his coat. (kukup·ᴀ·q is the name for a child's dress which is cut in precisely the same fashion as that of adults, with tails of fur hanging down front and back: otherwise, children when quite small generally wear a tunic cut straight off round the waist).

The little boy's grandmother often told them not to do it, because she had no more skin to mend his coat with, but no one paid any heed to what she said, and as they kept on cutting off the tails of the little boy's coat, the old grandmother at last hit on a remedy. She softened the skin from the head of a young seal and pulled it over the boy's face and head. She then spoke magic words over him so as to make him a seal, and then by means of other magic words made him dive down through a hollow in the bench, so that he came out by that mysterious road into the sea, and then she said to the boy:

"One day, when the kayaks appear off the coast outside our village coming to hunt young seal, you must dive down through this hollow, and come out this way into the sea, and then you must show yourself in front of the kayaks, and as soon as they see you, swim on ahead of them, now and then diving under water, but always keeping out to sea. When you have got a little way out, you must clap your hands and feet together and cry: "uɳa·, uɳa·!"

One day, when the kayaks were out as usual hunting young seal. the old woman set her grandchild out into the sea, and the boy, coming up in front of the men in the guise of a little seal, led them on and on out to sea, and so eager were the men in their hunting that they did not notice the seal was leading them far out to sea. Only when the boy suddenly began clapping hands and feet together, and crying out "uŋa', uŋa'" did the men discover how far out to sea they had come.

The kayaks now hurried at full speed in towards land, but just then it came on to blow. It blew a gale, one kayak after another capsized, and at last one man named Kivioq was the only one left. A heavy sea arose, and the waves towered so high that Kivioq, when a wave came, thought it was land in sight.

"There is the land, there is the land", said he to himself, but then the wave slipped away and vanished, and there was no land. There was nothing to be done. Kivioq drifted on, carried by the wind and the waves, but at last he came to shore. He rowed on along the shore. He saw a house, a shelter, built of turf and stones. He looked in through the smoke hole in the roof, and caught sight of an old woman scraping a skin. Kivioq spat down through the hole to attract her attention, and the moment he did so, the woman looked up and cut off a piece of her cheek with her knife, saying as she did so:

"That cloud that overshadowed me must have been very near!"

But Kivioq was so terrified at what she had done that he ran away.

Kivioq rowed on again and went on shore at another place, where he again caught sight of a house. He looked in, and when he was asked to come in, he went in. His clothes were wet, and the woman in the house offered to dry them for him. Kivioq clambered up on to the bench, pulled off his kamiks, and let her dry them. While he was lying on the bench, a meat fork suddenly appeared from the space under the bench, and began stabbing at him. He jumped up, and grasped at his kamiks, but could not get hold of them, because the drying frame rose up in the air, so that he could not reach them.

"Give me my kamiks, I want my kamiks on, I dare not stay here any longer, because a meat fork from under the bench comes and stabs at me, and because the drying frame rises up in the air when I reach out after my kamiks" said Kivioq to the woman in the house.

But the woman answered:

"It was I who hung up your kamiks to dry, and surely you can reach up to take them down".

At this Kivioq began saying a magic prayer:

"Bear, bear, come and eat up this woman!"

And a little while after they could hear a bear coming through the house; its growling came nearer and nearer. And Kivioq said again:

"Do give me my kamiks".

"I hung them up, so I should think you ought to be able to take them down," said the woman again.

Then Kivioq asked for his kamiks a third time, and now they

could hear the bear growling out in the passage. At this the woman grew frightened, and took down the kamiks and said:

"Here are your kamiks, here are your stockings."

Kivioq pulled on his kamiks and ran out into the passage. It closed up after him, but he was so quick that only the tail of his coat was caught and cut off. He ran down to his kayak, hurried into it and pushed off. Just then the woman came out from her house and said to him:

"With this knife of mine I came near to cutting you up."

Kivioq lifted his bladder dart, and threatened the woman, crying:

"I nearly harpooned you with this!"

The woman was so frightened at this that she sat down suddenly and dropped her knife, which rolled into the sea, and at once a thin sheet of ice formed on the water.

When the ice came spreading over the sea, Kivioq said a magic prayer, and a way opened in the ice before him, and he rowed on. He rowed along the shore, until he caught sight of a great tent. Then he came in to shore and went up to the place. A woman and her daughter lived there, and Kivioq stayed with them. He took the daughter to wife, and was wont to lie with her.

Outside the house there lay a piece of wood. Sometimes one could hear, while inside the house, a sound like teeth chattering. Then the old woman went out and fetched in the piece of wood, and when she laid it down, the wood shivered, and made a noise just like the chattering of teeth. This piece of wood was the woman's husband. There were a couple of large knots on the outside. Every morning the woman would take hold of it by the knots and carry it down to the water. Then it floated out to sea and came home in the afternoon with seals it had laid up on the knots. In this way it hunted and brought home meat for the woman.

The two women had a great number of beads, and Kivioq got them to make him a lot of mittens, and had all of them decorated with a border of bead work. Then he took the mittens with him and hid them far away, and when he came home again, he got them to make him some more.

Kivioq came to be very fond of his young wife, and was therefore very much surprised when he came home one day and found only one of the women. Her face was exactly like that of his wife, but her body was shrunken and bony. Thus he discovered that it was the old woman who had killed her daughter and pulled her skin on over her own. Kivioq then left that place, and went home to his own village. He rowed and rowed and at last recognised his own village, and when he recognised it, he fell to singing:

"asixai, asixai" (untranslatable).

Up in the village, people heard the song and the cry, and Kivioq's wife said:

"Kivioq is the only man who ever calls out "asixai, asixai!"

So Kivioq came home, and in his joy at having found his wife again, he let his neighbours share among themselves all the beads he had brought with him in his mittens.

Told by
Ivaluardjuk.

Meetings with strange tribes.

Navaranâq.

Navaranâq, an Eskimo girl, was adopted as a child by the Indians. And it was a habit of hers to excite illfeeling among the Indians against her own countrymen, saying that the Eskimos wished to kill all the Indians.

One day, when it was blowing from the south-west, and the ice was setting in towards land, the people of Navaranâq's old village went out hunting at the blowholes.

Navaranâq said to the Indians:

"When the wind is in that quarter, and the ice is setting in towards land, my countrymen generally go out hunting."

As soon as the Indians heard this, they made ready for battle and set off. On arriving at the village, they tore open the windows and stabbed the women to death through the window openings. The women then hit upon the plan of setting fire to their sleeping rugs, and this sent up such a stench and smoke that the Indians could not see. They had then to go in through the passage, and when they came in, there was a woman who bit an Indian's thumb so fiercely that she bit it off, and the Indian fell down and died. The Indians went on murdering, and when they thought there were no more left, they went off home. But there was one that had hidden in a dog kennel made of snow, and had closed up the entrance afterwards with snow, so they did not find her.

The men of the Eskimo village came home from their hunting, and could not make out where their women had gone. The woman who had hidden in the dog kennel was the only one who came out to meet them, and she told them what had happened. The men at once all made ready for an attack upon the Indians.

On arriving at the Indians' camp, all the Eskimos placed themselves in front of the windows and called in to them:

"Is there a woman here named Navaranâq?"

Navanaranâq, thinking no harm, called out at once:

"Here I am, here I am!" And she went out to the men. They caught her by the arms and carried her off, and dragged her so roughly that they pulled her arms out. But Navaranâq sang a song:

"The men tore off
My arms,
So sharp were
Their skinning knives."

And then she fell down and died.

The Eskimos now went home, but after having again made ready for battle, they attacked the Indians. This time they killed all in the camp, and then went home. On the way they found many Indian children that had gone into hiding. They lay on the ground pretending to be dead. But the Eskimos tickled them round the belly, and when they showed signs of life, struck them on the head and killed them. When there were but a few Indian children left alive, they drove these on ahead of them towards their village. The Indian children soon grew tired, and started moaning:

"Our legs, our tired legs. We also are accustomed to go out on hunting expeditions, but those who go on ahead at first are allowed to rest until the ones behind come up."

But every time the Indian children complained, they were struck on the head and killed. At last there were but two of them left, a brother and sister, and they reached the village alive. There they were kept as adopted children, and soon grew up and grew big, and the brother became a great hunter. All were fond of the young Indian, because he was skilful, and brought in much meat to the village. One day when they were standing about outside, they invited him to shoot at a dog with his bow and arrows. The young Indian would not shoot at the dog, but the men kept on urging him to do so, until at last he shot an arrow at it. He hit the dog and killed it. Then at once he fled away up inland, though all cried out to him to stay, and not to trouble about the dog, but the Indian continued his flight and disappeared up inland.

Told by
Inugpasugjuk.
(G.)

The dangerous nakasuŋnaicut.

A man once came to the dwelling of the dangerous nakasuŋnaicut. He went into a house, where there was plenty of room. A dog lay in the passage, with a litter of pups, and when it turned upon him as if to spring at him, he hurried into the house. Inside the house sat a woman cooking bear's meat, but among the pieces of meat in the pot he espied the forearm of a human being, with tattoo marks on it.

The woman said to him:

"Do you like bear's meat, or would you rather have human flesh?"

When he had eaten some bear's meat, he made ready to go, for he was very anxious and afraid, but the woman said:

"You need not be afraid. My sons will not hurt you."

The man was still sitting there when a young man came running into the house. His nostrils quivered, as he said:

"Smell of human flesh, smell of human flesh."

But his mother said: "There is no human flesh to smell here. It must be me you can smell."

And turning to her guest, she said:

"Now I suppose he has gone out to tell all the neighbours."

A little while after there came a creaking in the snow outside, and now the woman's sons came in, and she said to them:

"Here is a human being. He was very anxious and afraid, so I have hidden him away."

The two sons said:

"If there is a human being here, then let him come out." And the mother led the man forth from his hiding place, and her sons sniffed at him and smelt him and were glad he had not been killed. The sons said to the man:

"In a little while a big, strong, dangerous man will come in. He wil say something about how he longs for a good rich dish of meat, and he will challenge you to fight."

And the two sons gave the guest two stones, and said:

"Now when this man comes in through the passage singing, you must hit him with these two stones, first on one ear and then on the other, but be sure you do not miss. If you do, then you yourself will be killed."

A little while after, the big man came in through the passage singing, and when he had got far enough for the guest to see his ears, he threw the stones at him, and struck him on the ears, so that he fell down dead in the passage. He was at once dragged out and cut up, and part of the meat from the breast brought into the house.

A little later a youth came in, carrying part of the backbone and the head. He carried the head on one finger, stuck in at the base of the neck, and this youth then said:

"I thought father was thin. But there was suet round his kidneys all the same."

Towards evening, the woman's two sons said to their guest:

"This evening, when it is dark, you had better go out and cut the lashings of all the sledges." And he did so, but one sledge he forgot to cut. Towards morning, before it was light, he fled away from the village. One sledge overtook him. When it was near enough for him to reach the man's dogs with his arrow, he shot down the leader, and the team being then without leader, the driver could no longer keep them under control, and the dogs dashed off with him right out to the edge of the ice and over into the sea, and both man and dogs were drowned.

But the man came safely home to his own village and told of all that had happened to him among the nakasuŋnaicut.

Told by
Inugpasugjuk.
(G.)

The men who were carried out to sea, and met with dangerous folk.

Two men hunting at the edge of the ice were carried out to sea. They drifted about in the open sea, tried many a time to get in to shore, and when at last they succeeded, they were a great way from their village. They found some people in those parts, but they were not good people; they were evil and dangerous ones, and though one of the men proposed that they should make themselves known all the same, the other insisted that it was too risky, and so they went on again every time.

Once they came to a village out on a headland. The people here were skilful hunters, going out in skin boats that were driven with great speed. Here the two men could not resist the desire to make themselves known, and so they did.

But before doing so, they first hid close to the village in order to learn a little more about the people. The men used to go out all together to their hunting, so that the women were left behind alone.

One day when all the men were out, one of the two companions went down to the village and made himself known. But hardly had the men come back from their hunting and caught sight of the stranger, when they fell upon him and killed him.

His companion stood looking on, but did nothing. Not until all the men had gone out hunting again did he go down to the village, down to the women, to take vengeance for his companion. He flung himself upon the women and began murdering right and left, but when there were only a few remaining, he caught sight of the umiAq returning from a journey, and so he took to flight. The umiAq put in to shore, and the men in it went off in chase of the fugitive, and followed him for a long time, but at last all were tired, and only two kept up the pursuit. These also failed to overtake him, and therefore they too stopped, and cried out:

"When the young gulls are big enough to fly, you may expect us!"

The fugitive ran homewards at full speed. He came to a river, and began walking along the bank. Here he suddenly caught sight of two big people, a man and a woman, cutting up a caribou. He called out to them:

"Help me over this river!"

The two heard his voice. The man stayed by the caribou, the woman came down to the river, pulled her kamiks right up and began wading across. As soon as she had crossed the stream, she called the man to her, put him on her hand and waded back again across the river. Thus the man came over to the two giants, and the first thing they did was to put new soles into his kamiks; the soles were quite worn out, he had come so far. One day he said to the two giants:

"I long for my home, but now I do not know which way my own land lies. Perhaps you can tell me where it is?"

The two giants answered:

"Your land lies in the direction of the rising sun. You see those two peaks over there, far, far away; when you reach them, you can see your land from there." And they added:

"When we go that way ourselves, it generally takes us only a day to get to your land and back."

Then the man set out. He went on and on. It was autumn, and it passed into winter. Midwinter came, and he was still on the way homeward. At last he had reached so far that he began to pass snow huts on the road, but they were deserted. He slept in them now and again, and ate of the meat that was left behind. Once he came to a snow hut and found a great store of meat, so he stayed there to mend one of his kamiks. He wanted to make a good long journey the next day. While he was there mending his kamik, a sledge came up. He went out and saw two brothers who were out looking for the meat they had left behind. He joined company with them, and they went on homewards. As soon as they reached the village, one of the two brothers cried:

"We have found the man who was carried out to sea on the ice."

When they cried out thus, a woman came out from one of the snow huts and said:

"I was once married to a man who was carried out to sea on the ice."

When the mother had uttered these words, one of the men looked more closely at the man they had brought to the village, and recogniced his father's teeth. The father had come, but his wife had married another man. The man went to his house and said to the one who was now married to his wife that he could stay there all the same, they could quite well both be married to the same woman; and he said he would be very glad to have him there, since it was he who had brought up his sons. The man now settled in his own village, but it was not long before people began to whisper that he must have killed the man who had been with him when they were carried out to sea.

"Wait a little while before you kill me; wait until the young gulls are ready to fly. And if no one has come by that time, then you can always kill me if you want to."

It was getting on towards autumn, and all through the spring the man was busy making arrows. At last he had quite filled two pairs of kamiks with arrows and nothing else. It was spring now, and summer came, and soon came the autumn, and the time was come when the young gulls were ready to fly. As soon as he had seen a young gull flying, he was always up in the hills on the look-out. Sometimes he would be away all day. At last one day he caught sight of three umiAqs. They came in towards the village at a great rate. Then he went down to his neighbours and called out:

"Now your enemies are coming!"

All the men went down to the shore to meet the umiAqs, and when they were close to land, they began shooting their arrows out over them. They shot down all the biggest and all the strongest, and when only young men were left, these took to flight.

Thus the man who was carried out to sea on the ice saved his neighbours, though there was no one that would believe what he said.

Told by
Ivaluardjuk.

Tales of killing and vengeance.

Kukigaq, the manslayer.

Kukigaq was a terrible manslayer. He was so fond of killing people that no one who visited him ever escaped alive. Once a man and a woman came on a visit. In honour af their coming, Kukigaq built a very large snow hut. And this was because he now again desired to kill his guests. He had not yet managed to kill them, and they were still living as his guests, when he was suddenly attacked by some other people. When the attacking party approached, they sent an old woman who had never before undertaken any errand in vain, with a message to Kukigaq and his wife, bidding her say:

"There are some men coming to attack you, poor creatures they are seemingly of no great strength, men with ill-made weapons, men who could have no success in an attack."

The attacking party came up to the village and bade Kukigaq and his household come forth. It then appeared that the strangers had only brought with them the bows and arrows they used for shooting musk ox.

Kukigaq came out, and when he saw the company of men that had surrounded his house, he said:

"And I who had thought many men were coming to attack me. Why, there are not enough of you to darken the snow round my house."

"You and your party are not so many that you should wish your enemies to darken the snow round your snow hut."

Then they began shooting at one another with bows and arrows, and it was not long before Kukigaq had killed all his assailants. He himself had only received an arrow through the calf of his leg.

Kukigaq had gone back into his house when there came to visit him a woman who was unclean, and meant to harm him. Kukigaq lay crosswise on the sleeping place, one leg swollen with the wound from the arrow. Kukigaq found it wearisome lying there, and was glad of the woman's coming, for he thought she came to help him pass away the time, and he said to his wife:

"I am glad this woman has come to visit me. Give her some suet from the bag. It is in the nature of us human beings to be distressed when one of ourselves, one of those near to us, is attacked, but when it is a stranger, we never trouble ourselves. If now it should chance that any came to attack you who are in the house here, you have none to help you in the state I am now in." And the tears welled up and sorrow overwhelmed him, because of the pain in his leg.

Kukigaq had no idea that it was an unclean woman who had come to visit him; and there is this about unclean women, that their mere presence is enough to kill a wounded man. And again Kukigaq spoke up and said:

"Not until I am dead is the arrow to be drawn out from my leg, and if I die, people need not be afraid of visiting me in my grave, for I have always been very fond of my fellow-men."

And in the end it came about that the arrow in his leg proved the bane of Kukigaq, and he died of it.

Told by
Inugpasugjuk.

Qijuk, who stole Kíngusarârjuk's wife and was murdered.

There was once a man whose name was Qijuk. He was a strong man. But there was also another man who was strong. He lived in another village, and his name was Kíngusarârjuk. While out on a hunting expedition, Qijuk's wife died. Qijuk was now a widower, and made up his mind to kill Kíngusarârjuk in order to take his wife. Qijuk called for companions to go with him on the journey, and he collected a party and they set out. But it was a difficult road, with very rugged ice, a toilsome road, and most of Qijuks party turned back; at last there were only his two younger brothers in his following, all the rest having turned back. They travelled all that winter, and not until summer did they reach the place. Qijuk went straight in to Kíngusarârjuk's wife, laid his head in her lap and got her to pick his lice. Kíngusarârjuk was out hunting caribou. Towards evening, he came back from this hunting, with a caribou in his kayak. He was a skilful hunter. His neighbours greeted him on his homecoming and said:

"Qijuk has taken your wife."

Kíngusarârjuk burst into tears and said:

"The weak man never finds any to help him."

Qijuk heard these words, and said:

"Kingusarârjuk's teeth are crooked. When I fling him on his back and am just about to kill him, I shall laugh at those crooked teeth of his."

Kíngusarârjuk laid his kayak up on shore in such a manner that it could easily be launched again, and then went into a tent near his own. There was a man here, who gave him a knife with a wooden handle. Kíngusarârjuk then sang a magic song which sent Qijuk to sleep. Qijuk had pulled his arms out of the sleeves, and lay with his arms in under his tunic, his head in the woman's lap, while she picked his lice, and so he fell asleep. Qijuk's young brothers ran out and played games with the other young people of the village. But when Qijuk had fallen asleep, Kíngusarârjuk went over to his tent and looked in at him. He took his knife and went in. He cut the lining of his breeches and stabbed him, and went out again, his wife following. He leapt into his kayak and pushed off from land, with his wife in the back of the kayak.

But when Qijuk was stabbed, he jerked his arms under the tunic so violently that he tore it asunder, and then he set off in chase of the fugitives. He had nearly come up with them when he fell down and lay there on the ground, unable to rise. Thus died Qijuk, and his brothers were at once set upon, and one was killed, the other managed to escape. Qijuk's brother rowed home to the village, and here he was often urged to take vengeance for his brothers, but he did not think himself strong enough for the task, and therefore did not avenge his brothers.

Told by
Inugpasugjuk.

Aumarzuat and Atanârzuat.

Two brothers, Aumarzuat and Atanârzuat, lay sleeping one night in their tent, when they were attacked by enemies. Atanârzuat was killed, but Aumarzuat managed to escape and made his way home to his parents' house. His parents hid him under some seaweed, fearing lest his enemies should come in search of him. And this they did, but his mother then set about cooking some meat, so as to make it appear that she had no knowledge of their errand. They sought about everywhere, especially where the snow had melted away. They threw harpoons in all directions, but were forced to return home without having accomplished their purpose. Aumarzuat then lay for some time to let his wounds heal, and when he was well again, he kept to places far from the dwellings of men, and hunted game for his parents.

Winter came, and his mother made him a fine tunic, all embroidered with handsome white patterns. His tunics were always made like that, and when Aumarzuat had got his new tunic, he felt a great desire to set out and take vengeance for the killing of his brother. His parents sought to dissuade him but in vain, Aumarzuat held to his purpose, and since there was no help for it, they at last agreed to let him go off and seek vengeance for his brother.

He then went alone towards the village of his enemies, and when he came in sight, and people saw him, they said:

"It can be no other than Aumarzuat, for he is the only one who wears tunics like that."

And true enough, it was Aumarzuat, they could all see for themselves when he came nearer, and he came to the village and cried:

"I should like to fight while I am awake. Last time I was attacked while I slept. Let all my enemies come out if they dare."

They all came out, and the fight began, between that one man and his enemies. But when Aumarzuat had killed two men, and the others now saw the mighty strength of him, they ceased to offer any resistance; they were now afraid of him. The fight came to an end, since none would now strike in self-defence, and Aumarzuat took the wives of the men he had killed, and returned to his parents' house. Two men went with him on the road; they meant no harm to him. but all the same, when they were about to take leave of him, Aumarzuat killed one of them. He had, as it were, got into the way of killing; and thus he avenged the slaying of his brother.

Told by
Inugpasugjuk.

Tigganajuk, who killed the two brothers.

There was once a jealous man who had two wives. Whenever he went out hunting, it was his custom to lay soft, loose snow round his hut, so that if anyone came to visit his wives while he was away, he could see the fresh tracks in the snow.

Tigganajuk was displeased at this, for he knew that he was the one whom the husband suspected.

One day, when Tigganajuk was out hunting, he looked round and discovered that the jealous one had raised his harpoon to throw at him, but the moment Tigganajuk saw it, the man lowered his arm. Nevertheless, Tigganajuk moved off backwards, keeping his face to the other. He took a few steps back, and then with a run he dashed forward and stabbed the man to death. Having done so, he struck him on the head, and afterwards returned to the village.

The man who had been killed had a brother who was a shaman, and people now began urging him to take vengeance on Tigganajuk by killing him, and true enough, one morning the shaman entered Tigganajuk's house. Just by the window there was a knife stuck into the snow, covered with blood, and it was with this that Tigganajuk had killed the shaman's brother. The shaman now, on entering the house, took this knife, threatened Tigganajuk with it, and then went into the other part of the house, the second room, where some other people lived. Tigganajuk lay on his sleeping place calmly looking on. Hardly had the shaman moved away into the other part of the house, when he leapt up all of a sudden, grasped his knife, and stabbed the shaman to death.

Thus Tigganajuk killed the two brothers, and afterwards he took the wives of the jealous husband for his own.

Told by
Inugpasugjuk.

Strange stories.

Women become dangerous when they have no husbands.

In the days when there were many people living at Nuvuk (near Wager Bay), there were also two brothers living there, both married. They were bold and skilful hunters, and it was therefore not long before their neighbours grew envious of them. Once when they were out hunting caribou, both of them were murdered, and all the animals they had killed were stolen. After the killing of the brothers, the various men now lay with the wives of the murdered men. This the women did not like, and therefore one day they spoke to each other and said:

"Next time a man comes in here to lie with us, we will laugh him to scorn; one of us can pretend she is willing to receive him, but then the other shall come up and catch hold of him and make water in his mouth."

The night came, and when a man came along as usual to visit them, one of the women called out to her fellow:

"Ah, here he is!" And then the other woman came up, and they caught hold of the man, and one of them sat astride his head and made water in his mouth, and they kept on like that, until the man was suffocated. Then quietly they prepared to leave the place in the middle of the night, while the others were asleep, and fled away. They fled across the ice, and in the morning, when the neighbours found out what had happened, they set out in pursuit. The two women took with them their husband's mother, and when they perceived that they were being followed, they said to her:

"You know a lot of magic songs; sing a magic song that will break up the ice behind us, so that our pursuers cannot reach us."

"Yes, I know a little magic song, I will try it," said the old woman.

She then drew a line on the ice behind the uprights of their sledge, and recited the magic song, and at once the ice broke away behind the sledge, and the one in pursuit of them was so near that the leader of the team fell into the water, but the three women escaped, being carried out to sea. They came to Southampton Island, and here they lived all alone, and there were no other men there save their little sons, that they carried in their amauts. But now it was not long before these women began to long for men so greatly that they lay with their own children, and those little boys did not grow up because the women took all the strength out of them, and they stayed small. The women were therefore obliged to go out hunting themselves, and this they did by taking with them their sons, who were still carried in the amauts, but had the understanding of grown men, to show them how to manage. And thus they captured whales, walrus, seal and other animals.

But the shamans, from whom nothing is hidden, discovered them, and did not approve of the life they were living. But the women, who were skilled in shamanism themselves, found out that others were seeking to do them harm, and so they sang this song to their husbands:

"My husband I carry in my amaut,
love him and kiss him,
and hide him away now,
because he is hunted by one
who is not a real human being.
My husband I carry in my amaut,
love him and kiss him,
Ajaja — ajaja.

Walrus I hunt
With my husband in the amaut,
following his wise counsel,
loving him and kissing him,
and hiding him now
that he is hunted by one
who is not a real human being,
a shaman that seeks to kill him,
Ajaja — ajaja.

It is said that a real man once came to these women who had no grown-up husband of their own. The stranger met one of the women, and she took him in to her house at once and he lay with her, and when he got up to go, the woman said to him:

"Take this tent pole by way of thanks, for that you lay with me. lay with me who am lonely, having no husband to lie with me."

And the man took the tent pole home with him, that had been given him as a gift.

And another time, it is said, a white man landed on the island where lived the women without husbands. The women ran to meet him as he came, and so eager were they to embrace him, so eager to have him lie with them, that they suffocated him.

Thus women become dangerous when they have no husbands to lie with them.

Told by
Naukatjik.

The shaman who changed into a woman.

There was once a great hunter who when out after whale one day was thrown against the side of the boat and badley hurt. His genitals were crushed, and he was no longer a man. Since he could not be a man, he wished to be a woman, and got himself made a woman's dress. He rubbed away all the skin from his face, and people died of fright at the sight of it. One day, when he had got a new set of woman's garments, he went to his mother. When his mother saw him, she said:

"Is this really my son, the great hunter?"

At these words, he rubbed the skin off his face, and looked so terrible that his mother died of fright.

He was now a woman, and got a man to marry him, a poor unskilful hunter. But as soon as the unskilful hunter had taken him to wife, he suddenly became fortunate in his hunting, and they took in a boy as their adopted son and brought him up.

One day the neighbours had assembled for a song festival. The man and his wife thought they would like to be present, and went to the place. When the great hunter who had turned into a woman came in, the people began to deride him, saying:

"Take off those woman's clothes, do, and let us see if you are a man or a woman."

Then in his anger he began rubbing the skin off his face to frighten them to death, but the people ran away before he could get it down, and so he gave it up. But the adopted son grew up and became a mighty hunter, because he had been so well brought up.

Told by
Naukatjik.

The woman who turned into stone for grief at being rejected by men.

A man from Amitsoq (Melville Peninsula), who lived among the Aivilingmiut, was killed. As soon as his fellows at Amitsoq heard of it, a great number of men went down to Aivilik to avenge him. But all those men who came to take vengeance were themselves taken by surprise and killed.

But their women were divided among the men of Aivilik. Only one woman, named Inukpaujaq, who was getting old, was left without a husband, and when summer came, she took a dog with her to carry her belongings, and went off inland. She went on up country without rightly knowing where she was going, and came at last to Serluaq (Haviland Bay). Here she saw a man rowing in a kayak a little way out at sea, and when she had seen him, she called out to him and asked if she could be his wife.

"I dont want a wife who is getting old," answered the man.

The woman felt great shame at this. She could not walk the whole of the long way back to the village, so she sat down on a stone beside her dog. And she stayed there, sitting beside the dog. And as she sat there beside the dog, everything in her began suddenly to grow stiff with grief. So she turned into stone, and it is that pillar of stone that stands at the base of Haviland Bay and is called Inukpaujaq to this day, after the woman whom none of the Aivilik men would have for a wife.

Told by
Ivaluardjuk.

The old couple and their daughter, that were left alone in their village.

There were once an old man and his wife who lived alone with their daughter. The girl was of an age to be married, but there were no men to marry her. They had once had neighbours, but these had gone away, as they did not care about the old people, who were poor and could not manage for themselves.

Some time after they had been left alone in the village, there came a bear, and they could hear it moving about in one of the empty huts near by. The old man, who had once been a skilful hunter, but was now blind, took a tent pole and began making a harpoon. He was just fixing a harpoon head to the tent pole when the bear entered the house. It came in through the passage, and as this was close and narrow, the bear could move but slowly. At last it appeared at the entrance, exposing itself in a place where it could be severely wounded, and the old man stabbed it there with his harpoon. The bear uttered never a sound, but crawled out again. The man would have gone out after it, but neither his wife nor his daughter would let him go out. Nevertheless, he went out, and called to his daughter, saying:

"Little daughter, come out here, do, and look about in this dircetion."

The daughter came out and saw the bear lying out on the ice. The wife now also came out, and she spoke to the old man, suggesting that they should go over to where the bear was, approaching it from the front. The bear lay dead on the ice. They fastened a strip of hide round it and dragged it up to the entrance of their house and began cutting it up outside the house. While they stood here cutting up the bear, a strange man came up to them. The old man was frightened at this visit of a stranger, he was afraid they were now to be killed.

"We are just cutting up some meat," he said.

The stranger went into the house and sat down beside the daughter, and took her to wife at once.

And thus it came about that the old couple who were left behind by their neighbours, got both meat to eat and a husband for their daughter.

Told by
Inugpasugjuk.

One should not be afraid of worms.

Some people were out on a journey, and came to an island called Quvdlugiartôq: the place of many worms. Among the party was a man who was so afraid of worms that he dared not sleep there on the island, and when the others pitched their camp, he went off to another island to sleep there. And there he lay down to sleep, but was at once attacked by a host of worms, that crept into him through all the openings of his body, and killed him.

This story is told, because the old ones declare that it is the nature of worms to attack and kill all who fear them, whereas those who lie down on the ground without fear always escape. The worms do them no harm.

Told by
Inugpasugjuk.

The infant that killed its mother and killed itself.

A pregnant woman brought forth a child. The child was hardly born before it flung itself upon its mother and killed her, and began eating her.

Suddenly the infant cried:

"My mother's little first finger stuck crosswise in my mouth, and I could hardly manage to get it out again."

And with these words, the infant killed itself, after first having murdered and eaten its mother.

Told by
Inugpasugjuk.
(G.)

CONTENTS:

BV - #0062 - 091222 - C0 - 229/152/18 - PB - 9780282540715 - Gloss Lamination